Witchcraf Myth and Mystery and... Not Forgetting Fairies

Ralph Harvey

CAPALL BANN PUBLISHING

www.capallbann.co.uk

Witchcraft, Magic, Myth and Mystery and... Not Forgetting Fairies

ISBN 186163 284 3

Cover and internal images © John Hooper - www.hoopix-images.com
Cover design by HR Design

Published by:

Capall Bann Publishing
Auton Farm
Milverton
Somerset
TA4 1NE

Dedication

This book is dedicated to all the Witches who suffered so cruelly in the days of the hempen rope, and all those who suffered the torments of the Inquisition in those evil burning days.

I make a special dedication to Joannes Wierus whose attempts to stop the persecutions led to he himself ultimately being accused of Witchcraft after he courageously wrote his famous treatise entitled '*On Magic*' in 1563. He disproved the fallacies about us, such as flying on broomsticks, and changing into animals, incurring the full wrath of the Catholic Church in the process. His book was ceremonially burned in public as a rebuke. His second book '*de Praestigiis Daemonum et Incantisonibus ac Veneficii*' was banned also, remarkably he avoided the stake and the gallows tree, and was lucky to die peacefully in his bed at the age of 73 in 1588.

Most especially to my loving wife Audrey, who stayed the course over all the years, and who has never demurred in her love for me, and as I have in my love for her. With the passing of the years and now having celebrated 52 years of marriage, the bond is even closer as we enter the twilight years together.

To my five children of whom my only regret is they remained Xtians. In those early days when my first daughter was born in 1955 there was great prejudice in all levels of society, including schools; and rather than see them persecuted for their parents' beliefs we had them brought up as Methodists. The one branch of Xtianity that seemed closer to the original doctrine of their gentle messiah. They are in order:

Deirdre Susan
Martin Anthony Graham
Karen Ingrid
Vanessa Melanie
Wayne Ian Stuart

To Witches worldwide who have assisted me, and to all the covens who sprang from the loins of the Order of Artemis

To Levanah Shell Bdolack of the Clearsight organisation who sponsored my lecture tour of America in 2003, and introduced me to the shaman Eight Horses of the Navaho tribe, when we stayed on their reservation, and to the Navaho tribesmen who rescued us when our jeep broke down in the desert. Levanah also introduced us to the highly secretive Hopi who only accepted us when they knew we were pagan.

And last but not least to Lyn Baylis who shines above all the High Priestesses I have had over the years, and is now a pagan chaplain. A great step forward for the Craft.

Acknowledgements

To my wife Audrey who despite her failing sight read, reread, and edited both *The Last Bastion* and this book *'Witchcraft, Magic, Myth, and Mystery (not forgetting fairies)* and did a great deal of research on old fairy lore to aid me in that particular chapter and for a third book *'The Magical Realm of Faerie'* .

To Graham King, curator and owner of the famous Witchcraft Museum in Boscastle, Cornwall, for supplying some of the photos and prints within these pages, from exhibits within the museum, free of charge, in the furtherance of the Old Ways of our forefathers who followed the Old Religion.

To SN Emrys Grand Master of the Cromlech Covenant who wrote the wondrous foreword, a great magician in his own right with whom I have been proud to work on ceremonies at Stonehenge

To the Honourable Olivia Robertson, of the Fellowship of Isis in Ireland, and to the late Lord and Lady Strathlock. (Derry and Poppy) who opened their castle doors to us in Clonegal, and with whom we spent a wonderful five weeks seeking out the castle ghosts and phantoms, and who enlightened us on the phenomena we experienced in the fairy valley, and which encouraged us to add the 'not forgetting fairies' appendix to the title, and sowed the first seeds as to their existence once upon a time, it opened up the investigation as to their existence even now.

To Sir Lawrence Dean the well known paranormal lecturer, and psychic researcher, who read the original manuscript, and accordingly endorsed it prior to publication.

To John Hooper of Hoopix picture agency who took the time to visit me and photograph the great statue of 'Pan and Pard' and digitally create this book cover free of charge in the furtherance of the Craft.

Once more a big thank you to all the followers of the Order of Artemis and the numerous covens and witches world wide that helped with supplying material and enabled me to record disappearing ways.

Once more, a tribute to those Members of Parliament, Judges, Lawyers, Police Officers, Doctors, Nurses, and Magistrates who have accepted initiation into the Original Religion of this country, and who sadly still cannot openly profess their faith, for fear of persecution and prejudice in even this, the 21st century.

On a more positive note however I am pleased to report that some magistrates now openly extol their beliefs and have been accepted, plus now there are those of our people who have become Pagan Chaplains in Hospitals and Prisons, the first positive progress in hundreds of years.

To Merlyn of the 'Children of Artemis', and editor of *Witchcraft and Wicca* magazine for their previous reviews, and support for "*Witchcraft, Magic, Myth and Mystery (Not Forgetting Fairies!)*"

To Petra Ginman my PA for helping to format this book and juxtapositioning the chapters over a period of time, always without grumbling, but then after fifteen years with me as both PA, companion, and friend; she knows my ways!

Dr. Susie Iles-Jonas, a local magistrate who uncovered elements of fairy lore and a recent phenomenon. A lady of great potential, who has not been afraid to out herself publicly as both Pagan, Magistrate - and Witch!

John Eagle, the historian and expert on the Celtic period, who helped me in my research on the Iceni Queen Boudicca when I wrote the screen play. He also contributed immensely with his studies of the local phenomena in woodlands around his area, plus his knowledge of a sacred grove.

My neighbour Georgina Angele, who in Petra's absence spent countless hours teaching me the hidden workings of my computer at weekends - many thanks Georgina.

Previous Books by the Author

Travel
Brother to the Bedouin
Dowa for the Sheik

Short Occult Stories
Hobgoblin Hill
Sabbat, Solstice, and Equinox
The Witches of Warnham
The Black Egg
The Sculptor
Merlin
Earthforce
The Last Fairy

Satire
Hells Bells!

History
Iceni
Boudicca-Queen of Death
A Celtic Tragedy
Boadicea

Fiction
Sacre Bleu
Estelle
Maison d'Amour
Operation Pandora
The Sculptor
The Planter

Occult-factual
The Last Bastion - the suppression and re-emergence, of Witchcraft the Old Religion.

The Mystical Realm of Faery
Published under the 'Simply' series as' Simply Fairies'

Contents

Author's note

In 1951 the evil Witchcraft Act was finally repealed and with it a new age dawned. In England only seven families who knew the old ways had survived the holocaust of genocide that had been unleashed upon our people, but from these families, plus the few surviving covens and wise folk, a new seed was generated, and within a decade had prospered to such an extent that the Wiccan faith had spread across the oceans; and was over the next 50 years acclaimed as the fastest growing religion that was attracting worldwide, conservationists, animal lovers, and those anxious to see the Old Gods restored, with particular emphasis on the Earth Mother.

Overnight Xtianity went into a sharp decline from which it never recovered, and its male orientation swiftly faded as woman took her rightful place in the natural order of things once more. The Xtian religion had suppressed all that was feminine, usurping womankind's rightful place in the world. For centuries the established church had been a patriarchal, chauvinistic enclave, persecuting and suppressing all that was feminine.

Vainly they fought to prevent the upsurge of woman's newly-found emancipation, but they were fighting a losing battle, Within the span of a half century women were admitted into their church as priests splitting the traditional foundations of their faith asunder, only to be followed by the ordination of the first female bishops. The raison d'etre why the ecclesiastical authorities fought against a feminine priesthood was clear, for once they had ordained a woman to this privileged role she technically was not a Priest, but a Priestess, and that was Pagan!

Within the Wicca, we the Hidden Children smiled, for the tenet of our faith is the worship of woman, and although we have both the polarity of both God and Goddess, in truth, it is woman who reigns supreme within the sacred circle of the Witches. To us the sacred Earth Mother reigns supreme.

The hand that rocks the cradle rules the world. Thus it has always been and So Mote it Be - forever.

Final note

In my last book *The Last Bastion* I recorded that at the time of the repeal of the Witchcraft Act only six old witch families had survived; but since its publication in 2005 I am delighted to record a further two, making a seventh and eighth hereditary family existing at the time. I discovered that they still remain secretive in their ways and are wary of being exploited. I will amend this entry when the new reprint of *The Last Bastion* comes out, together with the reference to the Pickingill covens that contained a typographical error and should have read 'Before the First World War', as against 'before the war'.

Contacting the author

Ralph Harvey is always interested to hear of old customs. He can be contacted at:

Order-of-artemis@ntlworld.com

Foreword

Ralph Harvey must rank as one of the most extraordinary men it is my privilege to know. On the anniversary of his seventieth birthday, a time when most folk are thinking in terms of slippers and bus-passes, Ralph was to be found five thousand feet up in the sky strapped to a naked girl parachute instructor, swinging gently under a canopy in his first free-fall parachute experience. I mention this, not to be salacious, but because it illustrates his vivacious nature perfectly.

I belong to the Cromlech Covenant, where the emphasises is on producing what might be called "renaissance" wo/men - multitalented people with a wide range of skills and interests. My dear friend Ralph is just such a person, with skills as a horseman, actor, writer, stuntman, linguist and medievalist, to name just a few. It is a truism to say that truth is stranger than fiction, and Ralph's exploits throughout his life lend weight to that saying, however this brief preface is not the place to explore this aspect of the man: I merely want to cast a glimmer of light on the Witch and his milieu.

He has always been different to those around him. Even as a young boy, while his school chums played football and cricket, he would be found in the woods studying insects and other animals and indulging his particular fascination for amphibians. Continuously castigated by his teachers for his "strangeness" he eventually earned the epithet 'the wild boy of the woods'.

It was while wandering the fields of Berkshire on such an expedition that this young lad met a Romany Gypsy girl from the nearby encampment in Scours Lane or "Gypsy lane" as the locals dubbed it. She belonged to one of the few remaining tribes then still living in horse-drawn caravans. Every year they migrated to Tilehurst, alongside the river Thames, where they plied their pegs and palmistry to all. Perhaps the travellers saw something of themselves in the "wild boy of the woods": we shall never know, but for whatever reason, they made him welcome and before long the young Ralph's face became a familiar sight in their midst.

But this was in the gloaming of the Second World War: rationing was introduced within months of the commencement of that dreadful conflict and soon the people of Great Britain found themselves struggling to survive. Root vegetables became the mainstay of the diet, and cricket pitches, lawns and people's gardens were turned into vegetable plots. Any scraps would be fed to a scrawny hen housed in some makeshift coop in the hope that she would lay the occasional egg and thus introduce a little protein into the sparse diet. Nothing was wasted in those desperate times.

Ralph noticed the small ration of meat – two ounces (fifty seven grams) once a week – his family were allowed, but over in the gypsy encampment his friends fed sumptuously on rabbit, hare and pheasant. It was not long before they took him on their foraging expeditions and taught him the art of poaching. He learnt to study the striations in the grass that showed which way an animal travelled regularly, how to read spoor and how to set snares and nets. He was never keen on the use of the snare and he was taught the art of the catapult, silent and deadly, which soon became his favourite hunting tool. His friends introduced him to fungi and edible berries, and so it was that he supplemented his family's diet – and that of his neighbours – with a bountiful supply from Nature's parlour.

The war years taught him many other things at the hand of the Romany: these people were living repositories of the knowledge of the Old Ways. As medicines and other standard cures became difficult to obtain the urbanites suffered, but the gypsy women simply went into the country and came back with a variety of herbs and plants and made their own healing potions.

His role as "auxiliary" provider for the family came to an abrupt end when, at the age of at eighteen, he was conscripted into the RAF. He found himself rubbing shoulders with people from every walk of life, for the call-up knew no bounds of class distinction, rich and poor, they all ended up "square bashing" in the services. And strange to say many were glad of it, for the alternative was to end up down the mines hewing coal or mineral ores for the war effort, under the auspices of Aneurin Bevin, Minister of Labour.

At Padgate RAF training camp, he met many girls in the WAAF (Women's Auxiliary Air Force) and within a few weeks had formed a close friendship with Rachael, another Romany gypsy and also a former nurse called Anne. Old cures, medicines and folklore were a frequent topic of conversation amongst them, but it was the spiritual side of Rachael that struck home the most as he learned of old Witchcraft practices that were still retained secretly within the tribes.

In those days the foreign religion (Christianity) held absolute power, and being forced into church parades and compulsory church attendance did little to endear a free-thinking youth to it: in fact it simply reinforced the deep fear of churches that had been engendered in Ralph when, at the tender age of seven, he found himself locked in a church hall with many other children by a drunken (subsequently unfrocked) clergy-man. The trauma caused by the screaming and ranting of this "man of God", has echoed all down the years, and I suppose we should be grateful to the great Goddess who, in the guise of this priest, set Ralph on the Pagan path. But I digress...

Ralph was eventually sent into the desert in Aden in Saudi Arabia attached to the 4001st Armoured Car Flight, Aden Protectorate Levees, where he would spend long periods on patrol. In the way of soldiers everywhere the men grumbled and swore as endless vistas of sand, rock and scrub filled the long days and nights; books and letters were read and re-read; cigarettes ran out and utter boredom became the order of the day. But to Ralph, the desert night brought enchantment as centipedes, snakes, scorpions and spiders brought the apparently dead sands to life. His fellow soldiers couldn't understand how he could spend hours transfixed, watching ant columns as they traversed the desert surface. Here in the vast emptiness, he could feel his soul stir and hear The Lord whisper to him in the guise of desert winds, gently, oh so gently, touching his heart. Slowly but inexorably, the Pagan in him awoke.

Eventually demobbed he started to study esoteric religion, Paganism and folklore seriously. He went looking for his Gypsy friends, but they had moved on from Scours Lane as the large stadium complex nearby had encroached onto the lands they once occupied. He was never to see them again. Even their lane has long since disappeared, though the giant water trough carved out of solid granite for their horses still remained up until only a few years ago, bearing silent witness to a way of life long gone.

In 1954 he married his beautiful wife, Audrey. This was a strange match, given his leanings, for she was a practicing Baptist and Sunday school teacher. She accepted his practices because of her deep love for him, but would have no part of them, having been brought up to believe that everything occult was evil. This belief was not lessened when strange things started to happen around the house as Ralph experimented with the 'tele-sciences'. More than once, after an unsuccessful foray into the world of ritual magic, he would return from his temple despondent for having failed to move a single object telekinetically, only to find as they were about to go to bed, that wild poltergeist-like activity would become activated around the house. In time, as he became more proficient in these arts, she became more accepting of the result: unlike more than one Reading University student who stayed with them as a paying guest in those days, who packed their bags and left the "haunted house".

The couple had five children in all, and moved to a larger house in Blenheim Road in Reading. They found themselves living in an actual haunted house that had been the domain of a young woman who had died in the early 1900s and who had been the mother of two young children.

Appearing frequently to their own children, she was given the affectionate nickname of Fred, for she had mistakenly been taken for a male, but it was when the children started to speak of the 'lady' who sat and spoke to them at night, that it was realised that "Fred" was a woman and so was promptly renamed "Frederica". Frederica became so attached to the children that when they grew up and married she followed them from house to house. She still flits from one to the other as they in their turn bring up their own young families and theirs in turn; but she always returns to Ralph and Audrey where, to this day, she makes her presence felt by behaving mischievously, delighting in taking and hiding things then making them appear in full view, usually in an unlikely and prominent position. This has left many a visitor to their home dumfounded.

Her early, visible manifestations of her earthly form fuelled Ralph's fascination with the unknown. In 1952 this fascination, perhaps obsession would be more accurate, led via a very circuitous route, to his initiation into the Storrington witches' coven. These ageing witches who adhered strictly to the old ways were thought to be the remnants of one of the famous nine covens founded by the legendary Old George Pickingill, though in reality they had merely (though no less importantly) been guided by Pickingill from time to time.

By now the Harvey family had moved to Sussex and it was there that Ralph came to form his own order, which was to become the 'Order of Artemis'. He had realised that the Craft form known as Traditional Witchcraft, as practiced by his initiators, was badly in need of a "bit of a cleanup", albeit with a feather duster – in modern parlance: a slight "makeover" - to bring it into the Twentieth Century, just as Gardner was doing with his own branch of the Craft. "Artemis" gradually evolved into the form it is known today: traditional; adopting the middle way; letting go outdated tradition; but still retaining the innermost secrets, such as the passing of the secret names of the Goddess at the third degree. But more of that later...

With the passing of the years Audrey had become accustomed to coven meetings in the house, Ralph had abandoned High Ritual Magic and the accompanying disturbing phenomena had ceased, and he had successfully incorporated a lower grade of Ritual Magic into Witchcraft practises, with the emphasis on healing.

Thus it was that Audrey's interest grew, and she too turned her back on the foreign religion and sought initiation at the hands of Len and Anna, Wiccan Priest and Priestess, (descended from Rae Bone who had been Gerald Gardner's High Priestess) who ran the local Gardnerian "Acorn" coven. Sadly that group disintegrated when Len and Anna parted and before Audrey could take her 2nd and 3rd degrees, but Tom and Mabs Penfold who had both been initiated into Rae Bone's coven years before, and who now ran a flourishing coven in Hove, Sussex, invited Audrey to join them, and it was from Tom that she received her 2nd and 3rd degree. The transformation was now complete as a one-time Baptist became a Witch! Mabs and Tom were reciprocally initiated into Artemis and likewise Ralph accepted Gardnerian initiation at the hands of Mabs Penfold. From that point on the two traditions worked closely side by side for many years.

Now more than fifty years on, Ralph has become known as one of the brightest luminaries in the Craft; perhaps the leading exorcist in England; a regular contributor to the media, especially television; and he runs the largest coven in Britain, having personally initiated over one hundred ladies into the group, many of whom have themselves in turn founded covens worldwide.

In fact The Order of Artemis now has over two hundred covens in the USA, Canada, Australia, New Zealand, Germany, France, and other European countries, as well as Scotland and Wales. During his lecture tours to these countries he has met a large variety of covens, groups and solitaries both inside and outside Artemis, all avid for information on traditional British practises and lore. Hence this book.

Ralph's first book, chronicled how the Old religion of the British Isles rose, phoenix like from its own ashes, and how Sussex, the last bastion of the Native Religion in England became the cauldron of this renaissance of Witchcraft.

In this exciting new book, Ralph takes us on a helter-skelter ride through that book of shadows called his mind. Here you will find information about the Craft and its gods and goddesses; folklore; legends; sigils; ghosts; Wicca in the USA, Da-Vinci stuff, and much more than I can list, almost all of which has been forgotten (or sometimes hidden deliberately) and is chronicled here either for the first time, or shown in its proper historical context. The earnest seeker will find the answers to many questions, whilst the casual reader will find its information-packed pages a delightful treasure-chest full of esoteric gems.

Once more, his painstaking research, and knowledge gleaned from many decades at the forefront of "The Battle" shine through its pages, to bring back to life that which, but for him, through the grace of Her, would have been lost forever.

As I've said more than once: Pagan history will show what a dept is owed to this intriguing gentleman I am proud to call my friend.

Sn. Emrys

A G. M. of the Cromlech Covenant.
Rochford, England, Samhain, 2006

False and Forgotten Lore - Fith Faths and Fallacy

Much has been written over the years as factual with regard to Witchcraft practises, and much of this is erroneous as it has been written by biased clergy who have not only no understanding of Wiccan practises, but also have no interest in learning the truth.

We are all aware that the Xtian propaganda machine completely reversed most of the old practises of ours that were benign, and maliciously, with malice aforethought altered them into being interpreted as malign. It started with the identification of the Horned God of the Witches, the Lord Cernunnos, in all his forms from the Green Man of the country folk, to Herne or Pan, the Gods of the woodlands, and identifying them with a Xtian invention they called the Devil. Witches abhor the power of evil and do not believe in what the Xtians call Satan or Lucifer.

Once more this representation of evil was created by them in a number of forms and ranged from Lucifer - originally the Lord of Light (who gave his name to matches) and who apparently was a fallen angel whose sole crime was to question God's absolute authority - a grave crime! (No, as a Xtian there is one rule, and that is you must believe implicitly in what the priests tell you, and never challenge the Church's authority - period!) These entities' names ranged from Satan, Beelzebub, and Mephistopheles, the Infernal One and even Old Nick, to name but a few. I once saw a report where a Catholic Priest exorcised Satan from a bewitched woman in 69 different forms - plus he cast out several dozen minor devils as well.

Witches eschew this Xtian invention of what is usually referred to as the 'Devil' and dismiss the idea of a horned humanoid with a forked tail as a figment of their imagination. The early Xtians were aware that the Old Gods were all-powerful, and they had one thing in common throughout Europe, and that was they were all horned, horns being both a fertility symbol and representative of great strength and power.

The upshot was that originally their own deity, with all the hosts of Heaven together with his angels were equally depicted with horns, until they realised that this was just too, too, Pagan and had overtures of sex and erections as well, and so the practise had to cease. They really did have huge hang-ups! So henceforth the horns were erased from all things Xtian and henceforth they were anathema and were to be depicted as evil.

They then came up with the idea of creating a devil who would drag screaming down to Hell all those who did not unquestioningly obey the dictates of the church, and used this image to keep their congregations in line from that moment onwards. The image of this Satanic figure was now endowed with a vision of an infernal place of fire and eternal torment where demons constantly taunted those condemned to eternal fire. It was a big stick to beat recalcitrant churchgoers with and it worked for hundreds of years.

With this new image they now reversed all the Pagan practises that were associated with the Gods and Goddesses of the witches; while the witches worked for the prosperity of crops, they were now accused of blighting them, when they bestowed good they were accused of cursing, when they preached a love of the Goddess and nature, they accused us of blasphemy and imbuing evil, regardless of all the good we did.

The Church's propaganda machine sprang into action and said we disseminated all things bad from creating diseases and pestilence to poisoning wells. The Jews were equally accused of exactly the same thing. The burning days, and the days of the hempen rope, were just around the corner, it was now but a matter of time. The shadow of the hanging tree and the gallows grew ever nearer; and the heat of the execution pyre started to be felt.

Every artefact that could be found that they could exploit to drive yet another nail in the Pagan coffin was used; and top of the list was the poppet. Poppets were figurines that were created in the image or clothing of the person on whom the witch was working his or her magic. These could range from carved wooden figures to clay effigies of the afflicted, to rag-like dolls whose clothing emulated the sick person.

The name of the person would be incised on the doll and the sexual organs would be exaggerated as can be seen with the earliest depictions of the famed 'Sheila-na-gigs'. In the 19th to 21st century with the advent of photography, a photo of the person to be healed would be pasted onto the figurine, or in many instances just a photograph of the features would be glued to the head, making recognition perfect; a far cry from the old village wise woman who had to sculpt the features from memory and place a few hair or nail clippings from the potential patient (if she could obtain them) in the clay or wax.

Traditionally a pin of pure silver would be used to literally 'pinpoint' the area to be healed, although with the passing of the years just the colour silver came to be substituted symbolically, and ordinary pins of steel and similar materials came to be used instead.

It was not long before the old traditional healing art by the use of a poppet would become exploited by the persecutors, for with the first discovery of these they were held up for all to behold, "Was this not a figurine of X" they would cry "And low and behold is not X afflicted with a bad heart? And has not the area of the chest where the heart is been pierced by the Witch?" - and so it went on, if a pin was found in the eye of the poppet then clearly the Witch was blinding that person, the fact that the person had perhaps been born with an eye affliction never even entered the equation - it was always the Witch who had caused it.

Satanists I know have tried to emulate the Wiccan practice and use a poppet for evil and we have known of sheep's, pig's and ox hearts to be found pierced with an assortment of rusty nails and thorns. We are continuously combating these weirdo's whose practises do not work, and never will, for right always triumphs over evil.

Although poppets were used for healing they had other uses as well, and one old custom was to create a female one out of material and hide it away from sight in the bend of a chimney. Some chimneys were constructed with small fosses where a poppet could be concealed and would not be disturbed by the sweep's brush. These figures were hidden there to bestow blessings on the house and to bring prosperity to all within. A fine example that has survived the centuries can be found in a showcase at the Witchcraft Museum at Boscastle in Cornwall.

To Witches the poppet is known as a 'fith-fath' and means 'shape-changing' the pronunciation of which is 'fee-fo' and has passed into history as part of the Ogre or Giant in the classical pantomime of Jack and the Beanstalk who seeks Jack while uttering the words 'Fee Fi Fo Fum - I smell the blood of an Englishman'. He is actually bemoaning the fact that he cannot find Jack, and the inference is that Jack is able to change his shape and thus evade the Giant.

I am not going to give any secrets away here but I will give fellow practitioners a modern update that we have learned to do with the aid of modern science, but before I do so let it be known that if any should try to create a poppet with a malefice in mind, then the Wiccan law of three will automatically be invoked and their own evil intent will rebound upon the perpetrator, and note - if they should persevere in attempting an evil intent then it will hit them sevenfold - for this is the law of the Witch and is incorporated in the initiation oath of 'An ye Harm None.'

This warning is to the uninitiated for I have seen 'Voodoo kits'; being sold openly, both here and in America, and the creation of a voodoo doll is amongst its contents. Play with fire if ye will, but remember the consequences are awesome. No initiated Witch would dream of using a poppet for a malefice. These cheap and tawdry kits should be banned and have no association at all with the Craft of the Wise.

To revert to a highly effective method of Fith Fath healing we have evolved a method of 'charging' the doll whereby the life force is introduced into the doll and the healing powers contained within the ritual are enhanced several hundred per cent. We take a fertilised hen's egg and open up the chest cavity of the poppet. Modelling clay or wax is the ideal material to create this type of doll as the chest cavity can be plugged afterwards. Next the egg is blessed by a method that will be known to all Witches, then once it has been rendered sacred it will be broken and the fertilised section will be clearly visible, usually as a small red spot. This is the life-force within the egg we will use, where the embryo will commence. It is this living essence that is now drawn up into a hypodermic syringe.

Next an Akashic ritual is performed on the contents and the needle is now placed back upon the syringe - note you would not find it easy to suck up the fertilised section of the egg with the needle in, but it is simple to exert enough pressure to inject it later. The fith-fath is now ceremonially blessed and the coven will visualise the blue ray of healing apexing into the area of the poppet where the candidate's affliction is while the High Priest or Priestess utters the words of power and then injects the egg yolk into the poppet's chest cavity, it is then sealed with red wax.

The doll can also be sealed with scarlet candle wax from one of the ceremonial candles - red being symbolic of the life-force, and of healing. Only the initiated will be able to understand this ritual, and how to perform it, so no secrets betrayed. Remember that in Witchcraft as against ceremonial magic it is the intent behind the ritual that is all powerful, so woe betide any who should try to use a poppet or Fith Fath wrongly.

One thing that surprises me to this day is the amount of superstition that still abounds amongst farmers, and each and every time they will defend their beliefs with so-called 'facts'. In my forays in my youth, while pond-dipping I have seen farmers' faces crease up in horror to see me handling male newts, such as the common newt with its gloriously coloured translucent tail through which tiny bones can be observed. When asking why, one farmer urged me to kill it at once as they poisoned his cattle's water. He had found one of his cows dead and it had been seen drinking at the pond where he had observed newts, the association was clear, the newts were responsible!

The other thing that horrified him was the fact that I was fearlessly handling the 'eft' as he called it - the old country name for newts; he warned me that the bones that were clearly visible were in fact a vicious sting, and that I was taking a great risk of being stung. Naturally he knew of someone, who knew someone, who had been stung. Nothing I could say would persuade him to the contrary despite my handling it fearlessly in front of him. Of such things superstitions are born and perpetuated.

The superstitions regarding toads were endless but the most prevalent one of all was that a small ruby lay within the brain of the toad, but dreadful things would befall any who killed a toad and tried to extract it. I was once told by an old countryman that he had found a dead toad by a pond and that he waited for it to become a skeleton before removing the ruby, but when he did it was not there, the wee folk who were wise in all matters had beaten him to it. In fact, he told me, he did not know of a single person who had ever successfully removed the gem from a dead toad, but he had seen one squashed in the road and there was a small red mass exuding from its head where the ruby had been forming. Nodding his head he sagely observed "It must have been a young one because only adults have the ruby they say".

One old superstition that seems fact was that by rubbing a wart on a toad the wart would vanish, the belief was prevalent and widely used, always with positive results, again it is part of what in magic is known as 'like unto like' the toad outwardly is warty in appearance, and the magical symbolism is to transfer your wart to him.

Factually it is known that when threatened a toad will excrete a bitter acrylic substance that burns mucous membrane as many a dog or cat has found when seizing one in their jaws so it is highly likely that this self-same substance which is acidic, can destroy a wart. Even a grass snake will reject a toad, yet eagerly devour frogs. I have observed goldfish who regard tadpoles as a delicacy spit out instantly a sibling toad tadpole as the toxins are apparent as a protection even in the larval stage.

Many farms had both horse and ox or cow skulls mounted on barns to ward off ill and to attract luck. I know of no magical association with regard to bovines - but I am sure someone will undoubtedly enlighten me after this book is published. But horse skulls have been worshipped since time immemorial. The Celts erected them on long poles to oversee their encampments and so that they could look down on the severed heads of their enemies whose heads and skulls likewise ornamented the compound and were a warning to rival tribes to keep their distance.

I found that whole areas in rural Denmark displayed horse skulls and one particularly sacred area that was a water meadow had poles protruding above the water upon which skulls reclined, an ancient custom associated with the horse goddess Epona. The whole area was mysterious and the entry to it was barred by a broken-down old gate. Everybody who went to enter it was struck with a sense of awe, and felt they should ask permission to proceed further. Having requested it the whole atmosphere changed and the 'blight' that they felt there was immediately lifted and they wended their way safe in the knowledge that they had appeased the Gods. A similar area exists within a stone's throw of Hampton Court near the village of East Molesley.

A great many Wiccan practices were also affected over the years by the onslaught against their creed, and once more superstition enters the equation. Practitioners of the Craft are well aware as to the 'modus operandii' whereby we cast and purify a circle of magic prior to commencing a ritual, but part of the ritual involves holy water being used to sanctify it, plus incense etc - and without going into detail I will give just a couple of examples of this reversal of meaning that once more has been associated with us.

The holy water for instance that we use is stirred after an all-purifying ingredient has been added, with the sacred witches' knife known as an 'athame'. Once the final blessing has been delivered the sanctified water is used in purification rites within the circle together with secret incenses etc - simple enough? So how can this beautiful ritual that will subsequently be used to help and heal the afflicted be interpreted as evil?

Goodness only knows, but such were the machinations of the Xtian priesthood that anyone stirring a liquid with a knife was warned to cease such a dangerous activity. There was a dread superstition to the effect that 'to stir with a knife was to 'stir up strife' and more than one small boy or girl has been sent to their room as punishment for stirring with a knife as against a spoon, and would never forget the dire warning handed out by one's parents for daring to follow this practice. Naturally and in due course, they in their turn would impart this superstition to their own offspring once they entered adulthood. Thus superstition spreads from generation to generation.

Staying within the circle ceremonies (My goodness the evil we get up too - raising old Beelzebub - Orgies - getting plastered on ritual wine, is there NO limit to our iniquity?) I am going to touch on some of the salt rituals, a substance that is considered so pure that no consecration ceremony is necessary. Well yes, we do use salt within the circle and in a certain form it is used liberally to sanctify the circle, and yes, it does end up on the floor.

Now let a practising Xtian spill it on the floor - or more frequently the tablecloth and all hell is let loose (if you'll pardon the expression). Tradition rules that you must pick up a pinch of the spilled salt, spin your hand above your head three times with it, and then, with a suitable and righteous exclamation, throw it into the face of the infernal one, who has, of course, started to materialise behind you from the very first second the salt hit the deck - after all you DID summon him, and now you must repel him.

Fantastic stuff! Until I learned of this old practise, I was not even aware we had conjured Old Nick up from the depths to join us. Secretive old fellow we never even noticed him there, but I must admit the wine does seem to have gone down considerably, and on a recount I did make it 14 of us present!

Having mentioned obliquely the magical figure of 13 which convention says is a full coven (13 plus 1 to wit - the infernal one?). We could write volumes around this magical figure. 13 is the number of moons in a year, and is allegedly the minimum number required to be present at a Sabbat (Where we undoubtedly are up to all sorts of mischief) yet it was also the number of the Xtian Messiah's disciples - including him of course, under their logic 13 is a sacred number on the one hand and a wicked figure on the other hand - strange philosophy these Xtians have!

Thirteen men in Xtianity is a holy gathering, but thirteen women brooks evil. Come to think of it when you look at Leonardo Da Vinci's 'Last Supper'. Methinks that the one next to the Messiah is a woman - Mary Magdalene? O the hypocrites! Analysing the situation and given the choice of the 'goodie' one in their eyes, consisting of 12 men and a Messiah/Priest, and the 'wicked witchy' one where we have at least 6 girlies present, then as an honest to goodness hetero-sexual I must plump for the latter and go where the ladies are - and maybe a beautiful High Priestess as well. I plead no contest, and rest my case, for this is one anti Witch super-stition that will assuredly backfire.

Bellarmines, Bibles and Bewitchment

One of the first thing one learns in Witchcraft is self defence well, psychic self defence that is, for by the laws of the Craft we must abide by the law of 'An ye harm none' and so can do no harm. As Witches we are quite often the target of malefice particularly from evangelical Xtian groups and from mis-guided individuals, and when we are blighted by these in one form or another then we are permitted to deflect the evil and if it persists then we may invoke magic to rebound the malefice back onto the head of the one who has originated it. If it still persists then we can send it back threefold, sevenfold or even ninefold (never mess with a Witch!!) but the overriding factor is that the practitioner of Witchcraft must never, ever, originate it.

The methods of defence used are numerous and can vary from high-powered rituals within a circle to simple incantations in your back garden at midnight if necessary. But if you want to create a permanent barrier of protection around you then the good old-fashioned witch bottle is hard to beat. This old traditional method has been used from time immemorial and is well recorded over the centuries with numerous examples of these old witch bottles being found.

Traditionally a very specific ritual is performed prior to creating a Witch bottle, and a further ritual is performed at the time of the delivering it into the bowels of Mother Earth Needless to say I have no intention of writing these rituals here as they are part of the secrets of the Craft, but how they are formed and used is common knowledge and can be discovered quite easily in a variety of text books on magic.

The basic idea is to completely shred any bad vibrations, curses, or acrimony thrown against you, which is why a typical witch bottle today would contain nails, tacks, razor blades as well as pins and needles, plus shards of glass; a far cry from the horseshoe nails, thorns and holly leaves of yesteryear. A vital ingredient was one's own urine, and the most powerful one of all that could repel and destroy all evil and wrongdoing was one from a wise woman still in her fertile years to which a drop of her menstrual blood had been added, together of course with the correct words and ritual - and no, they are not going to be published here.

Originally they started off as old earthenware bottles, flasks and glass containers and now in the 21st century have altered but little, except for that most abominable invention of the 20th century - plastic! Plastic however is durable and serves its purpose very well. However, many years ago every self respecting Witch would obtain a Bellarmine jar and bury this artefact in secret for countless decades. So what was so special about these Bellarmine jars and why were they chosen? Certainly when I created my first Witch bottle I could not even find a modern reproduction, and eventually I settled for an old demijohn that used to hold acid and sealed it with a plastic insert (Ugh) and candle wax from the Altar of Magic.

Next stop was to find a secret place to bury it in where according to Wiccan tradition 'it will never be discovered'. In my book *The Last Bastion* I went into detail of how Witch covens scoured Chanctonbury Ring in Sussex after the Great Storm searching amongst the roots of mighty oaks and elms that had been laid low by the terrible forces of nature that had been unleashed that dreadful night, searching for any old Witch bottles that had been buried there over the centuries and might now be exposed.

Chanctonbury, we know, has been a favourite gathering place for Witch covens for centuries and its vast expanse had countless acres in which a Witch could bury their bottle in a spot that was decreed as being 'certain that in thy lifetime it will never be disturbed'. Well Chanctonbury alongside other landmarks such as Cissbury Ring etc were national monuments and protected sites under the auspices of various bodies so we all knew they would never be disturbed in our lifetimes.

The Great Storm upset all that, and within 24 hours of it raging, numerous covens had congregated on its slopes and were re-interring old athames, crystals and Witch bottles that had been uncovered, and all too sadly we found the smashed remains of these old bottles that had been crushed in the roots of the fallen giants. Many of these trees had been planted in 1760 by Charles Goring and had already - albeit unknowingly - been planted above many old Wiccan artefacts even then. Interspersed with these fragmented shards was also a great quantity of old Roman pottery, for a Temple to the Goddess Diana had once stood here.

For years Pagans had known the exact location of this Temple as rabbits were forever displacing fragments of its foundations together with a large amount of ancient broken pottery, and as a result this particular area while covering well over an acre was a favourite place for the burying of Witch bottles. Once these had been smashed in the storm their metallic contents would not survive long, if they had survived at all, and only the shards of glass etc would endure; there was nothing we could do. We found small pieces of a single broken Bellarmine jar which acted as a further pointer to the antiquity of the site.

Well, why Bellarmines? I hear you ask, what is so special about these jars that they were regarded as such a trophy by Witches? The answer is I do not know, but in all probability it was a form of resentment against the man who gave his name to these jars. He was a nasty character by any standards and he would turn in his grave if he knew how the jars named after him were used by Witches; so let us study the background to these jars to find clues.

Firstly Bellarmines not infrequently held alcoholic drink and this I feel is the first clue, for from the ritual wine used in all Witchcraft ceremonies; to the worship of the Old Gods who were not averse to a tipple is our first pointer. Well good old Bacchus was a prime example bless him.

So was it a form of rebellion against the man who inadvertently gave his name to the jar? Let us turn the clock back. Its namesake was one Cardinal Robert Bellarmino a hellfire and damnation Catholic and persecutor of all things Pagan plus Protestants too, who he regarded as equally ungodly. Must be a first to find us in bed with these as our allies! His main depredations seem to have been in what we call the Low Countries where he was universally detested. Sex (usual target) women and drink he considered abominations in the eyes of his particular God. Derogatory reports of him at the time describe him as being 'leane of body' and with 'a sharp little beard' (Mephistopheles?). Well he was outwardly a celibate teetotaller who continuously quote 'preached total abstinence'.

Reports of his death in 1621 (he was born in 1542) were surrounded by rumour, these vary from his dying of a heart attack from over sexual indulgence to alcoholic poisoning. Whatever the truth of the matter he was certainly a dyed-in-the-wool hypocrite and did not practice what he preached. The first bottles in quantity depicting 'his miserable little face' started to appear just after his demise, but the first recorded instance is listed as 1563 - in his lifetime! So he must have been detested quite early on as he was only 21 at the time when the first bottles appeared. The original bottles were soon considered too benign; after his death and by the late 1600s his 'mean little face' was remoulded by the potters into a snarl to show their continuing contempt for him. His grizzled countenance was also referred to as 'old greybeard' and over the years these bottles came to be called 'greybeards' as well.

It seems that using Witch bottles was not a prerogative of practising Pagans, and there are a number of recorded instances where the Church has used them too. In many instances the motive is unknown but there are clear indications that monks lower down the pecking order sometimes had it in for the Abbot who was oppressing them, and some cases are shrouded in mystery.

One famous case involves Michelham Priory in Sussex where a Bellarmine Witch bottle was found in 1973 while workmen were installing a new drainage system. It was just under an inner wall and we know from records that this wall was built in 1667. It was found in an upright position and had been carefully interred in a mixture of clay, sand, and gravel to stabilise it over the coming years - again showing a fair degree of knowledge in the maker's positioning by burying them in a place that 'will never (theoretically) be disturbed'.

By tradition we must presume that this old law is applicable for the Witch's lifetime. Most of us will probably over the years we practice Witchery, bury about four bottles in our lifetime in different remote areas, usually National Trust land that we know will never be built on or ploughed. We have all learned over the years to bury our bottles deep though, just in case, for during the war many a national monument was ploughed to raise crops, and even the parks were turned into allotments.

The bottle referred to at Michelham was sealed, but over the centuries water had seeped in. Archaeologists carefully removed the contents and subjected them to careful, examination. Inside was an effigy and pins. Microscopic examination was unable to determine the sex of the effigy but is presumed to be male. Rusted remains of 14 pin heads, and 12 pin points were differentiated together with an amalgam of material described as 'of a green patina', later analysed as bearing quantities of cupric oxide, zinc, and lead, twisted brass wire and other matter.

There are other reports of the contents written at the time and frankly they are in contrast to the archaeological evidence.

Since I wrote *The Last Bastion* I have been privileged to read the original archaeological notes and I have recorded these accordingly. Newspaper reports at the time stated that the jar contained a wax heart pierced with pins and thorns, this would certainly not have been Witchcraft, but black magic; but true to form is typical of how a reporter will alter the facts just to create a more saleable story.

There are a number of genuine contradictions here outside of what was published, for the remains of an effigy was found inside the jar though I know of no recorded instance where an effigy or fith-fath has ever been be placed in a Witch bottle. The whole purpose of a Witch bottle is to throw off evil emanations all round and this can take the form of anything from a psychic attack upon you to a psychic barrier being put up as a deterrent against something as simple as slander; it is a general all-round protection and is not directed against any specific individual. In this instance the monk concerned clearly had a bend against a specific person presumably within the monastery itself.

Also there is no known ritual whereby an effigy can be placed in a Witch bottle as this would contradict the ancient Witch law of 'An ye harm none' Defence - yes - retaliate - yes, - but from the formation of a Witch bottle and the way it is made, as I will explain later the contents would waste away the victim as the effigy of the personage inside would be eroded or dissolved over the years, and as I have said, this would contradict the laws of the craft of the wise by magically harming someone.

You might argue that the forming of a Witch bottle is an aggressive act in itself and will harm, but the answer is no for it will only direct evil against an evil doer and ceases immediately their evil stops. Most Witch bottles today are used as a rebound apparatus against Black Magicians, Satanists and the like whose practices are anathema to us.

This monk's knowledge as we can see was limited but we must presume that if the fith-fath was to work and the monk had intended harm then essentially it had to include fragments of such things as hair or nail clippings from his intended victim. The bottle when examined failed to show any trace of these as they had long-since perished and turned to dust. He obviously had access to such material within the Priory and logically could not easily obtain them from the local Witch if he suspected her.

Can you imagine him knocking on the local wise woman's door and asking 'Please may I have a lock of your hair, and a few finger or toe nail cuttings as I believe you have been doing naughties upon me - oh and a drop of your blood - preferably menstrual would be useful too'?

Monks regularly shaved their heads into the traditional tonsure, so access would have been comparatively easy in obtaining hair from his intended victim, and other elements from his body could logically be obtained too, such as wiping the moisture from a goblet where his lips had touched to incorporate in the fith-fath, these were essential ingredients in a proper fith-fath. So who was this man of God who used a most elementary knowledge of Witchcraft to bewitch a fellow monk or even the Abbot himself, we will never know.

The official story given out is that the bottle was undoubtedly fabricated by the monk as protection from a local Witch, or a safeguard from someone directing sorcery against him, but this does not collate, for the very presence of an effigy within the bottle shows that he knew beyond any doubt who his intended victim was, and as this was in the 1600s then it would have been a simplistic matter to accuse the Witch or sorcerer with the obvious result - for there could not have been an acquittal; one word of suspicion and the Witch would have been seized, these were dangerous times for us.

Curious? Well if you want to see a Witch bottle that has been excavated, there is a fine specimen on exhibition at the famous Witchcraft Museum in Boscastle in Cornwall. (Seen overleaf) I wish there was a record kept of Bellarmine Witch Bottles being found as although they should be buried, there are many reports, mainly from builders who state they often find them when laying pipes etc in old buildings, particularly the hearth, but occasionally sealed behind lathe and wattle walls as well. One found beneath a hearth in Ifield was well over 24 inches down beneath floor level before the top of the jar was revealed. It was removed intact and remains so to this day, regretfully the contents were washed out after it had been found.

Well from Bellarmines let us go to Bibles and explore some of the hilarious misprints that have occurred over the years that caused such consternation within the Church, and have led to them becoming collector's items in this the 21st century. Let us turn the clock back to the very first one the so-called 'Wicked Bible' printed in 1631 by one Robert Barker the king's own personal printer who when setting the text for the seventh commandment omitted the word 'not' with the result that the Bible when published urged all and sundry to commit adultery. Alas poor Bob, his Majesty was not pleased and Mr Barker was fined £300, a fortune in those days.

Previously the printers of the Geneva Bible had received a sharp rap on the knuckles in 1562 when they said 'blessed are the place makers' - not peacemakers and in 1653 a Cambridge printer wrote somewhat what we had all long suspected to the effect that 'the unrighteous shall inherit the Kingdom of God' omitting the word 'not'; now that did make sense - how else could all my enemies be so successful?

Printing was quite a precarious profession particularly if you were printing the Bible as befell a printer in the reign of Good King Charles. His crime was to cost him the absolutely mega sum of £3000 for misprinting psalm 14 stating 'The fool hath said in his heart that there is a God' - Wow a real corker and

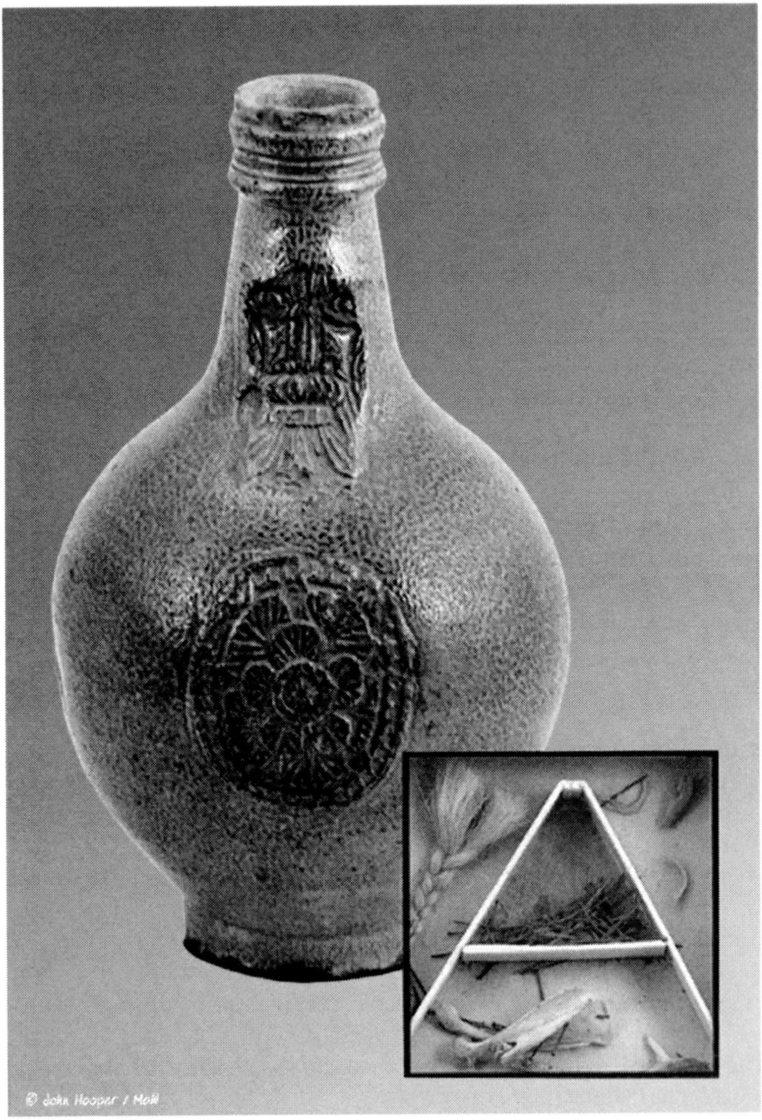
© John Hooper / Moli

Charlie was not amused at the omission of the word 'not'. 1716 saw the second Wicked Bible go into print when we were urged to 'sin on more' - a typographical error - the 'n' and the 'o' being reversed - and I thought my PA was the only one with ultra-quick fingers.

Do you think that this was the end of the matter? - No sir, for in 1804 a new print of the Bible read 'Thy son that cometh out of their lions' - instead of loins! - same fast fingers, but not quite so bad. The Murderer's Bible stated 'these are murderers' instead of 'murmerers' - quite a collector's piece today.

These of course are the accidental printings and are miniscule when compared to the deliberate erosion of a vast percentage of the bible, ranging from the excision of Lilith, Adam's first wife in Genesis, to the entire exclusion of close-on one third with the omission of the Apocrypha, not to mention the savaging it had under James the 1st.

The trend for centuries had been the denigration of womanhood under the Xtian yoke determined to impose a complete and utter patriarchal regime on all and sundry, and this was reflected under continuous revisions of 'the holy word' over the years. The wisest person in the known world was a woman, so the 1600 bible stated; a woman of such wisdom that Kings and Emperors did travel from far and wide to lay their crowns at her feet and seek her guidance, and it was written that she resided in the land of Endor and was known as the 'Wise Woman of Endor'.

When King James read this section he is alleged to have stated that if she was as wise as it was said then only Satan could have empowered a mere woman with such knowledge. In his revised version in 1611 she has become notorious and is recorded henceforth as 'The Witch of Endor' so in this instance instead of removing her he vilified her. This pattern is continuous throughout their sacred book. Only of late has challenge been made to it with the publication of such books as

Holy Blood and Holy Grail, *Bloodline of the Holy Grail*, *The Magdalena Legacy* and of course *The Da Vinci Code*.

Throw in the fact that much of the Bible was written from memory and hearsay evidence 400 years after the event, and it starts to become ludicrous when viewed in the light of modern analysis, and the prejudice of the hierarchy of the period at the time in its subjugating womanhood.

Witchcraft, Familiars, Brindle Cats 'n Hands of Glory

In my last book *The Last Bastion* I delt with Witchcraft practices over a span of 200 years from 1500-1700, cataloguing the trial and tribulations of our people who were so cruelly persecuted. I centred on Sussex and the South of England who fiercely resisted the imposing of a new religion that had landed on our shores, but who were eventually forced to succumb along with Devon, Cornwall, and the Isle of Wight, although stubborn, independent, Sussex was the last bastion to fall, and even then did not completely bend the knee, but beneath the surface remained Pagan.

With the great renaissance of Witchcraft in the 20th century following the repeal of the hated Witchcraft Act in 1951 it sprang to the fore once more as it faced a new and exciting future, and within its pages I explored many, many, avenues centred on old Witch ways, ancient lore and forgotten customs.

I embraced ancient customs that had survived, old cures that were the forerunners of today's modern medicines, near forgotten legends and folklore, right up to the 21st century - including modern phenomenon that had occurred whereby the Old Ones had shown us their power, and were pleased to have been awoken. So as we came into the last half of the 20th century it was no longer the twilight of the Gods, but the great awakening.

Within those pages I recorded many old ways and practices that are fading fast, particularly as since the year 2000 we have seen New Age Pagans rise in vast numbers whose roots are not established in the ancient ways we hold so dear, but seem hell-bent on sweeping away the old and on with the new. Regretfully the old ways are fading once more and must be recorded, and in my book *The Last Bastion* I did so.

Here within these pages I will continue to record old ways and old legends, try to separate fact as against fiction, and to explode many beliefs and Xtian fallacies about us that still persist today, and which have had such a devastating effect on our people over the centuries. I will tell of the Royal Order of the Garter that saved many, and how the Round Tower of Windsor was a Witches' circle once.

Some old ways are perpetuated in secret to this day such as the secret coin a member of parliament must carry if he is to succeed or to attain rank, and this self-same coin has crossed the boundaries and seas, and even ended up in more than one American senator's purse, but more of that later.

Legends, myths, old ways and ancient knowledge are contained here, but no secrets of the Craft are portrayed. Far too many have sold their souls to the God Mammon in the past, and broken the vow of secrecy that all Witches swear to abide by. What I want to record is a further history, of a bygone age that shows how the ancient customs are fast disappearing. At the same time, I hope to entertain you the reader with facts, albeit they be gory or gruesome, horrid or humorous, fact or fiction, they will be recorded as they were, and as it once happened. So tighten your seat belts as we take a journey to the far distant past!

In *Last Bastion* I explored the weird practises of the populace who actively sought particles of clothing and portions of the dead who had been hanged, and often gibbeted as well, some of these rotting corpses were condemned Witches, and if so, they said, then so much the better; for if the corpse was a Witch it made each artefact you stole from it, all the more powerful.

Those who reached the grisly, and often mutilated body first, scrambled to lift the hand of the dead man; these were usually barren women, who being childless, fought with each other to place the cold dead hand upon their womb in the belief that it would enable them to conceive. Men fought to lay the deceased's hand upon their own necks in the forlorn belief that it would cure goitre and scrofula, commonly known as the 'Kings Evil' now known to be tuberculosis of the lymph gland.

The only other cure was to get the King himself to lay his hands on your throat, or even touch you, not much chance I am afraid of getting even near his Royal Personage, let alone hoping that he would lay hands on one of the great unwashed. Most Kings and Queens shrank from touching anyone suffering with scrofula, yet there are cases of a small number of both Kings and Queens touching, and allegedly curing, the disease. Queen Anne is reputed to have cured in excess of 200 afflicted persons, and Charlie's are too numerous to record, but are listed as in their thousands. We have fairly accurate records of Edward the Confessor who must have had a scribe with him to record the king's good deeds, as he is recorded as having touched and cured 1,736 souls.

Well the chances of getting near a King were pretty remote and corpses were far more plentiful and easy to get to, nearly every crossroads or hilltop would be displaying the rotting corpse of some felon or malefactor, so why the rush, the cadaver was not going to go away was it? Well not exactly, but it did tend to disappear a bit at a time. You see nine times out of ten if you got there after dark you would find the hands especially were missing, cut off at the witching hour of midnight by a villager, especially on a bright full moon!

Had these been taken by some quack for their curative powers to make a small profit from a sufferer or a lady who could not conceive? The answer is no, they had been severed to be soaked in pitch or tar, have a wick placed upon the end of each finger and be made into the fabled 'Hand of Glory'.

The purpose? Either for their own illegal activities as burglars, or to be sold on to fellow housebreakers and the like. The 'raison d'etre' was that it was a widespread belief that if the hand of a hanged man so taken was carried on a burglary, then the inhabitants of the house would be magically entranced and would not wake to apprehend the intruder. Each finger, or rather the wick set into the tar on each finger had to be lit once the intruder was inside, and carried in the left hand if you were alone or by an accomplice if there was more than one of you. An old Hand of Glory was found behind the plastered walls of a public house in Hangleton in Sussex many years ago, together with a mummified rat, a glove, and an old shoe; they are exhibited there in a glass case to this day.

One housebreaker who stood upon the gallows cart awaiting execution named and shamed the malefactor who had sold him the hand. Prior to his being launched into oblivion he cried out that he had been sold the hand of an ordinary corpse, and that it was not the hand of a hanged man he had carried with him that night at all, otherwise he would not have been caught and be standing there on the hangman's cart that day. Apparently the owner of the house had awoken and together with his servants had caught the noisy intruder red-handed. What happened to the man who sold him the hand is not recorded. (Pity they did not have the Trades Description Act then!)

Some Hands of Glory were dried and leathered first and then magical and cabalistic designs were engraved on them, and tallow candles fixed to each finger afterwards. The populace, not Witches may I add, indulged in many unsavoury practices whereby they created talismans, not necessarily allied to the criminal classes. These were either to bring good luck to themselves or to avert bad luck, and avoid the theoretical baneful influence of Witches on them (we always get a bad press).

If your milk curdled, a cow dried up, a sheep died, or a crop failed, it was always laid at the poor Witch's doorstep, there is one case where caterpillars destroyed a field of cabbages - guess who got the blame for that? As you can appreciate, the scope for fetishes and talismans was vast as the villagers sought to avoid the 'evil eye'.

There was quite a ritual involved in creating one of these, and the prices of them when sold by one of the practitioners of the black arts (not Witches please note) varied somewhat. For example when the malefactors stole up to the gallows to take the hand they had to work fast in removing whatever bits of the body they wanted, or had orders for, or perhaps thought they could sell to fellow felons. But one of the best bits that fetched the best price was of course the culprit's hands, to be prepared as 'Glories' and sold on a thriving black market to the criminal underworld.

Right hands of the deceased fetched a far higher price than the left, as they were three times more powerful. Once taken, and the miscreants now safely ensconced back in their homes, then the awful business of preparing the hands commenced. When the hand was taken on a full moon they also had to remove part of the victims clothing that had absorbed part of his 'juices'. This in itself is interesting, as there is a widespread belief that at the moment of death or right afterwards the body will issue perspiration that contains elements of the very essence of the dying person as the soul departs. This, incidentally from a purely magical point of view is not so far-fetched as you might imagine, hence the cutting of a strip of clothing. A much-publicised depiction of this is of course the Turin Shroud, although this has since proved to be a medieval fake.

There is also evidence that the area where the 'juices' were most prevalent were the genitals, where you would expect to find the life force itself in the form of semen, for it is a matter of scientific fact that when a man is hanged and the spinal cord is snapped, he ejaculates in his last throes!, It is, as if in dying, the body makes one last vainglorious attempt to perpetrate the life-force.

Sometimes the hands would be taken after the relatives had removed the body after it had hung there, for the appropriate period, and they would then have to break into the relatives' home, this would be rare, as it is far more likely the corpse would have been passed over to one of the local women who specialised in the professional business of washing and laying out the body.

This practise of laying out the dead by a local woman continued right up to the 1970s to my knowledge and may well still be practised. I can recall as a child my own relatives sending for the 'washer of the dead' whenever there was a family bereavement, inasmuch the families would never dream of delivering the deceased to the local undertaker to prepare it for burial until it had been washed, cleaned, correctly laid out, and the eyes closed. Also there persisted the ritual of placing two old pennies on the eyes, presumably a leftover from the old practice of placing a coin in the deceased's hands to pay the ferryman when he took the deceased's soul across the fabled Styx to the netherworld.

One of the lowest crimes that could be committed in mediaeval times, was to steal the pennies from the eyes of a dead man, as this would swiftly inflame a mob if the thief was caught, and he or she would be strung up on the nearest tree without further ado. This crime has passed into modern parlance with the expression in describing a particularly obnoxious person as being so low that they would steal the pennies off a dead man's eyes.

If the hanged man's crime had been of a particularly cruel, or vicious nature then the courts would order his body to be gibbeted, a punishment for which I can find no record of ever having been passed upon a Witch, or a woman for that matter. This meant that the deceased once hung would never know a decent burial but that his body would be hung up enclosed in an iron basket-like frame, until it rotted away. It has been reported that even the most hardened of criminals wept, when prior to the day of their hanging they would be measured for their chains.

When a corpse had been so gibbeted it made the job of procuring the dead man's hands all the more precarious to achieve. Pirates for example, were hung much higher than ordinary criminals as a symbol and warning to all miscreants; also highwaymen and footpads would be gibbeted and exhibited on a high point such as a hilltop where they could be seen for miles - a powerful deterrent to would-be criminals

The notorious pirate Captain Kidd, they say, paled when told his lifeless corpse would be gibbeted, that was after it had been tied to a post in the sea, and left there until three tides had washed over it and the crabs had their treat. These gibbeted corpses would be regularly visited by scavengers, and provide a feast for both crow and magpie seeking the maggots, while the great unwashed and motley would gawk at the fearsome sight. Mothers would drag their mewling children to a gallows tree if they misbehaved and point out that the decaying corpse had started life as a naughty child! Whether these public exhibitions ever did deter them from a life of crime we will never know.

Anyway to revert to the Hand of Glory once more, from old records there are tales of the body having its hands removed while in the coffin awaiting interment, and of large strips of the burial shroud itself being removed at the same time. One must also consider the possibility that the washers of the dead may well have been part of this conspiracy, for to be able to mutilate the corpse for its parts would not present a problem, as they would have been aware of the movements of the dead person at all times,. Once the last of the relatives and friends had paid their respects to the departed then it would be her, or her and her husband who would nail the coffin lid down, so who would know if the corpse's hands were still there? They were the undertakers of the day and it was they who bound the cadaver in sheets, and ribboned the jaw; so even if the coffin was opened prior to the funeral, only the visage of the deceased would be seen, and the hands not missed. They would then be passed on to a known criminal who ran a thriving black market for Hands of Glory, and would pass them off as the genuine hands of a hanged man to professional housebreakers - small wonder that our miscreant cried out he had been swindled prior to meeting his death!

Let us assume that the perpetrators now have a pair of hands, then what next? Well there was a threefold preparation. First they would prepare an obnoxious concoction of a most foetid mixture of herbs, including asafoetida. Next, they dried the hand with the article of clothing or burial shroud taken, and placed the entire hand in a pot filled to the brim with this vile liquid, and there left it to marinate for the passing of a moon phase, or quarter to half quarter, usually agreed as being half a month, (records here once more vary) when it would then be dehydrated by desiccation in the sun or baked slowly in an oven. I gather the sun drying was the most favoured (not that I have ever made one may I add) then it should be wrapped in pure white linen together with vervain and fern leaves.

The next stage was to use some of the fat taken from the dead man, mix it with tallow and sesame and form a candle of it, this would be severed into five parts and a wick inserted into each part, and then each section affixed to each digit of the hand. Now the Hand of Glory was ready and could be sold to a burglar with impunity, enabling him to enter any house without fear of being detected - in theory that is!

The *Libellus de Naturae Arcanis* by Alberto Parvi Lucli that emerged in the 1500s went as far as to publish the formulae to create a Hand of Glory - even going so far as to instruct you to remove the hand of a hung felon while the corpse is still on the gallows tree. It instructs you 'wrap the criminal's hand in a scrap of funeral pall' as soon as it has been severed from the body. A strange reference then follows that I have not come across before whereby in tells you to squeeze the dead man's hand. Perhaps it was to shake hands with the dead for some inexplicable reason, but I would imagine it was an instruction to squeeze out all the last remaining remnants of blood prior to the embalming process.

It then gives a quite specific formula to mix together in a pot and to place the appendage into it, this being a mixture - quote - of Zimat(?) , Nitre, Long Peppers and Salt; and left there for half a moon phase. What was supposed to happen to it in the intervening period is unclear as the next instruction is to place it in strong sunlight on the 'dog days' these being July 3rd through to August 11th to dehydrate it. If the hand was cut off say in the winter as an example, then after the two weeks in the pot of salt and nitre etc then there would logically be some wait to begin the next process. All I know of these so-called 'dog days' is that they commence when Sirius known as the 'dog star' rises over this period and sets with the sun - presumably on the last day, so the evil hand has to be exposed to its rays then logically for 39 days- i.e. 3 x 13?

The ritual even goes so far as to allow for inclement weather during this period as it states that the hand may be baked slowly in an oven together with vervain and fern. The usual procedure is now followed as you next take some of the fat of the felon (Why did they not mention this at the time the miscreant was cutting his hand off?) and mix this putrefying lard with some sesame and peony. Next make this appalling mixture into five candles with pure beeswax fix it to each finger of the dead man's hand and off we can go a-burgling. Another French ritual instructs you to make a single candle and fix it inbetween the middle fingers of the deceased to form their equivalent of 'Un Main de Gloire' so obviously this evil custom was used on the continent as well as here.

The Italian Jesuit and demonologist Martin Antoine Del Rio speaks of all five fingers being lit in the *Disquistitonum Magicarum* published in 1599, the first recording of its being used is in the 1400s by Petrus Mamoris. A relic of the ritual accompanying it goes as follows:

Let those who rest more deeply sleep
Let those awake their vigils keep.
O' hands of Glory, cast thy light.
And guide us to our spoils tonight.

There are many cases where the intruder has been taken in the act of stealing having awoken the occupants of the house, yet rarely names the infamous Hand of Glory as being the cause of his downfall. Tending instead to blame his apprehension on the fact that the house owner had probably sought protection from his depredations by consulting the local Witch, who would have supplied the house owner with an unguent made of the fat from a white hen, the blood of an owl, and the gall bladder of a black cat etc., and instructed him to anoint all the entrances to the house with it, including the chimney, a sure-fire magic countering of a Hand of Glory's effectiveness.

You couldn't do better than consulting your local Witch in those days; Bat's blood beat a fossilised hand every time! A counter spell against a lit hand if the burglar was disturbed was to throw milk over it as this was supposed to be the only way it could be extinguished.

Robbing body parts from a gibbet was not confined to stealing the hands and parts of the clothing, No way, penises and scrotum of the deceased were also favourite targets to be dried and ground up to make aphrodisiacs. The taking of these was certainly quicker and easier. The taking of the head was also a nasty little habit, and once secreted away would be boiled and rendered fleshless. It was the top of the head, the cranium, that was the target, and this would be sawn off. This section would then be left in a pile of rotting and damp logs top upwards until moss grew on it, then it was ready to be used as a cure for wounds (note - NOT a Witchcraft cure!, we used honey and cheese mould - and it worked). I would imagine it was not an easy task to steal the head from a man hanging on the gallows, as he would be hanging by the neck and the sudden disappearance of the corpse on the skyline would draw attention, mind you the rest of the body would be there lying on the ground (probably with his trousers around his ankles).

The reason that gallows were a favourite target was that the cranium, had by tradition, to come from a man who had died a violent death, so a hanged man was perfect. Some old records state that it should come from a 'A mann slayne in Battel'. Well battles and skirmishes were two a penny in those days, so such a cadaver should have been much easier to obtain. Also they could be dug up from old battlefields a plenty, after all no one out there died of old age did they? I guess that any body found from someone who had parted this life from a blow from a battleaxe to the head was not a great deal of use, as the cranium had to be watertight as we shall see.

After the bone had accumulated a suitable amount of moss on top, you took the skull top and scraped the moss off, then mixed it inside the cranium, using it as a cup, together with newly dug up earthworms and red wine - some cocktail! This was then applied to the wound, scientifically moss certainly has therapeutic qualities, and the alcohol in red wine would act as an antiseptic, I am a little bit doubtful as to the earth-worms though as the earth could easily introduce tetanus. I wish there were more accurate records. For instance, were the worms being washed first? Many a cure involved earthworms in those days, and some old recipes do say that they should be washed in white wine first.

On a historical note once again, the Scandinavian toast of 'skoll' comes from the tops of skulls being turned into cups/goblets, and then filled with wine. At the great Viking banquets when the cry of 'skulls' was given, only those warriors who had killed and taken a head in battle, and made a goblet from it could stand, skull tops in hand, and drink. From the cry of 'skulls' the Nordic 'skoll' evolved.

One of the more unsavoury practises of this period was to bury a cat alive under the front doorstep of a new house to banish evil influences and deter burglars. These misguided people sincerely believed that it would bring them luck; although being a Witch and an animal lover I cannot conceive of a much greater evil than confining some poor feline to a narrow subterranean space to die of thirst and starvation, but it was a quite common custom both here, and in Europe. Cats were associated with Witches and occult forces, and the taking of this magical animal and keeping its body under the front door was considered a powerful talisman.

Cats and Witchcraft have always gone hand in hand, and no cartoon of a Witch would be complete without a black cat, together with a tall pointed hat and broomstick, again based on fact as I shall explain later. Over the centuries the Witch's cat, so often her familiar, has changed colour, and over the passage of time has come to be shown as an all black, or sable animal, this dark shade obviously to represent darkness and the powers of evil, yet the truth of the matter is quite different for the true Witch's cat is actually a brindle, a mixture of colours, not unlike a tabby but with more shades.

This mysterious animal, who was a creature of the night and could see in the dark, was held dear to all practitioners of the Art Magical, and would often be captivated by Witches and made into the 'Familiar' of legend. Old testimonies refer over and over again to Witches' familiars, and as a result absolutely any creature could stand accused of being a Witch's familiar. Old records have turned up numerous cases of hens and cockerels being put on trial, plus pigs and goats - an obvious target! There is also an account of a cow being hanged. Even a fly was once captured and condemned as having been seen trying to get to its master incarcerated in an underground cell. I would love to see if it there is a record of its confession.

Amongst the old records Artemis holds to this day, is a very powerful spell of enchantment whereby an animal, any animal may I add, can be bewitched to form an even stronger rapport with its owner. I myself, have raised a kestrel from an abandoned chick, and made her my own familiar very successfully; she became part of the household and was much loved.

I have occasionally found an injured bird brought to me that refuses to leave, even after being returned to the wild. These animals have unintentionally become humanised and regretfully become partly or fully dependent upon their benefactor. I note with interest that in this day and age there has been an intense scientific study to return animals back into the wild, as it has now been recognised as not being an easy task.

Once an animal has become so humanised then it is a perfect candidate to be ceremonially made a Witch's familiar. The bond between the Witch and the animal is strengthened further, but the Wiccan rule is that all efforts must be made to return the animal or bird to the wild. If the familiar is kept, then it can never be confined, the opportunity to go free must always be there.

It is however extremely rare for a bird to become fully dependent upon someone provided they are not confined; all of those I raised or treated were freed at the earliest opportunity, and would return only if they wanted to. With my falcon Ella, she roamed free and could even identify my car, even when I changed make, model, and colour, she would fly in the car window to go for a ride and perch on my shoulder looking out of the open window as we travelled, but Jenny, a foundling starling whose parents had been killed by a cat, roamed free and would fly in any open door or window of our house to be fed. All attempts to ignore her and force her to feed herself were of no avail. She would sit on the typewriter carriage as either my wife or myself were writing, and mew piteously as the carriage moved back and forth until you gave in, and took her into the garden. Once there, we would lift leaves and she would peer underneath as we did so and gobble up woodlice, which she adored. We used to stand her by another leaf and leave her there, but she would mew continuously until we returned and lifted it for her again. We even used to scratch the dead leaves with her little feet to encourage her, which turned out to be just a big game to her; she would fly where she wanted all day long and only return for food. On one occasion my wife Audrey was shopping in the town centre when Jenny suddenly landed on her shoulder and cried for food, to the amusement of passers by. Audrey was forced to go to the local park and feed her, Jenny never ever learned.

One day she never came again, and we never knew her fate. We can only hope she found a mate and that at long last the call of the wild drew her back to her roots, Jenny incidentally, was not a Witch's familiar: but we also had another completely wild starling who would come whenever we called her, she was always in earshot. If you love animals, as all Witches do, and you have the patience, you can tame any animal. All you have to do is gain their trust so that they identify you as part of their kingdom.

To this day my neighbours are intrigued to see the local Witches, to wit myself, and my wife Audrey, continually visited by a succession of animals and birds. Squirrels come in the house and sit on the desk as I am working, and also completely accept Petra my PA as part of the scene - provided she has food may I add! Robins sit on my shoes as I am digging, awaiting a juicy worm to appear, and a pair of doves seem to regard me as their daddy. People would stare as we left the house to walk to the car followed by not only the two wild doves, but also later on their offspring as well, who would follow us in crocodile fashion. We currently have an entire flock of starlings, known as The Mob, and a Seagull who knocks on the door with his beak, nicknamed Percy the Pelican.

Nothing enrages followers of the Old Religion more than spurious tales of Witches and animal sacrifice spread by evil rumour mongers. Animal sacrifice is perpetrated by Satanists and the like, plus followers of Voodoo, it has no place within the

Wicca. Locally, we have a rabid animal lover, so-called, who every time a moggie goes missing in the neighbourhood (usually to return within a week) she screams from the house-tops and to the local press that it has been taken by the local Witches. Regretfully it is difficult to control such fanatics, but fortun-ately the local press and police know her as an eccentric, and she is largely ignored, she has cried wolf too many times thank goodness to be taken seriously, but to anyone who will listen she will exude pure vitriol and lies that have more in common with the works of Dennis Wheatley than fact.

How anybody could harm one of the Gods' creatures such as a cat beggars belief, and all Witches deeply resent the spurious tales of animal sacrifice so wrongly and falsely attributed to them. No Witch would harm an animal as they love all things in nature, and incidentally, for good measure, this is one of the oaths they have to swear at their initiation.

As it is not my intention, as you know, to print any of the internal secrets of the Craft of the Wise in this book I can tell you no more except that the love of animals and 'All things in Nature that have been created by the Gods' is a solemn oath that is sworn during the ceremony (I believe income tax inspectors are not included though). Joking aside, in fact a leading Income Tax inspector I know is also a leading Witch within my coven, and practises the Craft in his everyday life, he is sympathetic and kind. We also have a high-ranking RSPCA inspector in our midst who originally met us during an investigation. We helped him track down the culprit he was seeking, and he eventually became one of us, a very stable ally in combating the false and erroneous stories so often attributed to us.

Cruelty to animals was prevalent in the Middle Ages, and it was said on the Continent that the suffering of animals was of no consequence, as they had no souls. We have even had to combat this in more primitive countries with the argument that whether they have souls or not, may be debatable, but they do have feelings. One of our coven has been avidly involved in the saving of donkeys in particular, in the Middle East, and another of cats in Sicily; and although I would not normally use a book to promote a particular cause I will break my rule and ask any animal lover or reader to help a most wonderful charity called the Brook Trust, that provides treatment and succour for animals in the Middle East in particular, where veterinary surgeons are thin on the ground. You will find details of this animal charity at the end of the book. Many of the dumb victims they have saved have been subject to terrible injuries, these range from a donkey who had its eye poked out with a sharp stick by its irate owner when it was unable to cope with an extra heavy load, to another one that had its ears cut off by yobs for 'fun'. Terrible reading, for which I do not apologise. The Brook Trust also helps to educate these people in animal welfare.

At the time of the persecutions when so many of our people were burnt at the stake it was also a common practice to hunt down the Witch's cat, or any stray cat for that matter and burn it alive in a basket. The crowds seemed to draw more entertainment from a cat burning than a human, as the animal's hideous screams were heard. This, it was said, was the Devil trying to escape, but as the basket had been sprinkled with holy water beforehand, the Devil in the form of a cat, within the basket was trapped.

Logic does not seem to have entered the equation, for if you have destroyed Satan so completely, then why continue to torture the animal? It was sadism pure and simple. The reason is that by the medieval definition of the Devil, they are in fact referring to a devil or imp. i.e. an emissary of the Infernal One, These devilish little creatures were said to be numerous, and a witch's house may well harbour a number of them. In the *Last Bastion* I detailed the trial of two witches who 'after being 'put to the question (a sanitised way of saying tortured) confessed to having nine animal familiars and imps by the names of Ilemauzar, Pyewacket, Pocke in the Crowne, Griezzwel

Greedigutt, Jarmara, Vinegar Tom, (who had a cow's head), and an evil pair known as Sacke and Sugar, plus another called Newes.

By a strange anomaly of the Church at the time it was quite in order for school children to attend a Witch burning, or a cat burning. One belief prevalent at the time was the Witches' ability to turn themselves into a black cat at will, but at Hallowmas it was said all Witches would turn themselves onto black cats in order to sneak to the great Sabbat surreptitiously, (Strange people - don't they know that we always use broomsticks and fly by night?) The result was that on October the 31st any black pussy in sight would be caught and at midnight tossed into the bonfire, they all knew that its screams were the Witch trying to escape, while a cat burning in a basket was said to be the Devil screaming - and any old moggie would do for this. This ritual was in order that they could see evil punished, and the Devil dispersed, Canon law however expressly forbade them to attend a racetrack or see any form of gambling. Their Xtian priests were all heart.

We referred earlier to a popular belief on the continent that animals did not possess souls, which in fact invites discussion. I do not know if there are supposed to be animals in the Xtian heaven, or in the Wiccan Summerlands, and if my fellow Witches care to summon me on the Sabbat of Hallowmas when I have passed over, I will return for that night and let you know.

In trying to establish the truth of this conundrum I have used my investigations into paranormal sightings and hauntings that I have personally experienced over a 50 years plus span of time and the results are extremely interesting; leading me to conclude that undoubtedly there is a soul force in animals, but it seems to be allied to the intelligence of the animal concerned. For instance, sightings of ghostly apparitions and wraiths of dogs and cats abound and have been substantiated time and oft.

I personally have seen the shades of both dog and cats on numerous occasions so therefore have no doubt on this issue whatsoever. There are also numerous sightings of horses, but never of cows to my knowledge. Equally, as we go down the scale of animal intelligence, not size please note, we increasingly find the absence of phenomena as we reach the lower levels of intelligence. There have never been substantiated reports of creatures such as mice and lizards, snakes or shrews, guinea pigs or rabbits having appeared as wraiths after death to my knowledge, leading me to the conclusion that a soul force as such is associated with the degree of intelligence in the animal concerned, and not instinct.

We cannot claim that insects, slugs and snails are intelligent, nor creatures of instinct either, nor can we with creatures such as sparrows and starlings for example, clever yes, intelligent? Well to a degree. Having said that let us examine still higher intelligences in the bird world such as the owl, whose wraiths have often been seen throughout history.

When my own familiar, my falcon Ella, died at the grand old age of nine I embalmed her in the Egyptian style and buried her deep in the earth in the centre of the sacred circle where we worship and conduct our rituals in secret. Shortly afterwards, a pure white kestrel appeared on the scene and has frequented the coven site ever since. Coincidence? I think not, for I have never in my entire life, ever, seen an albino kestrel. Whenever we arrive there strangely this white kestrel appears, and perching on a nearby tree watches our activities late into the night, then as we pack up to leave, it flies away into the depths of the wood.

Dogs and cats on the other hand are creatures of extreme intelligence, and therefore there is every reason to conclude that their soul force may well survive death, and maybe even be reunited with their owners. Again, out of academic interest I have heard of the phantoms of other creatures being seen, such as a phantom elephant, said to roam spectrally on the plains of

Africa, but do not have substantiated information to verify the absolute authenticity of this. Again, if we use the intelligence theorem then the elephant phenomena becomes highly likely to be a true rendition.

There are also reports of primates being seen long after they have passed this world and against these criteria of animal intelligence that I have used, we must essentially consider emotion as well, i.e. whereby one creature is able to show affection or their own form of love to another of the species, such as the great bond between elephants. I would be very interested.

Goddess Birds - Robins and Wrens - and Ladybirds Too

Lady Lanners. Tommilidens an 'ole Jenny
Or Ladybirds, Robins an' Wrens as we know them.

The lore of the Witch is the lore of the Goddess, and she like the God is personified in all things in Nature, she is identified with trees such as the Silver Birch, known as the moon tree, The Lady of the Moon tree, or by more common usage, The Silver Lady, silver being the element of Magic used in the craft, and held dear by its practitioners.

As She is to the Moon, so the Sun is to the God, as is personified in the famous words of the Witches' Rune as they recite their ancient history enshrined in its words at Sabbats.

"The Golden Sun King of the Morning.
"The Silver moon Queen of the Night,
"Enlighten our Destiny's doorway,
"Made up of the dark and the light.

And to quote another profound verse from it

The Dark and the light in succession
The opposites each unto each
Show forth as a God and a Goddess,
Of this did our ancestors teach.

Trees, rocks, animals, they have all been associated over the years with the Gods. North American Indians identified the forces of nature with the animals of the forest and prairie, and created totems in their image. In the wilds of Africa the indigenous population followed these self-same practises that respond to some subliminal call, that made even primitive man aware of hidden forces around him, and with which he swiftly associated a divine element.

Even as the centuries passed this base instinct did not diminish but rose as an awareness of the occult permeated all aspects of peoples' lives, usually inspiring them with a sense of awe of these all-powerful energy sources just waiting to be tapped, but sometimes with fear of the unknown and the unseen. It was the latter, at the instigation of the Church that led to the persecutions that still rankle today. Stone circles, and circular groves were created by those who recognised specific power points, usually where major ley lines crossed, and it was these that became the focus of their worship.

Again what is not generally known is that even insects were worshipped, and identified with the Gods, and by strange coincidence in some instances even influenced the economy, as I shall explain shortly. While the North American native identified for instance with the mighty eagle, his British counterpart identified with the simple robin, and even here what started out as a straightforward worship of this bird, became contaminated when the Church once more lambasted it from the pulpit and relegated it to become the spawn of the Devil and a creature of fear as well.

The result was a complete contrast where in one part of the country the robin would be venerated, and in another, usually the towns where the Church held sway, the local population would reverently cross themselves when they saw it, much like people do today when they see a magpie. Once more with this highly intelligent bird, it depended upon one's background and indoctrination as to how it was regarded, and the attitudes of yesteryear have passed down over the centuries into a bastardised form whose origins have been long forgotten. Its distinctive colours of black and white, were regarded as epitomising night and day, the dark and the light, and latterly the powers of both good and evil, which when you look back you realise as to how it came to be regarded as a bird of ill omen, albeit obscure and nonsensical. This image of this lovely bird was not helped by the fact that it was an inveterate scavenger, and could be seen hovering around execution sites, and gallows trees. When you consider that its colours represent both good and bad (in theory) and are equally balanced as is darkness and light in nature, as well as the seasons of the year, only then does the true significance of the magpie evolve

It was against this background that the modern-day greetings to the magpie originated. The country folk of old greeted this old scavenger of carrion with affection referring to a pair as 'your Lord and Ladyship, God and Goddess' while others referred to them as 'Mr and Mrs Magpie'. The former was a greeting to this bird that was a respected symbol of the Old Gods, while the latter. was an acknowledgement of the evil forces thought to be contained within the bird and was greeted almost fearfully by many who hoped that by acknowledging it whenever it appeared that the bird would pass them by as they had shown it respect.

Many gamekeepers will not shoot a magpie. An old friend of mine was Commander Abrams who was Captain of HMS Magpie, a British warship during the war, he was a keen sportsman and shot with the Burghfield gun club, but when game shooting he would never shoot a magpie even if it was robbing pheasant eggs, but simply wave his hat at it to shoo it away.

It is amazing how over the years symbols of good become symbols of evil without any help from the Xtian church who have practised reversing all the benign pagan practises and depicting them as malign, but in this instance the magpie has evolved, probably as a result of its being seen on battlefields and gorging itself on all things dead -as a 'bird of ill omen'

I myself was taught to greet a magpie with the rejoinder of 'good morning your Lordship' - strangely enough a single bird was always presumed to be male, while a pair would be greeted joyfully as a good luck sign and be greeted as 'your Lord and Ladyship'. By contrast those Xtians who feared the magpie would cross themselves in the traditional genuflect but still greet it by calling out 'good morning Mr Magpie', or 'good morning Mr and Mrs Magpie'; if it was a pair or a group, one was bad luck and had to be averted, two was good luck, but if there was a small flock, usually the parents with their young, then they would acknowledge and swiftly look away, not daring to count, for seven meant a Witch was around. This attitude was reflected in the 16th century with the following rhyme that was used as a guide to country folk who saw them in numbers such as the following.

"One be for sorrow, but two be for mirth, three be a wedding, but four be a birth. Five be a christening, six a death, sevens Heaven, eight be Hell, and nines the Devil his old sel'

Another version that was also common was.

One for sorrow, two for mirth, three for a wedding, four for a birth, five for rich, but six for poor,--but sevens for a Witch, I can tell you no more.

As we approached the 20th century, and the latter part of the nineteenth the following came into its own.

"One for sorrow, two for joy, three for a girl, but four for a boy, five for silver, six for gold, seven for a secret never to be told, for eight make a wish, but with nine you must kiss, and ten is a bird that you should not miss.

You will observe that various numbers evolve over the years as a degree of logic overcomes superstition, six for example becomes downgraded from death to just simply poor, and then becomes a luck sign with the symbolism of gold and good fortune. Eight which in fact is the sign of the Goddess in numerology (888) is hell in the 16th century alongside 666, but 888 is a lucky wish now! While seven, regarded as a luck sign is the sign of a Witch a hundred years later, and in the 20th century becomes a great secret, this surely cannot be a coincidence, for if we examine the evidence on the 17th century version the words are clearly ambiguous, for the number seven, that says it is for a Witch, concluded with "I can tell you no more" it is not fearful. surely it is representative of the hidden secrets of the Craft.

But let us turn next to the robin that much-loved and most revered of British birds, that ornaments so many Xmas cards and has come to represent the season of goodwill, but was it always that way? Many legends have grown up around it over the centuries and since the advent of Xtianity in particular. In fact the robin has been recorded in British folklore since time immemorial. The robin is prolific throughout Europe and also the USA, but it was in Scandinavia in particular that many legends grew up around it.

In Norse mythology it is a major player in the death of Baldur, the Norse Sun God, who it is said was killed by a single sprig of mistletoe. In fact it is believed that the well-known nursery rhyme *Who Killed Cock Robin?*, is in reality the expounding of the slaying of Baldur; and it is more than probable that this refers to the myth of robins always covering the face of a corpse, and in many versions of Baldur's death, it is said that a robin covered up the Sun God's face. This legend of a robin covering the face of a corpse is engrained in British folklore, but with the passing of the years has all but faded. Legend has it that if a robin discovers a body it will gather up moss and cover the face of the corpse with it. It is also widely reported in history that they have been known to cover the entire body, (with not one single truly recorded instance incidentally). Having said that there is an old manuscript, still in existence, where it is said on good authority that a robin had been observed placing morsels of moss on the open staring eyes of a dead man, and in another manuscript we find the robin referred to as the 'Sexton Bird'.

Another legend that goes back to prehistory, states that if a robin discovers a body, it will mount the corpse and sing to draw attention to it, and it will remain with it until such time as it is discovered and buried. When we analyse this behaviour which may well be based on fact, it is far more likely that the decaying body provided a good food source with its attracting myriads of insects, and later of course, an interminable supply of maggots.

No one quite seems to know how this delightful creature ever came to be called 'Cock Robin, for years ago our little redbreast was called 'Tommiliden' or 'Bob' robin, or even just Bobbie.

The old version of the *Babes in the Wood* fairy story depicts the two babes as being dead and the robin has - or is, covering them with leaves in this instance. An old rhyme of this event reads:

"No burial this pretty pair"

"From any man receives"

"Till Tommilide piously" - (another version reads""Till Robin Redbreast piously")

"Doth cover them with leaves"

'Bob' Robin has many more superstitions associated with him but the constant theme throughout revolved around luck at the time, bordering on the misfortunes that would befall both man and beast should either of them harm one, even accidentally. There is a story of a robin nesting in an old jug in a farmyard that was moved by the farmer who needed the space, it was said that he blamed his subsequent crop failure to this event, and he directly attributed his subsequent misfortune to this deed.

The robin has a reputation as a bird without fear of man, who will ferociously defend his territory against all comers (other robins). In mediaeval literature they speak of its valour and of how the robin would hop in-between the legs of gardeners as they dug, snatching worms and grubs as the workman's spade or fork exposed them. I myself have personally experienced this while digging and have even had a robin sit on the blade of the spade as I dug, peering down continuously in its search for food, then fearlessly snatching a worm beneath the very spade itself as I dug. If you are prepared to be patient you can tame a robin quite easily with food and it will soon accept earthworms from the hand. It is a bird that implicitly trusts humans as there is some inexplicable link between us and it. Human nature is both base and cruel but it is rare to find an instance of a human harming one. Whether this be from the inherent love we find for the robin or the superstition that still prevails, that death or injury will befall all who harm the bird is debatable, this same superstition incidentally also applies to the wren. An old rhyme runs as follows.

"He that hurt either robin or wren.

Will never prosper - boy or man."

Another version exists in the plural and goes as follows

"He that hurts either robin or wren"

Will never prosper- boys or men."

The raison d'etre was simple, if you harmed one of these birds you would fall into the hands of the Devil, or the local Witch coven would get you. The punishment would be like on like, if you broke a robin's wing you would suffer a broken arm, if you broke a wren's leg, then you would break yours too, kill one and you would die, or be blighted for the rest of your miserable life.

Another old adage says quite specifically "Thy cows shall give forth bloody milk, thy barn will burn down, and the thatch on thy house will catch fire, thy hands will develop the trembles and thou wilt shake so that thou canst work not." Strangely enough this curse was also directed against any cat that slew a robin, it is fact, and it has been shown, that cats will hesitate before attacking a robin upon sight of its scarlet breast, and equally robins upon seeing a cat stalking them will turn and display its breast provocatively as if challenging them. Nine times out of ten this gives the robin time to escape. It has also been recorded that there are many instances of cats being seen to turn away. I once saw a sparrowhawk swoop on a robin only to break his 'stoop' at the last moment as the robin turned and his red breast became visible.

The curse of bloody milk we now know was mastitis in cows, but the curse of the barn or house burning down is undoubtedly vested in the tradition of how the robin got its red or scarlet breast. Fire plays a significant role here, for it is said that the robin brought fire to Guernsey where it was unknown, by carrying a smouldering ember in his beak. Xtianity was quick to embrace the robin into its own theology to counter the reverence in which the robin was held by Pagans, hoping to attract more converts. This replacement theology was quite successful here as the robin became entwined with the Xtian Xmas message and was widely portrayed on cards etc. It is at this point that many written documents on the robin were wilfully destroyed becoming lost for ever.

For every legend lost; the Xtians created a new one, and knowing the reverence amongst country folk for this bird they corrected them and expounded the origins of this bird as being 'blessed by God' they explained that the robin got its breast scorched as it flew through Hell to try and alleviate the suffering of the poor damned souls there. Apparently it tried to carry a beak full of water to them, but found its breast feathers blazing. Another version says it was a jenny wren that carried the water into purgatory but caught light, and the robin's breast was scorched saving it.

Xtians however, in adopting the robin into their own culture under the doctrine of replacement theology, strangely enough also feared it. We all know how our sacred sites were requisitioned by the ecclesiastical authorities, and where the Pagans gathered and met for the great Sabbats, the Xtians built their cathedrals and churches on this Pagan ground to deny the populace access to them. Even going so far as to inter the Pagan altars into the church foundations, or beneath the flagstones in the North, was the most favoured method.

Looking back as to how in those early days the newly built churches were divided into two sections, the North side being for the indigenous population who could continue to worship the Goddess of the region there, and the Eastern portals for the 'new religion' that had invaded the land. We know that the two sides lived in reasonable harmony for a long time, until the Church, finding itself the stronger, evicted their rivals and took over the whole building, now referring to the section where the Goddess of England was once worshipped as the 'Lady Chapel', and placing a figurine of the virgin Mary there where once a statue or depiction of the Goddess had stood.

Suddenly in history we find that the robin becomes feared by the Church and that a robin flying into one of them was a sign of impending disaster. Even worse was to follow, it is said, should the robin alight on the Xtian altar, and an even greater disaster is on its way should this Pagan bird start to sing! Legend? Well let us see, for I will recount a local incident, well recorded here. The scene is Hurstpierpoint College in Sussex. It was here that a robin flew in during a service and alighted on the high altar whereupon it started to sing most joyously. Immediately both the Priest and the entire congregation fell silent, for in Sussex the superstition is rife, For interminable minutes the robin sang merrily then abruptly stopped, At that precise moment the passing bell of a nearby church started to toll for a local boy who had died. As the first peal rang out, the bird exited; but the pastor declined to continue and, clearly unnerved, brought the service to a close.

Robins are a contradiction in folklore for many of the so-called 'bad luck' superstitions were only believed in and observed for eleven months of the year. To give you an example of this, should a robin fly into your house, then as with a church this was a sigil of impending disaster or even death, but if it flew in during November (The traditional month of death, and the death moon) then it was considered a most lucky omen and one that was a harbinger of prosperity and good fortune. Strange old world is it not?

The King of the Birds in folklore is in fact the wren, alongside the robin, and the swallow, and all three birds are very sacred in Witchdom, and outwardly in country lore as well, but this king of birds has suffered the most horrendous persecution right up to modern times. How strange that a sacred bird, loved, venerated, and worshipped has been hunted for its magical properties. Witches can never understand how people can possibly think that they can receive benevolence or receive luck from a creature they have cruelly murdered? Do they really imagine that some poor little creature such as the wren, will bestow a blessing on them for hideously killing it?

Pagans for hundreds of years have deplored these stupid superstitions that have arisen over the centuries by church going folk. These can range from the slaying of the wren for luck to the killing of the simple rabbit - then cutting off the feet as lucky charms, Do they really think that having a so-called lucky rabbit's foot in your pocket or purse is an asset - remember the dead rabbit had four of them and clearly 'it' was not lucky!

I could write volumes on the hunting of the sacred wren, and its being tortured, but it is so disturbing it would sicken your hearts with the details; all I will do is outline a few examples, some of which still exist. Hunting the wren on the Winter solstice is still perpetrated in Ireland and the Isle of Man.

A ceremony called 'Deckan' o' the wren' used to take place in Galloway in Scotland, and is the only place in Scotland where this comparatively benevolent ritual took place. On New Year's Day gangs of boys sought out wrens and captured them. The wren on this occasion is not hurt, but multicoloured streamers are tied to its neck and legs, and then it is freed. A sharp contrast to the Scottish custom of spilling a wren's blood to ensure luck on New Year's Day, then afterwards any small bird would be killed together with any other creatures that crossed the gangs' paths.

In the Isle of Man whoever killed the King of Birds on a saint's day, by custom St Stephen's Day was honoured as a leader and would proudly perambulate around the town with the dead wren on a pole garlanded with ribbons. In fact this garlanding of the wren seems to have been a common barbaric mediaeval practice. The wren would be accompanied by two boys with blacked faces carrying a bunch of leeks like a tail behind them. Part of this evil ritual was the plucking of the bird and the distribution of its feathers for luck. Then the plucked corpse would be buried in the churchyard. The feathers were sold to sailors as luck charms. I am happy to report that this practice in the Isle of Man is now outlawed.

This parading of the corpse seems to have been a universal practise, sometimes the live bird would be carried through the village in a cage before being killed. An old song of the period says in the melody that it must be killed with 'sticks and stones, to break its bones' and another says that it must be slain with cannons. This came in during the 1600s. Another song tells how the little bird must be chopped up with hatchets and boiled in a brass pan.

At Epiphany in France, whoever killed a wren on New Year's Eve could attend the Bishop as he conducted High Mass, and the culprit would walk before the Bishop and the church and local dignitaries carrying the dead bird on a beribboned pole. Again this fortunately has now been suppressed.

Witches adore and worship all animals and the slaughter of a little bird like the wren and to use it in Xtian ritual is anathema to all Pagans, and I am happy to say most Xtians as well. I would say that it is high time the Catholic Church in Ireland spoke out against the gangs of boys who still beat the hedgerows in the infamous wren hunts there at present, but the reason it is tolerated goes far deeper, for legend says when Jesus hid in the Garden of Gethsemane it was the wren that betrayed where he hid, by calling trilling, and attracting the attention of the searchers.

This is also why the bird is hunted by churchgoers and killed on St Stephen's day, for again legend says that St Stephen was escaping from where he was incarcerated and had almost succeeded in escaping, when a wren alerted the guard by flapping its wings in his face. They have needed much less to find reason to hunt us.

It is part of a bloody past where cruelty was afforded to all: from the barbarous torture of our people, to so-called 'sports' like cock fighting and bear and bull baiting. In Horsham in Sussex in the market square the old ring where bears were tied down is still visible. It was where miscreants from all over Sussex were taken for public execution and rejoiced in the name of Hangtown.

Well, from birds such as the robin and the wren, to the insects, yes, a sacred insect that was identified with the Goddess of the Witches. Undoubtedly that will surprise you, but the humble ladybird was once called the Lady Lanner, and was symbolic of the Goddess. Not only that, but when the dreaded doctrine of replacement theology was invoked, the Church of course immediately identified it with the Virgin Mary! Honestly, is nothing sacred?

I am writing these anecdotes into this book for they are an essential part of Wiccan history. To study the background of the witchcraft of yesteryear then you have to study everything of yesteryear, one cannot cherrypick for just the salient points and ancient rituals that are so dear to the student of our ways.

The ladybird is an essential part of our heritage for strangely enough, as I referred to earlier, it also had a strong influence on the economy; but more on that later. Once more like our friend the robin it was considered unlucky to kill or harm one. In perusing old documents you would more be likely to find her referred to as the Lady Lanner, as against Ladybird, and in old Scottish writings there are many references to them under this heading where they were used in love spells by Scottish and Northern Witch covens. Part of the ritual (please note, part only) was to gently procure a Ladybird and place it in the palm of the hand, telling our lady that you wished to evoke a divination of love.

Now apparently at this point it is essential that you treat the Goddess ladybird with great respect, and must remember that you are huge and she is very, very tiny and your voice would be like thunder to her, so it essential for you to whisper, in an extremely low voice the following .

"Lady, Lady, Lanners-
"Lady. Lady. Lanners.
"Take up thy Clouk about your head.
"'An flee awa' to Flanners.
"Flee ower River, flee ower Sea.
"Flee ye east, or flee ye west.
"Flee to him that loves me best.

This ritual to our Lady was particular to Scotland and the accentuation is obvious from the words. Apparently in Kincardineshire the ritual was exactly the same but at the end it culminated in the ladybird being lifted up in the palm of one's hand and raised to the petitioner's lips and very gently blown into the air with the following words added, the sex of the Goddess ladybird now becoming masculine, and it is now representing the God force. Suddenly the Goddess Lanner becomes the God Gollow, for the invocation now continues as follows, but this time it is sung merrily.

"King, King Gollow
"Up your wings and fly awa'
"Over land and over sea
"Tell me where my love can be.

Then followed the cry that we all know from our childhood, for as the ladybird becomes airborne the invocation continues:

"Ladybird, Ladybird, fly away home.
"Your house is on fire
"And your children all gone"

Another version ends

"And your children at home."

I have studied ancient Gods and Goddess's and the names by which they have become known in different areas, but have never traced the origins as to how the Goddess became known as Lanner, and the God Gollow. The usage of these names is certainly particular to Scotland, and to Kincardineshire. If any reader can enlighten me as to their origin I would be much obliged. Certainly names of insects evolved independently from region to region as did local superstitions.

In Northumberland there is a quite different species of Ladybird indigenous to one area that was once marshland and it is known there as a 'Reed Lodger' now in this area it is – or should I say was, used to influence the weather. The ladybird would be lifted up on one's hand and blown into the air as was customary, but this time the invocation was.

"Reed Lodger, fly away and make the moma sunny doy."

I have found ancient interpretations that show that doy is quite clearly day, so the chant here is for a sunny day, but the exact translation of moma is unknown to me, again if anyone from Northumberland knows, I would be pleased to hear

In finishing the lore of the ladybird in this chapter, I will just add a few more legends:

In the West Country our beautifully marked little insect, which just for the record feeds upon aphids, as do its larvae, is called Bishop Barnaby. There is once more an old rhyme used by young girls to foretell their wedding, We know that a girl had to catch the very first ladybird she saw - she was not allowed to select one, as the number of spots on its carapace was indicative to the number of months the girl would have to wait before she would be married.

As we all know the ladybirds' spots can vary from two to nine, the most common being the seven spot ladybird. Lucky the girl who found to her joy that she had captured a two spot insect. Proudly she could tell her fiancée that she had adhered to the old ritual to the letter (now regretfully lost) and that it was the will of the Gods that she should be married two months hence. (This ritual does seem to lend itself to a little cheating here, but surely ladies, be honest; you wouldn't cheat - would you?

I have just mentioned that the full ritual seems to have died out, but I have found the original words. What I do not know is how the ladybird was ritually launched into the air as apparently you multiplied the spots on it by the number of times you had to blow - each one growing in intensity until it decided to take off - again how easy to cheat" You can imagine a bride-to-be saying to her beloved "I only blew once dearest - ever so gently and dear Bishop Barnaby took of at once, would eight weeks from now be convenient sweetheart?"(Only joking!) The words recited are as follows.

"Bishop, Bishop, Barnabee
"Tell me when my wedding will be
"If it be tomorrow day
"Then take your wings and fly away

It was considered to be a lucky sign if a ladybird alighted upon you, if it did you could not disturb it and it must be allowed to fly off of its own accord. Another thing that was indicative on a ladybird was the deepness of the red of its carapace, as it was considered that the deeper the hue, the greater in intensity would be the degree of luck coming to you, and again the number of spots on it would indicate how long you would have to wait for your good fortune.

In Dorset, farmers used the ladybirds' spots to forecast the coming price of wheat - each spot counting as a shilling a bushel, a practice that had a profound effect on the economy. If the price was high then many would buy up all stocks to make a profit, perhaps there was a black market for seven spot ladybirds. I think we may take it for granted that two spot insects were welcomed by the populace, but were not exactly popular with the farmers.

In Somerset we find a most unusual naming of the Ladybird where it is referred to as 'God Almighty's Cow' - and a strong superstition to it locally to the effect that this holy insect must never be harmed - in Somerset it was revered.

It is amazing as we traverse the country to find how many legends are attached to this humble creature, and the various names by which it has become known. Up in Newcastle it is captured and then set free to the chant of:

Ladybird, Ladybird, fly away home
Thy house is on fire
And thy children all roam
Except little Nan who sits in her pan
Wearing gold laces as fast as she can.

Some old documents are difficult to decipher and I am inclined to believe that this should read 'Weaving gold laces as fast as she can'. Intriguing! Well finally sportsmen and women consider it lucky if a ladybird settles on you before a race or match - it means you will win.

Strangely enough, one bird that was revered by Xtians was the bee eater, for the plain and simple reason that it ate bees - and bees were evil! Well I always knew they could sting you but in all my years I never have been stung by a single one and most certainly evil they are not. In the eyes of the Church though, they are harbingers of evil, servants of Satan, and emissaries of the infernal one. The old documents on these hard-working, honey producing insects would run to volumes, and just how this association with the black arts came about I do not know; maybe if we delve into history we will, probably find that some clergyman got stung on the lip by a bee while extolling some anti-Goddess, or anti-Pagan vitriol during a hellfire sermon.

Well let's be honest, could you think of more conclusive evidence that this was a premeditated attack on a man of the cloth. When he had retired to the sacristy to place a blue bag on his nose (an old cure for bee stings, it was a small bag of an alkaline with a blue die, hence its name) it probably dawned upon him that old Horny was behind the attack, and a legend was born - well it's as good a theory as any I reckon, but it is a fact that bees were regarded as insects of ill omen.

One thing that intrigues me and that nobody, not even apiarists can answer is" Can or do bumblebees sting? Whenever they have flown into the house and are found buzzing angrily in the window I have never hesitated to gently enclose them in my hand (buzzing and protesting all the time) and then free them back into the garden. My father handled them as did his father 'afore him, and they were never stung. Nor have I been stung; and neither have I ever heard of anyone ever being stung by a bumblebee, so the question dear reader is, do you know, or can you answer what naturalists and beekeepers cannot, and that is - do bumblebees sting? You can e-mail me at the address at the end of this book. My own conclusion is that in all probability - yes they can, but don't. I have never been tempted to tease one to find out.

Witches see beauty in everything in nature, from the adulation of the robin, to the worship of the ladybird, and naturally what is probably one of the most wondrous creations of the Gods, an insect of scintillating hues has of course not escaped their attention. One of the beauties of this particular creature is the fact that absolutely nothing adverse has ever been associated with it to my knowledge. I am, of course, referring to the butterfly which is always associated in ancient yore with good luck. The lucky omens that have followed its sightings vary from the numbers seen together, to the actual colour of the butterfly itself - and even the season. Country folk smile if they see three revolving around each other, as it is a sign of benevolent fecundity for a good harvest, being two agile males laying courtship to a female, it is also the sign of a good day. The first one you see in summer is also of significance and has great meaning too. If it is a white one then the omen is that you will eat white bread that year, white bread being traditionally the prerogative of the prosperous and wealthy. Should you see a brown one, such as a fritillary, it is not a bad sign, on the contrary, rather it shows it will still be a reasonable year but you will have to work hard. Nevertheless brown bread will be your staple diet, which is coarser bread. This old superstition is what has led to the expression 'It will be a brown bread year' i.e. you will have to work hard in the coming months. All sightings of butterflies are considered lucky but the brighter the butterfly, the brighter your luck.

Even moths have not escaped superstitions surrounding them, and, like the butterfly, they have a good press. If one persists in flying around you it is said to symbolise a personal letter, nothing new in that nowadays, but turn the clock back over a hundred years or so ago and a letter was quite an event. Oh, and a large moth meant a large letter. It is strange how these creatures of the night have always been associated with messages for people. Witches were alleged to receive messages from them, and Witch covens sent messages to each other via moths, which is undoubtedly where the modern-day myth originated; for instance if one flies around your lamp it was said in Victorian times that you would receive a post card from far away, if it flew around twice it was a letter, and three times was a parcel. Of such things, based on old Witches fables, are legends made.

Bees however are a completely different picture, for they have always been associated with the occult and are linked to countless old beliefs outside of the Church's horror of them. One could write endlessly upon the many tales associated with them, but probably the most predominant of them that span international borders worldwide is that of the apiarists themselves who keep their hives.

No apiarist (bee-keeper) would dream of not going from hive to hive and telling the bees of major family events. Superstition says the bees must be informed, for if you neglect to keep them updated they will leave you. This is particularly important for all births, engagements, and forthcoming weddings within the family, the bees have to know what is happening; but most importantly of all they must be the very first to be informed of a death. After hundreds of years this custom has persisted right down to the present day. My grandfather kept bees and within minutes of his last breath my grandmother went down to the hives to tell the bees of his sad passing, they were always the first to know.

It is considered extremely lucky to find a swarm of bees, and unlucky if they should desert you for no reason (maybe it was something you said, or forgot to say!) If a bee should fly into your house it is a lucky sign, but only if you leave it to fly out of its own accord. I have heard it said that they were Witches' familiars seeking their mistress, and if you were sensible you would leave them alone lest they got the idea you were evicting them, no way would you upset a Witch's familiar. If it should settle on your hand it was a sign that money was forthcoming, and if on your head then greatness would be bestowed upon you. If you were a mother and the bee circumambulated your new-born baby deosil, and provided it was asleep, then it was heralding a happy and prosperous life for the infant.

One old name that our honey-making friend was called was Melissa, which is Greek for honey bee, and the bee has been linked over the aeons with Lemon Balm which has had the same properties linked with it as the fabled royal jelly of the bees. Which in turn was one of the ingredients of the wondrous 'elixir of youth' another name for Lemon Balm (*Melissa Officinalis*) is Bee Balm, and this once more has the same healing propensities as honey. Old-fashioned lemonade was made from Bee Balm, and although it is not 'Craft' I feel this old recipe should be recorded. I have incidentally brought the measurements and wording up to date.

First you will need four large fresh lemons, 5oz (150grams) of granulated sugar, 2 pints (1.1 litres) of cold water.

Peel the lemons then place the lemons whole in a glass container or jug - i.e. with the rind added. Add the sugar, and then pour sufficient boiling water to dissolve it. Next add the lemon balm leaves, stir and leave to cool, when cool squeeze all the juice from the lemon pieces and ad to the syrupy mixture-pour in the cold water and cool. Finally, remove all the debris of the balm, Strain the mixture add some fresh sprigs and the ice cubes. If the lemonade is to stand for any length of time, then remove the lemon peel. Add more sugar or lemon juice to your individual taste.

One could write endlessly on Witchcraft legends and lore associated with all manner of creatures and plants but they are far too numerous to go into one book so I shall finish on a mammal, to wit the horse, so sacred to the Celts and the Goddess Epona.

Epona - The Cult of the Sacred Horse

Many are the legends associated with the horse, and as the years pass the old legends that were associated with them, like so much ancient lore, is fading from memory. The horse; a majestic animal once worshipped and, to many, worth their weight in gold. A prize stallion could be a worth king's ransom. "O' If wishes were horses" so an old saying goes, for wishes are a form of magic and mind power can make them come true, and the horse of course was a magical animal.

One Goddess is uppermost in our minds when we think of the horse, and that of course is the Horse Goddess herself - Epona - worshipped and revered by the Celts. No one in those days would harm a horse, for to do so would inflame her anger, and formidable would be her wrath if this most noble creature of hers was harmed.

The mighty God Odin rode the Heavens on a dappled grey, and to see or meet a dapple grey when travelling was a harbinger of luck that day, and was also considered to be a sign of portending prosperity. This sighting of 'dappling' was not confined to horses alone, for I remember as a child my father beaming when we went for country walks when he had just seen a Dalmatian dog, he went home on a high; and in the school playgrounds youngsters would speak of having seen a 'spotted dick' the name by which the Dalmatian was fondly known. The 'brindling' on a cat, the true Witches' cat being a brindle and not black, was considered a lucky sign if roundel patterns could be seen in the fur.

We of the Order of Artemis are aware that our own deity was also closely associated with the ever-sacred horse. It is a fact that everything associated with the horse is lucky, and of course its horseshoes are much revered being one of the sacred symbols of the Craft.

There has, by the way, been much debate as to which way up a horseshoe should be hung and I can clarify this as being in the upward position whereby the points are skyward. If you should find one in the road while travelling it is a lucky sign, and in a short period of time, traditionally considered to be seven days, then bountiful luck would follow. The ritual was that they would be nailed up with two alongside each other and one in the centre above on the next full moon

Witches used them as a cure, and would nail them in the two down and one up position above the sickbed of the afflicted as shown:

U
UU

Despite this being 100% Pagan and its association with Witchcraft, the clergy eagerly absorbed this ritual into the Church, and like the Witches before them would visit the sick and nail three horseshoes in the identical pattern above the bed, but with the following words.

"Father, Son, and Holy Ghost"
"Nail the Devil to this Post"
"Thrice I strike with the Holy Crook"
"With this 'Mell', I thrice do knock"
"One for God - and one for Wod, and one for Lok.

It is interesting to note that they still used the Pagan entities in the ritual, probably because they knew the people had great faith in them, but wishing to take a percentage of the acclaim they simply added the Xtian God to this ritual. I have studied old records here and it is clear that they are invoking Woden and Loki, but as the years passed it would appear that the 'one for Lok' came to mean 'and one for luck' while the Mell referred to it seems was the bishops crosier or holy crook as one might think, and also were not Xtian; but referred to the Hammer of Thor, the Yggdrasil, a mighty emblem of old in the form of a tree that was alleged to connect both Heaven and Hell by its roots and branches.

Otherwise the ritual was identical, with one exception, the priest charged money for it, while the Witch or village wise woman was happy to accept half a dozen eggs or a small loaf. In the 19th, 20th and 21st century the horseshoe became a favourite to be immortalised in horse brasses, and the old triple horseshoe was prevalent under the Victorians with farmers who incorporated one at least onto every dray or carthorse, together with a highly-polished crescent moon, associated with the Goddess Diana.

No, the Old Ways had never died out and could still be seen in everyday life and items such as horse brasses. This refusal to bend the knee to the ecclesiastical authorities was depicted everywhere, whether it be on the drayman's horse and cart, or the God Cernunnos skillfully worked in by the masons among the cherubs and gargoyles on a church in the form of the Green Man. The Old Religion, particularly amongst country folk was there, all you had to do was scratch the surface.

Jingling alongside it there would be a heart-shaped brass that was sewn in to the leather as a protection to the owner. The Unicorn was a pure white horse that displayed the horn of power on its forehead, and we see the legendary Pegasus as a pure white horse who could fly, so outside of the lucky dappling referred to, the white horse runs a close parallel alongside it. Technically, before some practising equestrian writes in and chastises me, there is no such thing as a white horse, (but there is in legend!) for the presence of one single dark hair deems the animal to be a 'grey', but for the sake of this book we will refer to these as white for the old tales do refer to them as white.

To give an example of this, in Devon 'white stockings' on a horse is a good luck sign and a white leg even better. At horse sales in Devon if a horse came under the hammer that had patches of white on its legs, or better still if it had white socks (White hair from the hooves up) it would be eagerly sought after by the bidders, who wished to take the luck home with them.

On another note which I know that all animal lovers will want to hear, there is an old superstition of Romanies, and that is they will not put down a horse with white socks. This superstition should be spread at the iniquitous horse sales of the Dartmoor and New Forest ponies that take place annually where so many healthy animals are purchased by unscrupulous dealers for either export to the French abattoirs as a delicacy, or, if old, slaughtered to be processed as dog food. So get your paint brushes out girls and paint 'em white in the night.

If you see a white horse ask its blessing and make a wish, the same applies to the dapple, and to a piebald. The piebald is the Witches' horse that is a panacea for the curing of ills, the old village wise one would take the sufferer of whooping cough to one or bring the horse to the sufferer's door and there breathe in the air exuded from its lungs, and why not? I have never known a halitosis horse!

Sacred white horses abound on hillsides throughout the hills of Britain and many have been ploughed over or desecrated by zealous Xtians who are hell-bent on destroying all traces of the old ways. Recently some of our people had to maintain vigilance at the Rollright stones and the Merry Maidens stone circle after Xtian evangelists vowed to destroy them one night.

We have already seen many monuments desecrated such as Avebury where paint has been poured over the stones, irreparably damaging them and destroying rare lichens and mosses in the process. There would be an outcry if we were to start chipping bits of the church door would there not? But have no fear Xtians; we are conservationists and not vandals.

For luck or fertility stand in the eye of a depiction or carving of a white horse on a hillside, and there repeat the old words "If wishes were horses" then make your wish. If you want to conceive, make love in the eye of the horse at midnight (when none shall see you) and at the supreme moment of conception name the sex of the child you seek to conceive. This ritual is still performed to this day on the full moon by child-seeking couples, if not on the white horse's eye, then in the groin of The Long Man of Wilmington or the Cernunnos Giant.

Magic 'n Magicians - Sigils and Signs

In Witchcraft there are three sigils that are associated with the Witch which have persisted over the centuries, and they are the cabalistic Celtic (even sided) cross, the pentacle or five pointed star, and the 'U'. Or 'horseshoe-shaped icon. We will analyse these in detail, then revert to the Pentagram that is in usage today.

Firstly the cross was not a Xtian symbol but a Pagan one, and this persisted despite being usurped by the Xtian church right through to the present day. Once Xtianity came on the rise the legend of crucifixions being enacted on a cross came to the fore (whereas, as we will show in another chapter, it was performed on a stake) the Celtic or Pagan cross was the perfect icon for the spread of the gospels, simply apply the rules of replacement theology and keep the symbol but lengthen the base to form a crucifix.

The further you delve into the past and examine ancient religions you will find the Celtic or even-sided cross occurring time and again throughout numerous religions, invariably being a symbol of the moon. The Xtians had other reasons for usurping the cross as their emblem as well as the obvious and that was the fact that both Sun and Moon played a major role in the Old Religion that they were attempting to extinguish. The moon being the female and thus Goddess faction threatened the slowly growing Xtian faith the most and therefore became a primary target. So they emphasised the cross in their teachings knowing that it would be symbolised to the Pagans as a symbol of their Goddess and the Moon.

The subterfuge went even further for the holy day of the Goddess was a Friday. (Freya's day) and the son of the God they were promulgating died on a Friday - and is subsequently resurrected on a Monday (Moon's day) - subtle! But this was not the end for they now went back into an old Scandinavian legend that was told to children, and therefore was known to them just as we were told fairy tales, (although there is a possibility that this ceremony could be based on fact, but if it did ever occur then it has most certainly died out.) This was of course the legend of the Moon ceremony where a man, a volunteer may I add, agrees to be a ritual sacrifice a year hence.

His reward is that he has a wow of a time the preceding year that makes it all worthwhile; just imagine a year of utter debauchery, with wine, women, and song. No girl will refuse you, and at the end when you do get topped, you enter into a wonderful Nirvana for close on twenty years or so until you are reborn into a far better life, plus your head will be a topic of conversation for ever as it ornaments the Chief's palace. Anybody who was anybody always got their head on a stake, especially their enemies, an absolutely charming old Celtic custom. Now that is what I call fame!

This seems just too good to be true, so what was the catch, and more importantly did they tell the poor devil beforehand? All he would probably know is that a year hence he buys it representing the Sun God, on a Friday (Freya's day) and the jolly old moon comes along and resurrects him on the Monday (Moonday). If he is wise then he should tank up on mead, and whatever spirits were distilled at the time, plus a really good intake of magic mushrooms or whatever. So when the great day eventually comes he has to represent a menstruating woman and fertilise the land with his blood, but how? The answer was quite simple really you simply cut his testes off and give a quick slash upwards of the knife in between where they used to be; in fact you really had to remove the entire unit down below so to speak.

I suppose this was the very earliest sex change in history, even if it was of comparatively short duration. (Have we progressed much since I ask you?) Well, I doubt he knew much about it when his testicles were passed around and everybody had a little nibble in the belief that their own sexual performances would be enhanced, plus the luck that would surely follow. Old records fail to mention if they were roasted or not, and if he was allowed a sample!

What is the purpose of this story in this book? Well the whole legend became entwined in Xtian gospels some 300 years after the event, which is when the descendants of those who had been present at the crucifixion decided to write them down, the details having been passed down by word of mouth in the 300 year period inbetween, and by now were fragmented as to what happened. Matthew, Mark, Luke, and John, were dust by then. (I find it strange that the other nine did not contribute to the Gospels, but it is commonly believed that their own reports were out of step with what the established Church wanted and so they were excluded, it was one of the first forms of censorship). Moon worship was still prevalent at the time, the Pagans were still dominant, and the Old Gods continued to be worshipped and revered.

Now, with a master stroke, the Catholic Church absorbed the whole story into their own culture, and Holy Communion (Eucharist) was the result. Their God dies, and three days later returns to life. In the original Pagan story the Sun dies and is resurrected by the Moon three days later. Throw in a little bit of ceremony and you have the same ritualised cannibalism when they symbolically drink the wine which is supposedly turned into blood at that moment, and eat the bread in the form of a wafer that is transformed into the flesh of their saviour. Well, I am no Xtian, but methinks the reconstituted story has got the edge when you think about it, and our illustrious ancestors took the dash of plonk and a biscuit rather than a nibble on someone's gonads and a somewhat sanguine drink.

All you have to do now is set the happening by the moon and call it Easter, then for good measure make sure it becomes known that it is also set in the period of the Goddess of fertility, Eostre, from which the word Easter is derived and you have absorbed the original story lock, stock, and barrel into Xtianity and proclaimed it as original. There is one factor here that seems to have scant records, and that is how the present story shows the resurrection taking place on a Sunday, as against the original Moonday. I have been unable to trace this transformation period or find when it first appeared. Presumably it was well after the new religion had firm roots that the 'third' day became the Sunday.

In analysing this we know from old records, and these are set in stone so to speak, that the crucifixion took place on a Friday, for the following day was the Sabbath and that the holy period started at sunset on the Friday. And three days afterwards the resurrection is said to have taken place - a Monday! This ties in with the concept of the moon and resurrection of the Sun under replacement theology, then an undetermined period of time later, probably at least three hundred years or more this becomes 'and on the third day' making it a Sunday, which henceforth becomes the Sabbath. Well this is all connected with the Moon symbol of the cross, but let us proceed to the pentacle.

With the pentacle they attempted to show it as a star, and once more associate it with various factors of their religion such as the three wise men following it etc, but only with a limited degree of success. For the Pentacle, which they referred to as the 'Goblins' Cross' was never absorbed, and remained the main symbol of Wicca right up to the present day having survived the persecutions. The main reason for this is its association predominately with the Goddess herself; the five points, known as the five paths of wisdom, were also the body of the Goddess in the Star Goddess position, with the head dominating the top, the two arms to the side representing the arms of the Goddess, and the legs apart being the base of the pentacle.

The third sign was the 'U' or horseshoe shape which was never absorbed by the Xtians in any form whatsoever, and which came to be known as a Witches' luck sign personified in legend with the lucky horseshoe. One of the main reasons behind this was the worship of the horse itself as a symbol of the Goddess Epona, the horse Goddess, and this in turn became eternally enshrined with the magical unicorn.

Many are the legends associated with the horse, and there are many instances of them being enchanted and becoming Witches' familiars. History abounds with stories of Witches having absolute control over horses by the use of words of power, and secret scents. The famous horse whisperers knew these arts, and they are still used today. I knew one who could subdue the most ferocious stallion in minutes and have seen it follow him like a dog, nuzzling him as he walked.

Old George Pickingill, that great master of magic to whom so many covens turned in those early years, as the Guru of Gurus, was an adept and delighted in showing off his powers to any who crossed him. There are tales of him stopping tradesmen's horses and carts after a dispute with him, and he refusing to utter the magic words to make them go until they had apologised to him. Old George was a master of what we call silent magic; he did not even have to say anything, he could just glance at the animal and it would move, or simply make a hand gesture. This is the silent magic to which I refer, a system of magic that can be imparted to the focus of your intent by thought and mind power alone. An art that can be inherited without the gifted one often even knowing at first that they 'had the power, and had been born with it'.

These people are natural Witches and many have never been initiated into covens and received the stringent training that every neophyte and acolyte receives. But if and when they do, then these become masters and mistresses of the secret art and can reach the exalted rank of ipsissimus (I will go through these grades and explain them at the end of this chapter), normally only acquired by ritual magicians who have gone through the ranks. Silent magic is a highly potent force and has to be controlled. It is this 'gift', if you call it such, that has lead to the superstition of the evil eye, regretfully something that factually exists, but please remember and digest that this has nothing to do with the actual practice of Witchcraft.

I feel at this point I should clarify exactly what this is, and strangely enough you, the reader may be able to identify with it, and realise the hidden power that is enshrined within you, and the formidable power of the mind you can exert, albeit unknowingly such as the evil eye so widely feared, and also make things happen, or bluntly, wishes come true, for this is 'silent magic' and one must consider that a few trials may have been based on the fact that someone within a community could unknowingly blight someone. Witches are trained in magic, i.e. a latent power, pure and simple, that can only be used for good.

I will here quote part of the creed of the Witches that is emphasised in their initiation. "That I will suffer no creature to be harmed, either in our mind, or in our will." And a further part that they recite - "To love all things in Nature". As you will see this runs in tandem with the ongoing oath of "Eight words the Wiccan oath fulfil, an' ye harm none do what ye will" The whole basis of Witchcraft is the control of power, a latent power that the Witch uses to help and to heal, but like all power it can be used for evil as well, which is why Witches make it so difficult - or should - for anyone to join their ranks.

Each candidate for initiation is examined for a year and a day by the elders as to his or her suitability to be brought in to the coven, and to make sure that if, and when, they do become Witches they do not abuse or misuse the power. It is not generally known to those outside of the Craft that for a minimum of a year after initiation (following on the year they awaited admittance while they were examined) they are denied any real Power until they achieve the exaltation of the 2nd degree. Then and only then is the 'power' transmitted, and the power supreme is given at the 3rd degree. Once more this power will depend upon whether the 3rd is given whereby the initiate becomes a 'true Witch' or a 'Witch in true' this expression will only be recognised by the fully initiated, but regretfully nowadays few Witches become a 'Witch in true'.

Artemis is different to most covens inasmuch as we are not averse to incorporating a degree of ritual magic into our ceremonies, particularly when a great deal of power needs to be generated for instance in the case of the afflicted being seriously ill. If we should attempt this then the magic circle has to be doubly sealed, not only by the normal casting, but also by sprinkling salt copiously around it as well. Then the defence ritual would be used to exclude all malign influences and a very heavy ritual would ensue to give absolute protection. This would entail raising the Ruler of Tempest in the East, The Lord of Lightning in the South, The Ruler of the Deep in the West, and the Dark Ruler of Mountains in the North.

These are but a few of the titles that are afforded to these mighty entities whose powers are legendary. I decline for obvious reasons to give this ritual out in full within these pages, nor the opening identities associated with them as they could be read by anyone, but if any healing coven should seek this knowledge, and can prove their credentials as bona fide worshippers of the Old Ways then I am prepared to impart this esoteric knowledge to them. The same ritual can be used as a defence against psychic attack which contrary to popular belief, is as rare as snow in the Sahara, and normally only exists in the realms of fiction.

In all my years I have only known two truly Satanic groups who for reasons unbeknown have decided to conduct a little 'muscle flexing; and as good always conquers evil, they end up with the short stick every time. Out of interest to the readers who are often bewildered by magic the grades are as follows. I will give these out with the degree order first, followed by the Sephiroth, then the all important grade of Magical ability, next the associated Scandinavian God or Goddess, and finally the Egyptian God or Goddess for those who use Isian rituals incorporated into their Magic.

Magical grades

10° to 1°.	Kether -	Ipissimus -	Wotan	Ptah
9° to 2°.	Chockmah	Magus -	Odin	Tahuti
8° to 3°	Binah	Magister Templi	Frigga	Shu
7° to 4°	Chesed	Adeptus Exemptus	Wotan	Maat
6° to 5°	Geburah	Adeptus Major	Thor	Horus
5° to 6°	Tiphareth	Adeptus Minor	Ra	Osiris
4° to 7°	Netzach	Philosophus	Freya	Hathor
3° to 8°	Hod	Practicus	Odin or Loki	Anubis
2° to 9°	Yesod	Theorecticus		Isis
1° to 10°	Malkuth	Zelator		Seb, or Nephthys

The lower grades of Theorecticus and Zelator have no distinct Scandinavian Gods or Goddess's associated with them that can normally be used in ritual. (Note. The highest obtainable grade is that of Ipissimus and is rare - Aleister Crowley was reputed to have reached this grade but failed to use it for good thereby precipitating his own down-fall.)

These grades of ritual magic are quite separate from Wiccan invocation, and are related in progress to the Cabbalistic Tree of Life. The main difference is that with Witchcraft it is the intent behind the ritual that is all-important. Should the High Priest or Priestess make a mistake in the ritual whether by a wrongfully placed word, or gesture, then it is not of the uttermost importance, the Gods will understand, all that is necessary is that the intention behind the ritual is made absolutely clear from the start.

For example. "I Selene, High Priestess and *****, have summoned the coven here on this full moon to invoke ******, to aid us in a healing ritual for Mary Jane *** who has cancer, etc etc, (these are not the exact words that a coven would use but gives an indication of the style, and how a ritual would start, so it is perfectly clear to the powers that are being raised what the purpose is, for the summoning of the deities that the coven is calling upon - hence if she should stumble in any way, the Gods or Goddesses in spirit form know why they are there. Wicca is a really beautiful religion that works in harmony with Nature and the spirit world, with a great and awesome respect, but devoid of fear.

The world of the ritual magician however is a whole new ball game, for he must be occultist, mathematician, and possessed of an infallible memory as well. It is rare for a high-grade magician to resort to reading from a parchment or book, for he dare not risk losing concentration for even a second, but must keep his mind focussed on the geometrically prepared area where he will invoke a spirit to obey his bidding. His circle must be geometrically perfect, as must all aspects of the Cabbalistic drawings within it. While the Witch has the power to create an instant circle with a sweep of her arm if needs be, what we call 'casting at switch'.

Do not, dear reader even dream of taking up the path of the ritual magician unless you are young and possess the qualities mentioned, and achieve the supreme accolade of your profession only when you are mature or even old. It is a lonely path. Before anyone takes this up and inundates me with e-mails screaming why am I using the idiom of 'he' in the role of ritual magician, it is because ritual magicians have always by tradition been male, and all the great ritual magicians in history have nearly all been men. Equally so, the most powerful Witches time and time again are female, such as the all-powerful Wise Woman of Endor, who the Xtians delegated to become known as the Witch of Endor. Notwithstanding this I see absolutely no reason why either sex should not take up the traditional role of the opposite sex. In fact Witches for example are both men and women although women essentially predominate, but most covens in this day and age tend to try to achieve a balance of both sexes within the group.

Having said that I still state that the role of the ritual magician is predominately masculine, but I do know of one exceptional lady who is a practising magician, and a highly successful one too. The 'raison d'etre is quite clear and I must admit is an unfair one bestowed upon womanhood by nature, but the fertility cycle of a woman is a factor that could be against her whereby a man does not have this problem and therefore is able to adapt into the role of Witch or magician whereas a lady can be handicapped.

You can imagine the difficulty a female magician could face if attempting to use a particular moon or astrological phase only to find her cycle of paying her tribute to the moon was against her or too close for comfort to the required date. When it comes to study then the easier path is Wicca, and by the simple harnessing of the forces of nature you can achieve marvellous and outstanding results, I have trodden the path of the magician and do use it occasionally but unless you are prepared to spend years of study then leave it to the zealots.

For example the Witch has only three grades to achieve, the ritual magician has ten. The Witch if he or she is able could reach the 3rd degree of magic in as little as three to four years, while the Ritual Magician will look to well in excess of twenty years or even more. He will start off at the lowest grade of Zelator having already progressed from the lower realms of acolyte and neophyte, where his training would have been most vigorous before he even started up the rung of the ladder of mystery. In the Cabbalistic tree he is now on the bottom rung in the sphere of Malkuth, probably under the surveillance of the Egyptian deities of Seb, or Nephthys. His power would be limited to one degree to the power of ten.

The next stage if he succeeds in mastering this degree, is the grading of Theorecticus, and in the cabbalistic tree he is now off the bottom rung and on his way, having now achieved the realm of Yesod, He would be limited to Egyptian deities most likely, and be overseen by the Goddess Isis in all her forms. His power would now have risen to two degrees to the power of nine.

Now he would have to face his first major task, for he would now be entering into the realm of Hod in the Sephira, and have to face the first of most daunting tasks as the theoretical training would now be behind him as he laboured to be a Practicus and must tread warily. His mentor's eyes would now be fixed upon him looking for the slightest mistake that could endanger him.

Now he has come under a different pantheon of God and Goddess forms as he struggles under the watchers in the forms of Odin, Loki, and Anubis, it is at this point that most fail, but if he succeeds he will now have the degree of three to the power of eight. Although this is a major step it is still virtually the beginning of supreme knowledge, for he has simply proved that he can conquer the meticulous formulae required to practise the supreme art. It is his first major hurdle to overcome, and the path has been a hard one, but now he has achieved practical magic.

Compare this to the Witch who would be at his or her 2nd degree after a year's waiting and becoming acquainted with the rudiments of the Craft, and who would now have been in the coven watching and learning and now eligible for their second. There within the circle of magic the High Priest or Priestess, would be placing instrument after instrument in their hand and commanding them to use them while the whole coven watched. Here there is no supreme loneliness, for there would be at least twelve to help and advise one who would shortly achieve the power and join them on their way to being part of a supreme healing coven.

So our Practicus will now look forward to achieving the rank of Philosophus. He can even teach the lower grades such as neophytes or acolytes the first rudiments of ritual magic for he has mastered them. He will seek to achieve a higher degree now and raise his ability to four degrees to the power of seven, and climb the Tree of Life into the realm of Netzack. Within this realm he will be embraced by the Goddesses Freya and Hathor. There will be no male entity to help him in mastering this degree. He is on his way.

All being well he should find the next stage an enlightenment as it is one of supreme beauty, there are ever harder tasks ahead, but I regard the realm of Tiphareth which he is now in, as a more gentle learning curve at this stage. The Gods will be kind to him for having come this far, and will help him achieve a degree of five to the power of six as he be progresses towards his goal.

His next achievements must essentially be to proceed from an Adeptus Minor to an Adeptus Major and acquire a mastery of magic to the degree of six to the power of five. He is now into the heavier stuff, but there is a rocky path ahead. He has reached half way up the ladder and will be wearied; most decide to rest their laurels at this point. Why go further when the going is so hard, for they have entered the realm of Geburah and have mastered it with the help of Thor and Horus - most powerful entities? I have found that few progress beyond this point, for a degree of this status and of now being an Adeptus Major, is an achievement in itself, and few want to face even more years ahead of such an intense study.

A few stalwarts will take the next step and enter into the realm of Chesed as they seek to become even higher in the Cabbalistic Tree of life, and go for the accolade of seven degrees to the power of four, if they can do this and become an Adeptus Exemptus then they can go to the very top. Wotan and Maat now become their Scandinavian and Egyptian Gods - but can they reach the eighth rung and become a Magister?

I do not refer here to a Magus but a rank of Magister Templi for this is governed in the great Sephira by Binah, Here within this lofty realm is the possibility to hold a degree of eight to the power of three, and know that both Shu and Frigga have shadowed your faltering footsteps this far. Here you will learn the power of sex magic and how to control it. There are now only two hurdles to the top but rare is the one who does not fall down now but rests on their laurels.

Chokmah! - One from the top, but the chances of ever acquiring the final tenth grade is low indeed, In over fifty years I have only found three, and for the record they all were Jewish. But here we reach the rank of Magus, a true master of the occult, and where the Gods Odin and Tahuti reach out to you a welcoming hand. One to go in the Sephiroth for you now have nine degrees to the power of two, you are a MAGUS.

The final stage is the hardest of all, for as I have said I know of only three who have ever reached this most lofty realm. This, if reached, is the Accolade Supreme for the Magician has absolute power and has entered into the realm of being an Ipsissimus, the most powerful rank to be known and enshrined in the novels of authors such as Dennis Wheatley, who love to empower the Ipsissimus in their novels as being able to kill with a glance or thought. Well this is more than just a little bit exaggerated, but this is the very highest degree and is ten to the power of one.

He will now have reached the Godhead within the realm of Kether and have been welcomed under the auspices of Wotan and Ptah. It is the most exalted rank. There seems to be something in the Hebrew background that lends itself to the full mastering of Kabbala (Cabbala) and on a point of interest I have never known anyone who did not have Jewish blood in their veins to become an Ipsissimus.

At this stage only, many years beforehand the witch would have received the third degree, but like the master Jewish magicians, only the most able ever achieve this within a coven. Regretfully some covens award this degree prematurely before the Witch has truly proved his or her mastery of both magic and ritual.

It is sometimes tempting to become a 'Witch in true' to achieve the power as against a 'true Witch', High Priests and High Priestesses of this rank will understand. It is a moral dilemma that must be analysed thoroughly by the parties involved.

Ancient Law and More, With Brothels, Bawds and Besoms!

One of the strange anomalies of English Law is that absolutely anything you want to do is legal provided there is no law specifically against it, this has been used as a successful plea many a time and oft including Witchcraft.

One famous precedent in the burning days was the trial of one Jane Wellman who stood accused of Witchcraft, and was sent for trial at Gloucester. But when the trial commenced the only evidence of her sorcery were witnesses who each swore they had seen her fly, a sure sign of the Witch. There seems to have been great confusion in the legal arguments proffered as to whether poor Jane had flown 'under her own steam' so to speak, or whether she had used a broomstick. After hearing the evidence the judge, a most learned man by the name of Justice Powell decided that regardless of HOW she flew, the whole case rested upon whether she flew by any means, or what. Looking at Jane he asked her directly "Tell the jury prisoner - can you fly or not?" Jane Wellman looked him straight in the eye and answered "Yes, my Lord" There was a gasp from the jury at this sudden admission, outwardly the case was sewn up, for by her remark and admission she had pleaded guilty. Then to their surprise Judge Powell exclaimed "Well then you may, there is no law against flying".

Here was a case that was a contradiction in law, for on the one hand the accused had pleaded guilty to the charges before her, while on the other the Judge decided that there was no crime involved, and therefore no case to answer, and he accordingly instructed the jury to acquit her, which they did.

It was this same law that was a precedent, which led to the legalising of cremation, strictly forbidden under ecclesiastical law, but yet to be tested under common law, the law of the land. In this memorable case, burial was the norm for all Xtians as this ensured the corpse was ready to be resurrected and rise up on the Day of Judgement. So deeply was this engrained into the common people in the Middle Ages that by the 19th century the God-fearing Victorian society even saved amputated limbs to subsequently be interred with the deceased. It was a facet of the staunch Xtian belief of the age that an incomplete body could not, and would not be resurrected; apparently based on a ruling by the Council of Nicea which created a paternoster to be intoned to the effect that the wording 'we believe in the resurrection of the body' was to be henceforth included. It came to be accepted as part of the 'Nicean Creed'.

It was a great Victorian eccentric by the name of Dr Price, who created a near riot when he cremated his son, (whom he had irreverently named Jesus Christ) and who had sadly parted this life at the tender age of a bare five and a half months. Price, an 'odd ball' by any standard, continuously shocked all those around him by his outrageously eccentric and odd behaviour. He walked around barefooted everywhere, believing that socks suffocated that part of the body, whether he visited a library or a general store he was always barefoot. Living in a strong Xtian community in Wales, the local populace were strong Chapel; he stood out a mile with his unkempt appearance. In fact his whole dress attire in general was decidedly odd, with brightly polished brass buttons on his ordinary clothes. Plus, his insatiable sexual appetite shocked those around him as he fathered a number of bastard children from a string of mistresses and married none of them. His naming of his latest bastard 'Jesus' was the final indignity to those godly folk in whose midst he lived, and the untimely death of the boy was to subsequently provoke mob vengeance.

As the Church awaited instructions to bury the poor lad, the news leaked out that Dr Price intended to burn his deceased offspring in a giant bonfire on a nearby hilltop. Incensed, a mob gathered to prevent this desecration of a body which violated their belief, but as they furiously marched towards the hilltop they were greeted with the sight of the funeral beacon already blazing in the night air. Reaching the cremation site they angrily recovered the charred remains of the young boy and drove Dr Price off, one man remained there, swearing he would personally throw Dr Price himself into the inferno should he dare return.

Doctor Price was arrested and charged with creating a public disorder and accordingly sent for trial, naturally he defended his actions and himself. Challenging the judge on this selfsame point of law he scored well, for the judge within minutes announced that there was no law AGAINST burning a body and ordered the jury to acquit him. It was not long before cremation in the light of the ruling, slowly crept into fashion as a cheap means of disposing of the dead legally.

Cremation remains an issue amongst Witches to this day as many resent this method of disposing of their earthly remains, it being reminiscent of the burning days when Xtian zealots would gather up the ashes of the pyre and cast them into the nearest river so that not one single element of the Witch remained. Even the pulverised ashes of the Witch were considered to have evil powers in case the wind might blow some of the deceased's ash into your garden and thus blight you or your crops. We were mightily feared then, either dead or alive, unjustly so, as we know.

The Witch ideal is for their earthly remains to sleep peacefully in some woodland glade close to nature and provide nutrient for the soil in the process, usually with an oak, rowan, willow or silver birch planted above as a marker. I am reminded of the words of Omar Khayam whose 247th quatrain reads:

I sometimes think that never blooms a rose so red
The rose as where some buried Caesar bled
That every Hyacinth the Garden wears
Dropt in her Lap, from some once lovely Head

So sad, but this is mortality. I am pleased to report that Witches are combining and also individually finding money to buy woodlands where they can worship with the coven and which will also become their ultimate resting place. I know of some who have been cremated and the ashes either cast around the sacred circle or even buried near it.

In *The Last Bastion* I depicted a beautiful ritual I had created that combines with the retaining of the ashes, and mixing them with flower petals, incense and earth and ritually incorporating them into a tree or rose. It has become very popular over the last few years.

The Witchcraft Act of 1951 swept away the last vestiges of the persecutions outwardly, although close on 50 years were to elapse before it became acceptable. On a legal note once more, the first overtures towards legalising Witchcraft was with the Witchcraft Act of 1736, although this was not the intention! For the very phrasing of it shot the legislators in the foot, so to speak.

The wording of this act is as follows, and states it to be an offence (quote) '*Shall pretend to exercise any kind of Witchcraft, sorcery, enchantments, or conjuration, or undertake to tell fortunes, or pretend from his or her skill or knowledge in any occult or crafty sciences, to discover where or what manner any goods, chattels, supposed to be stolen or lost may be found.*" They were to suffer a year's imprisonment, with an hour in the pillory every quarter. By an anomaly of law, once again it is this selfsame act that also declares and prevents '*any prosecution, suit or proceeding against witchcraft, sorcery, enchantment or conjuration, or charging another with any such offence.*"

The operative word in the first part of the legislation clearly rests upon the word 'pretends' so my legal mind says that provided you were not pretending, and genuinely thought you were performing sorcery for real, and could prove you were a Witch, then obviously no offence was being committed.

The 18th century was an age of enlightenment and the manic Witch hysteria had started to abate, In remote rural areas the peasantry were still ingrained with superstition and prejudice, and there continued to be Witch ducking and swimmings, but the authorities were clamping down on such practices now, and those who perpetrated such unauthorised crimes were sentenced. There were even cases that where mob rule had subjected a suspect to an ordeal whereby they died in the process, the ringleaders were hanged in public. Sanity was slowly dawning at long last.

The 'legal' persecution of Witches, if you will pardon the expression, we know started in 668 AD when Theodore, Archbishop of Canterbury brought out the '*Liber Poenitentialis*' with mild punishments for basic Pagan practises, including sorcery, and Witchcraft. These early persecutions were basically to deter the populace from the frequenting of stone circles, sacred groves, plus holy streams and springs. Besides, the Church had already got its eyes on many of these sites with a view to Xtianising them, and where possible to build their churches on them and thereby prevent the peasantry from being able to get onto the sacred land - unless of course they were happy to enter the church to do so which was their intention from the beginning!

Remember, dear reader that many sacred groves of oak and yew had already had these structures erected in them against the wishes of the locals who saw this as a sacrilege and desecration of the sacred and holy sites. These early days of penalising the Goddess worshippers who revelled with their God in the woodlands and forest were not a great worry to them as mostly the Church's punishment decreed for continuing to follow their age-old faith, was simply a period of fasting; and once in the seclusion of the woods what clergy would know what feasting went on.

These penalties remained in force until 735 AD, when, not to be outdone, the Archbishop of York, one Ecgberht, stepped into the picture and produced his updated edict the 'Confessional' which came to be known as the '*Confessional of Ecgberht*' he suspected that sorcery was at the root of many unexplained deaths and increased the period of fasting from one to seven years for 'murder by incantation'

Sorry to divert from Witches to whores but it was King Aethelred who put us in the same category so to continue. Not to be outdone in 925AD King Athelstan went one further and abolished the penalty of seven years of fasting for murder by incantation, and introduced the death penalty for same.

Well, by 865 AD King Aethelred, King of Wessex and Kent put Witches into the same category as whores or 'bawdy women', (I still cannot fathom his reasoning, but perhaps it was our fertility rites that were the common denominator). He was determined to make his mark on history, and show his power to the Church at the same time.

In his infinite wisdom, his 'Coup de Grace', he decided to exile both Witches and whores together. Oh how I would like to be able to throw my mind back to those heady days when all we Pagans suddenly had all these myriads of loose women thrust upon us! I guess we must have somehow magnanimously absorbed these ejected maidens into our community, after all somebody had to give these poor fallen women a home, (and a bed to sleep in) and we Pagans are rather munificent in such matter, are we not!

For pure hypocrisy you cannot beat the moralistic hell-fire teachings on the sins of the flesh that was expounded from the pulpit of churches the length and breadth of the land, while along the Thames embankment all the brothels, bordellos, and cat houses called 'stews' were owned by the Bishop of Southwark including the most infamous prison that bestowed its name to history and was called 'The Clink'. This building, still standing near the Thames at Southwark, is open to the public as a living history of what prison life was like years ago. Its history is amazing when you look back, for while the churchmen were screaming morality at the Witches from every pulpit, nauseated that we worshipped the Old Gods as nature made us, (and this dear reader is not a sexual frenzy or orgy, just a simple and moving ceremony), and accused us of sexual frolics and immorality, the local diocese there under the auspices of his supreme eminence the Bishop of Winchester was busily raking in the mazuma from a string of brothels he owned that stretched from London Bridge to Blackfriars.

The entire area was one massive and notorious red light district where every conceivable act of utter debauchery could be purchased for a price. As far as sexual frolics were concerned then, the activities of the hundreds of doxies that plied their trade there could have added another thousand pages to the *Karma Sutra*, and would have shamed the bordellos and girls depicted on the murals of Pompeii's erotic scenes. 'Oh ye devout Xtians what does your holy book say about 'He who be without sin cast the first stone'?

The Church grew rich on the immoral earnings of its unfortunates and made the hypocritical Bishop a mega-rich man while the ecclesiastics grew fat on the immoral earnings, as well as savouring the delights of completely freebie romps with a selection of buxom beauties whenever the inclination came upon them. I mean after all there have got to be some perks if you are a celibate man of God, and a man of the cloth to boot.

This mega-pimp the Bishop, would unhesitatingly throw any of his captive prostitutes into the Clink if they failed to earn sufficiently or were suspected of holding out on his worshipfulness. There was even a list of the punishments laid down for disciplining his whores including branding on the breast with a red hot iron for a second offence. Part of the decree, engraved on the wall (still there to this day) stated that the executioner was to make sure when branding, not to mar the girl's beauty, for she was a valuable commodity and if pretty could earn well for him. For a first offence she would be severely whipped and if she got caught a second time, branded as we have just said. If she still continued to withhold any part of her earnings, including 'tips', given over and above the statutory charge levied by the Madam (Well Bishops do wear a dress like garb. Don't they?) for not giving Caesar his dues then her 'career' was finished and she was back on the streets to ply her trade for a few farthings a time in the back alleys servicing the beggars and itinerants, but now with a deeply imbedded scar in the shape of a 'W' for whore on each cheek, applied there by the public executioner with a hot iron. The bishop's control on these women was absolute.

This was a warning to all the other harlots not to renege on their obligations to the Church, oh and by the way do not think that this poor broken-down prossie would now be off the hook so to speak. Oh no, not if she still plied her sordid trade along the Thames embankment a percentage of her meagre earnings would still have to be paid to His Grace the Bishop, and a further offence of not paying 'rent' for her pitch, would bring the red hot iron to her breast yet again. I have looked for some saving grace for the Master Pimp of all Whores who revelled in the title of the Bishop of Winchester, trying hard to find one single credit to his name, and I am pleased to be able to tell you that there is one saving grace on record. His girls were not allowed to work on the Sabbath - amen.

These massive collections of houses of ill-repute were called 'stews' which gives a completely different aspect as to what a stew pot really was. This vast area started its career of infamy when King Stephen gave the area over to Henry de Blois, who leased it to the Church as a going concern. The ecclesiastic authorities were swift to cash in and immediately saw a goodly income to be achieved by licensing all the stews and bawdy houses and putting taxes on inns and drinking dens. This was swiftly followed by increasing the list of entertain-ments to be licensed such as badger-, bull- and cock-fighting, and bear-baiting, the list was endless. King Stephen by passing this goldmine to the Church was simply following the tradition of the area, for it was a an area of ill-repute where one could satisfy all their carnal desires as in Roman times.

902AD saw the introduction of the '*Canon Escopi de Sancre*' as the screws started to tighten in the suppression of the Old Religion. But this was only the beginning as far worse was to come, but for a small respite in 1066.

It was about 1067 that William the conqueror, a gentleman not particularly known for either mercy or charity, decided that the death penalty was far too severe for such a crime, and he ordered that sorcerers who theoretically killed by magic should be banished and not executed. (Incidentally it was dear old William who gave the bordello and red light area of Southwick to his successor King Stephen.)

If the Witch did not want to be banished he or she - usually a she, could claim to prove their innocence of such a crime by requesting trial by ordeal, which in the Middle Ages evolved into 'trial by combat' when a lady could seek out a knight willing to fight for her and champion the justice of her cause (we've all seen *Ivanhoe*).

Odo, a great chieftain of the time, and warrior saw his wife Agnes accused of sorcery, and to the surprise of everyone she picked up a red hot iron in the Church and walked the statutory distance holding it as required. Her hands were immediately bandaged after the ordeal, and three days later, before the assembled clergy they were unbound to show her burns had healed, so thus no case to answer as was the law, Agnes was accordingly acquitted.

1464 saw the first sinister beginnings when the vile pope of the time Pope Pius VIIIth instructed two men to develop a stronger and more intense persecution of everything Pagan. He also issued a Papal Bull to all German Catholic priests to reinforce their inquisitional powers and to use burning as a method of execution. His chosen vehicles for his murderous campaign were two men by the names of Johannes Gremper (described as a 'Priest of Constance') and the infamous Dominican monk by the name of Jacobus Sprenger. These two stalwarts wrote *'The Fortalicium Fideo'* apparently this remained in force from 1464 until 1485, when Pius the VIIIth felt that Johannes Gremper was not enthusiastic enough for the job, and it is at this point he disappears from history. So exit one Priest of Constance and enter another Dominican monk of as vile a disposition as that of his Dominican counterpart Jacobus Sprenger. The name which would pass into infamy alongside Sprenger was Henry Kramer: between them Kramer and Sprenger rewrote the earlier treatise between them from 1485 to 1486. This diabolical duo intensified the punishments and tortures in the name of their all merciful and loving God to his eternal glory as was normal and produced the most horrific and beastly tome ever; that went under the name of *'The Malleus Malleficarum'* to become known as the *'Hammer of the Witches'* this evil document led to one of the most hideous persecutions ever known.

The instruments of torture that were invented to put people to death in the process of interrogations, or inflict the most excruciating agony, defy the imagination of even the most depraved mind. As Witches we are not anti-Xtian, but what the Catholic Church has perpetrated in the name of an all-merciful God should condemn them to their own hell-fire.

The following 56 years saw a wave of hysteria as the persecutions mounted, for each time a so-called 'Witch' was seized they were tortured until they revealed the name of another, and another, for it was deemed you could not be a Witch alone; as a result sometimes whole villages were decimated, particularly in Germany.

One would have thought that nothing could be worse than this mass slaughter of innocents but in 1542 the pressure increased with a new edict that widened the variety of offences that could send you to the stake, or the hangman. Even 'unlawful' love was included! By 1547 Henry the V111th had been caught by the grim reaper and sent to his own private hell, and Edward the V1th had ascended the throne and promptly repealed the act, England could at last relax; the hysteria had abated. This period of stability was not to last regretfully, for within a few years Mary Tudor followed and, being a staunch Catholic, promptly burned everybody who was not of her chosen faith, swiftly engendering her reputation with the name 'Bloody Mary'. This period of bloodshed was to come to an end within five years with her passing over to join Henry the V111th in Hades. Most of her victims were Protestants who she saw as worse than Witches it would seem.

Under Queen Elizabeth, we see the punishment for Witchcraft downgraded with many ending up in the pillory, as against on the end of a hempen rope. 1560 for example saw two priests convicted of Witchcraft being merely pilloried. It was a conspiracy by the Countess of Lennox against the Queen that set the ball rolling again, for part of the charges of treason laid against her and others, was that in plotting against Elizabeth she had sought out and consulted wizards as to when the Queen would die.

Sir Anthony Fortescue, an astrologer, was arrested and charged with casting a horoscope of Queen Mary Tudor, a charge that would be repeated in modern times when R.H. Napier was indicted for the self-same offence in 1930 for daring (with unerring accuracy may I add) to forecast the future of Princess Margaret Rose, and found himself arraigned for Witchcraft before the Old Bailey This was not to be the last Witchcraft trial for 1944 was to see one Helen Duncan accused of Witchcraft, convicted of same, and in the 20th century imprisoned!

Elizabeth acted fast and immediately sought to revoke Edward's revocation, and re-implement the act, but failed to get it reinstated. The time had come for a new law to condemn us and by 1562 yet another act was passed suppressing us for a number of practices, including healing. This act was widely supported and encouraged by the medical authorities who saw it as a way of ridding themselves of the traditional healers, and herbal-dealing old village Witches, and wise women who were renowned for their skills and healing powers. This act was once again all encompassing but was reinforced in 1581 by being expanded to cover fortune-telling and horoscopes (hence the 1930 trial). Even so the courts were far more lenient than in times of old and saw only 82 executions for Witchcraft during Elizabeth's entire reign.

With the death of Elizabeth in 1603 a new wave of terror was about to be unleashed as James the 6th of Scotland (James the 1st of England) took power and, influenced by his mother Mary Queen of Scots in his early years, who was a staunch Catholic and an avid Witch hater as well (she had been executed at Fotheringay castle some years beforehand) prior to her death had urged her son in his capacity as forthcoming head of state, to throw the net wider still and thus entrap more Witches and sorcerers.

James being an avid Catholic as well, agreed, and in 1604 was instrumental in engineering a new Witchcraft act which was duly passed. This was the vicious egomaniac who also edited the Bible once again and created what came to be known as the 'King James' version. His ascent to the throne of both England and Scotland was a dark day for the peace-loving worshippers of the gentle God and Goddess. For the age of enlightenment was still to come, eventually it was repealed in 1736, and the burning days were over - but not the persecutions, for the act was invoked as we have seen in both 1930 and 1944 in two famous trials. Only in 1951 were we finally released from bondage, with the dawn of the Aquarian Age.

With our new-found freedom we must strive for two purposes now, one to see the original religion of England, now called the Old Religion, restored and officially recognised as a religion, and the image of the evil Witch of history abolished. To this day we are depicted as evil in film, television, and cartoons. If such vitriol were to be thrown at any other class of society whether it is Hindu, Moslem or Jewish for example there would be an outcry. Society must recognise that the Human Rights Act covers all Pagans and that includes we Witches as well

So mote it be.

Sex in Witchcraft!

Fact as against Fiction, and the Child of Promise

Wild orgies! The Wild Hunt culminating in one great sexual free-for-all, wear a blindfold and choose a partner by touch? Oh dear, with my luck I would probably find we were one girl short and some bastard had brought a blow-up doll along. (I did hear tell of a quite simple soul who had this pulled on him and thought he had found the perfect woman who never nagged, and docilely accepted every advance he made, apparently he wanted to marry her but he couldn't get her to say "I will") but seriously over 95% of the sex in Witchcraft is symbolic.

Does sex take place in a circle? Well let us examine the acts and practices of yesteryear, and compare them to today. First you must take into consideration the fact is that we are a fertility cult, always have been, and always will be. In all magic it has long been realised that sex is a powerful force and if the power of that powerful sexual explosion can be harnessed then it can move mountains, but that does not mean one wild orgy - far from it.

I will turn the clock back later, for the present I will go as far as I dare in explaining much the sexual activity that takes place within a circle in this the 21st century. I will NOT be giving out words of power nor will I go into the ceremonials leading up to what I will describe. And of course will not be going into detail as to what follows in the ritual; but any initiated witch reading this book would know the truth anyway, for that is not what this book is about.

Let us start at the beginning at what we call the welcoming; this is a beautiful ritual where each Witch stands in a line outside of a magic circle awaiting entry. The circle once consecrated and reinforced to keep any floating spirit or evil entity out, must now be ceremonially opened to admit the coven. Each Witch entering will be challenged and will give their secret name which will be known to both the High Priest and High Priestess. Inside they are blessed and purified according to ancient rites that go back into the beginning of time itself.

Wow! that should really wet your appetite for a wild orgy! Why? Well have you not recognised that we have started off the evening meeting in one massive demonstration of sex! It is rituals such as this that gets the *News of the World* reporters slobbering at the jaws to run an expose of a group of dedicated Pagans, consisting of your local Bobbie on the beat and the indigenous bank manager from the village. Plus the butcher, the baker, the candlestick maker, an' old Uncle Tom Cobley an' all (not forgetting Martha the local postmistress who keeps the records). And they are all nude, so logically in Xtian eyes, it just HAS to be an orgy of the widest propensity. You still don't get it? Well let me explain. The Circle is symbolic of the womb of the Goddess; it is the entry point of all life and the queue of Witches in a limp irregular line outside awaiting entry suddenly come to attention and form a straight line which is of course a phallic symbol. And this phallic line enters the circle! Now let's be honest, you cannot get any sexier than that can you? Is that it? Goodness gracious no. For now we get down to the real sex as we consecrate the wine and bless the salt, I will take one example only and this is not the revealing of a secret, it can be found in countless books now regretfully.

You see the Priestess will present a goblet of wine to the Priest and to the accompaniment of magic words he places his athame (a magically powered knife) in it, sheer, utter, unbridled sex, being performed in front of a group of avid voyeurs. Well the Priestess's cup is obviously a female receptacle, and the knife entering it - it doesn't take much imagination does it! No wonder the 'Sundays' are after us - and it does not end there, no sireeee.

We will see the power of sex in increasing intensity as the evening draws on, it's just got to get better, If it's a healing ritual as most coven workings are, then we will use a really huge cauldron for it, out will go the bat wings, frogs, toads and puppy dogs tails plus the poisonous toadstools, alongside all the un-baptised babies gathered over the year. (absolute essential to any self-respecting coven - all the 16th century books and the Church say so.) and in will go aromatic herbs and incenses. The cauldron is the Earth Mother's womb and the High Priest will be held back by the coven who will be restraining him, such is his eagerness to put his stang in it, (no I will not tell you what a stang is - look it up.)

In this state of near-euphoria he will be put in the centre of the circle and all the coven, to the accompaniment of drums, tambourines and fifes, will dance deosil around him merrily to symbolise the quickening of the womb. OK, so it's really a symbolic orgasm, but who cares, we've raised the power and we can now heal up to three people. Just think what we could do with the Band of the Royal Scots Guard present. Now do not start to condemn us dear reader for such clear unbridled licentiousness, for we at least do not perform our sex acts in front of any old Tom Dick or Harry like the Church does, it also has the effrontery to invite most of the village in to witness an absolutely blatant sex act as well. O' Xtians cast thee not the first stone!

Sex in a church? Why yes, it's enacted regularly. There before an invited audience the groom performs a symbolic sex act by placing a ring on a finger of the bride, the finger is the phallus and the ring the womb - now we all know what that means symbolically don't we? On a more serious note though, it is in fact just that, and again is an old Wiccan practice that once again has been absorbed into the Church. It was symbolic of the consummation that would follow the wedding nuptials. (*News of the World* please note - with marriages you could get a lascivious story every week). On a historical note, early wedding rings were made of iron not gold.

In prehistory there was an even greater symbolism, and caves where rituals took place bore many explicit symbols that could be deemed literally pornographic. The well-known figurines such as the female Sheila-na-gig were common, and the female Yoni was openly displayed in carvings, including many carved inside the churches themselves. Undoubtedly there were many of these depictions carved into trees where their ceremonies took place, but with the passage of time these have rotted away, but many a rockface still shows lurid and unashamed sketches etched there by our ancestors.

We know that when the High Priest took his place in the north of the magic circle he represented the female clitoris, and that the circle was the vulva. There was a moon God called Sinn as well and he represented the female clitoris in ritual, and it was not long before his name passed into the language as representing evil in the form of Sin, for sex itself had essentially to be solely for the purpose of procreation in Xtian eyes, and any indulgence other than for this purpose was a mortal sin. Sex must never be pleasurable.

I am reminded of the story of the pious clergyman entering into his wedding night with trepidation that what he had to do was sinful, but necessary. The following morning he asked his young bride if she was pregnant, and upon being told that she had no idea, remarked "Oh dear, don't say we have to go through all that again tonight." (Amen) do you really wonder why Paganism has survived?

Woman was believed to be the very foundation of original sin by the Church, after all it was her that ate the apple not Adam, and it was she that succumbed to the wily old serpent. She was ever the temptress, and exploited man's weakness. It was said that God cursed her, and inflicted the menstrual cycle upon her, hence why the menses are referred to by Xtians as the 'Curse of Eve' and the modern-day Miss quite openly explains her indisposition, by saying she has the 'curse'. In Witchcraft, if a girl within the circle wears a robe we acknowledge the fact that she is in all probability ‘paying her tribute to the Moon’ a far nicer way of respecting her cycle. Within Artemis a small proportion of our ladies always wear robes, that is their right if they so desire. Their initiation is conducted ‘skyclad’, but after that they may be robed thereafter at any future Sabbats. The exception would be when they were elevated to the second degree, and eventually their third.

The gutter press have sought for years to infiltrate an initiation ceremony, but have always been repelled, although much of the ritual has been written in explicit detail in books, and has even been televised. There is no sex in an initiation, other than symbolism, but to the uninitiated the ritual could outwardly be said to have sexual overtones. If you think this is so, then I challenge you to ask any Witch as to how they found their initiation, and the usual reaction is ‘It was one of the most moving experiences of my entire life’. I rest my case.

With the rebirth of Witchcraft in the 1950s much was made of a ritual when the sex act was enacted factually by some covens, and which came to be known as the Great Rite. This was factual, and was performed at great Sabbats and at elevations to the 3rd degree - a ritual where the passing of supreme power took place, which again goes back to the days of persecution. The normal procedure within the Craft is a slow and gradual training and slow acquisition of power by the Witch over a period of many years.

From their initiation of the first degree, the training begins, and the power is not passed until they are worthy of elevation to the second degree, note, we are speaking of power here, not the supreme power that was engendered by sexual induction. Nothing sexually overt takes place at either of these rituals; it is the supreme power that is passed by the act of coitus at the elevation to the third degree that has been the subject of so much speculation.

What is not generally known is that woman herself, as a Priestess of the Craft (all women become Priestesses at their initiation, not to be confused with High Priestesses) is in complete and utter control of her own body at all times. It is she and she alone who will determine the issue, as to whether she will become a Priestess in True by sexual induction or a True Priestess by going through the rite in token only, I do not intend to go into further detail other than to emphasise that sexual intercourse does not take place with a True Priestess.

Why, you may as,k was this old rite practised, and why has it all but disappeared in the 21st century, and what does happen now? We have to turn the clocks back to the burning days when the Craft was almost exterminated, covens were decimated and often wiped out completely, but sometimes one or two escaped the inquisitors and in their turn founded new covens.

Now if we go back to the original tri-gradal structuring of the Craft we see that the degree system was reversed, and the degrees were 3-2-1 - not 1-2-3 as today. As we no longer fear persecution we are able to take and train an acolyte or neophyte gradually teaching them how to conjure safely and perform magic, and at the same time keep them on the right hand path. With each coven meeting their powers would grow until they reached the second degree and then the third. At that point, they outwardly would be expected to 'hive' (break away with members of the coven and form another group and thus perpetuate the Craft). Training started at the first degree and was gradual.

The power that sexual energy creates had long been known to magicians and occultists and what they have done is literally harness the power surge and utilise it. Moralists will undoubtedly throw their hands up in horror at this archaic rite, but the fact of the matter is it works. In the burning days if the sole survivor was a low grade Witch then his or her ability to start again would be hindered by their lack of power.

Sexual rites have been practised by societies in nearly all countries since time immemorial; in fact, I am almost inclined to say all countries, for I cannot think of a single abstention where sex has not been part of their culture - until the coming of the Xtian church that is. If you turn the clock back 2,000 years you will find many records of sex rites from the sacred prostitutes of ancient Rome, an honoured profession in their society, to the fabled Hieros Gamas of the ancient Greeks, the words being translated as 'sacred marriage'. This sexual rite was a supreme dedication of worship and is akin to the Great Rite of the Witches; the whole ceremony is beyond sex and was a sacred consummation whereby the participants raised power to achieve a specific result.

In the Hieros Gamas the object was to control the orgasm mutually and culminate at the same time whereby a mighty spasm could be achieved and for a few fleeting seconds as the mind left the body in the supreme ecstasy and the participants communed with the Gods at that moment, or ventured into the vast beyond and saw the other worlds. The old writings still exist in the original Greek detailing the 'modus operandii' as to how to commune with the ethereal world via sexual union and its climax.

The Great Rite of the Witches is far more finely honed, and is rarely performed as only the most skilled can undertake this sublime act if it is to be used for a specific purpose. This would usually be a highly-charged healing ritual and the participants would spend a long time in meditation envisaging the implications of the rite beforehand. Thus training and preparation is essential if the purpose of the rite is to be achieved for at the moment of the mutual orgasm and the split second later that the mind becomes disembodied from the physical body they must both visualise in that minuscule period of time the purpose for which they have jointly engaged in the rite.

This usually would be in one of two forms. At that moment, they must in unison visualise the image of the person for whom the rite is dedicated, or they must see the purpose they have worked for. Let us take two scenarios here. If they were working on someone, shall we say, who had a cancerous growth then at the magical moment they would together see an image of that person and direct a blue healing ray to the infected area.

If as an example they were working for a brother and sister to be reconciled they would envisage them embracing and smiling together. Outwardly simple, but no, for this is where the training comes into play and only a 3rd degree Witch would undertake this. For essentially they must be disciplined, to hold the image in their mind at the moment of power, for woe betide them if an alien image should slip into their minds at that moment and the power be negated or driven elsewhere, this could have disastrous effects. So when this now rare ritual is enacted you will understand that this is beyond sex and physical desire but is a finely honed ritual by two participants who are using tantric energy to a purpose. Together they would have found a spiritual and ethereal oneness with the God force and would have harnessed it.

Rituals could be both learned and acquired over the years from other covens, but one secret that was taught was the way to harness magic simply. So if a Witch was alone, he or she would know at least the principles of harnessing a degree of power and how to utilise it. For example a spell cannot be cast unless it is in rhyme and this would be influenced by fluctuating tones of the voice that resounded in the ether, even a first degree knew these basics. The adage of all Witchcraft goes back to the principles of 'In Herbis, Verbis, and Lapidimus, Magna Vis Est." - Sometimes written as Lapidibus, both these spellings are to be found in old writings, but I personally favour the Lapidimus as the more correct. Translated this is 'In Herbs, Words, and in Stones doth lie the Great Power'. Herbal concoctions correctly balanced were powerful agents to raise power by incense, and could also be used for cures, and ailments, It is in words we see the greatest emphasis laid on words. Only those who have seen the circumambulation deosil of a circle of Witches starting the Witches chant of:

Darksome night and Shining Moon.
East, then West, then South and North
Hearken to the Witches Rune,
As here we come to call thee forth--------etc, etc, etc

As this chant gathers in intensity we see the magic of words as the cone of power starts to form in the centre of the circle. Throw in the magic being worked in a power seat such as the centre of Stonehenge, Avebury, or say the Merry Maidens and you have a mega energy field that can be formed into a blue light cone and directed like an X-Ray to a sufferer. This is real magic!

If the survivor from a coven had the full power to make magic from the beginning then he or she were as a Magus, and a new coven would form around them all the quicker, and swiftly grow in power. Therefore when the burning and hanging days were at their height, the power was passed by sexual induction between man and woman, and woman and man, and as they achieved a mutual orgasm the power was now vested from one unto the other. Study the old alchemical works and you will find how the sages of old would seek these sexual excretions to make magic. The fabled Serpents egg could not be made without it; and it is the base of the legendary 'First Matter'.

With the dawning of the 21st century a new era commenced and the Craft faced a far greater threat than the Churches could devise, by now we had reverted back to the original graded structure of one, two, three, and third degree was merely an option to those who wished to take it, I would imagine the percentage nowadays who attain this degree is between 8-10%. The majority of Witches take the power of the second degree and remain there for the rest of their Wiccan lives. This threat to the old ways came in the form of Aids, a sexual time bomb that could be carried in the body unknowingly for years, so now, unless it is performed by consenting couples already in a relationship; the old ways are almost certainly dead. This is as a result of a modern evil, that had reared its head in the 20th century, and has done in a few years what over 500 years of Xtian persecution had failed to do.

In *The Last Bastion* I explained how after years of research, and it was years, we discovered a great Tantric ritual hidden in a series of books by the late Dionne Fortune and sought to synchronise these into an alternative to the Great Rite whereby the power could be passed by body contact but through the hands. This is a most powerful and actually hypnotic ritual and culminates with the pressing of palms together while the power is passed like an electric current between them. It worked the very first time we performed it, and as a result Witchdom came into the 21st century. One door had closed, and another one had opened.

The Great Rite is symbolically enacted each Candlemass and Hallowmass, and occasionally we have a consenting couple to perform the rite as of old. Otherwise all the so-called sexual activity with its stories of orgies etc are completely and utterly false. If, and only if, the Rite should be performed it will be no more than twice, possibly three times a year (the spring equinox being the other) and even so years can pass without it happening at all, and if it is then it is in private with only the maid of the coven in attendance, to conform to certain niceties that must be observed, and even she will leave before the moment of consummation. There are no voyeurs in Witchdom. It is a sacred moment.

If you throw the clock back a thousand years you will find that this revered ceremony was conducted factually, specifically to create a magical child. A chosen and consenting couple would seek to conceive within the Circle of Magic, and as a result bring forth a baby to be raised by the entire village, this child would never want for anything as the villagers would feed, clothe, and educate the progeny over the years, until he or she, (they would pray for a girl child) became a priest or priestess in their own right. This magical human came to be known as the 'Child of Promise' and was the result of sacred sex I am often asked if the expression 'Old Horny' the name so often associated with the God of the Witches is a phallic likeness and if he is identified with the God Priapus, that most magnificently endowed God - we should be so lucky! Although this phallically endowed deity I know is not every young girl's cup of tea. A well-known society lady whose husband was renowned for both his affairs and a somewhat small member, despite his not being as well endowed as one would have thought; replied to the effect that in her youth she had lain with men of Priapic proportions and those who were somewhat diminutive, and said with alacrity 'If you are given the choice my dear between a Bull and a Chihuahua, take my advice - go for the Chihuahua every time.'

Well the answer here is twofold for the magnificent horns of the Lord Cernunnos, Pan, Herne, or Boreas for example are both fertility symbols and symbols of power, and thus synonymous with each other. But horns have always been regarded as symbols of strength and virility, when primitive man observed the deer locking antlers, and subduing their rivals for the choice of the females in the herd - and then seeing him proudly displaying his horns to all the hinds in his group. Our Neanderthal ancestors marvelled at him, but this quickly turned to admiration as the animal commenced the rut and proceeded to mate with 20-30 of them in a single day! Clearly the horns were the secret, and so when he hunted and slew the deer he would eat its heart for its strength, and make a headdress from the horns to parade in front of the women of the tribe as both warrior and potential mate.

It was the early depictions of primitive man wearing antlers in cave drawings etc that gave rise to the personification of the God Cernunnos in the form we identify him to this day. The reference to the Horned God of the Witches as Old Horny is both a reference to his sexual prowess, and also to the great spread of horns on his head. They ooze sex as a sacrament - and as a celebration.

What is not generally known is the Xtians looked upon this in the very early days when Xtianity was embryonic and realised the people admired horns and their phallic depiction, they were stiff, upright, and ever-ready in a permanent erection; and the populace identified with them; in fact it is specifically mentioned in the Xtian Bible under 'Kings 22-11 Deuteronomy 33-17 and Psalms 22-21.

The very first depictions of both Christ and the angels, whether it be in paintings or statues have a common heritage inasmuch as they were all shown with short horns protruding from their foreheads, Their Messiah having slightly longer ones as the head priest, Jesus Christ had now taken the place of the Horned God worshipped by the Pagans!

After the Reformation, the Catholic Church decided that horns were too Pagan, and as sex was now taboo and priests were celibate (theoretically) they advocated abstention. Sex as a means of communicating with God was anathema to them. It was a wonder the Xtians as a sect did not die out within a few decades for failing to reproduce - but then you get backsliders in all societies don't you?. They desperately wanted to stamp out the beliefs and customs of yesteryear when the coupling of a man and woman was regarded as a spiritual rite and that henceforth those who had experienced each other carnally were now the more powerful for it.

To the Church horns were a symbol of both power and fertility, you could not have one without the other. Their Messiah they decided must be celibate and so the horns must go, no longer could they substitute their God and cast him in the image of the Pagans' great horned one as before, for by now the people had realised that this was merely transubstantiation and this new God was being slowly forced upon them.

Within a few years the horns were chamfered off the statues and the horns in paintings were extended to form a circle, which came to be known as a halo. What is generally not known and which I now intend to clarify is that the word Halo means Horns, and is derived from the Latin '*halos*', the same word is almost identical in a number of languages and there are variations in the spellings from halus and holus to halous, and mean horns in every instance.

There are many old customs that featured horns that still exist to this day in fertility rites and can be found in the re-enactment of old Pagan rituals such as the Abbots Bromley Horn dance, plus many Morris Dancing groups utilise stags' horns in their dance sequences, and there are hundreds of these perpetuating these ancient rites throughout the length and breadth of the country every weekend to popular acclaim.

In Sussex the vestiges of a Pagan ritual are enacted every July on the 25th of that month in the little hamlet of Ebinoe near Petworth, a horned sheep is roasted on the village green and at the end of the day the horns are ceremonially presented to a villager (Could it be the local lothario?) Ebinoe is described as a little village locked in time that for years has refused to enter the modern century, and up to the early 1930's boasted neither an inn or village shop. Technically Ebinoe is a hamlet, not a village for it does not boast a set of stocks or pillory to place miscreants in, a necessary requirement by English law to qualify for 'village' status, still un-repealed.

In Southern Ireland there are areas that ritually elect and worship a horned billy goat for the day, he is ornamented and even given his own throne, an old custom that predates Xtianity when the Horned God was worshipped universally. The strong Catholic Church has never been able to stamp this custom out, and are remarkably absent that day. Such rituals as these are not confined just to England but are widespread on the continent as well. They are all vestiges of ancient fertility rites.

In villages in France during the May Day festivals sets of horns of all descriptions are taken out of lofts and attics and dusted for the big day when all the young men of the village will wear them, then at a predetermined time they will suddenly set upon the village girls (who have been waiting for this moment of course) and rush upon them, naturally the timid creatures run screaming into the woods where they are pursued by the boys. Reminiscent of deer and hinds as they are pursued by the rampant stags? A remnant of yet another old fertility custom.

Old Horny of course was known by many other names not least of which was when he appeared in the form of Herne or the ever virile and somewhat lecherous Pan. I cannot tell you how many male witches want to be known as Pan after their initiation. Now Pan really was a horny old so-and-so, he had a continual ache in his loins and was ever ready to copulate. This lust of his was often seen in old depictions of him when he was shown with a massive erection and probably gave rise to a rather vulgar expression that a quickening of the male phallus has come to be known as.

The great God Pan was never happier than when he was engaged in his favourite pastime of copulation, and would pursue any little nymphet that crossed his path ablaze with carnal desire until he had his wicked way with her. The most famous depiction of him is in the form of the Greek God Priapus where his penis is shown as long and as thick as his arm (complete fiction alas ladies). In his more idle moments Pan would play his fabled pipes, luring young maidens to him with his enticing music. I tried this once in woodland on a village outskirt, but all I got was an inquisitive rabbit and an odd look from the local farmer, but then I never was much of a musician.

So let us conclude and clarify once and for all, 99% of sex in Witchcraft is symbolic and sex rites are in the whole carried out in token. By answering honestly we can now state that sex is as rare as snow in the Sahara but the rituals are there and can be used, albeit rarely. The majority of Witches will spend the whole of their life of Witchdom and never celebrate a sex ritual nor ever observe one. So let this fallacy be laid to rest once and for all.

Freemasonry, Druids and the Old Religion

So much of Witchcraft itself has been lost with the passing of the years, but one has to realise that the Craft itself is a non dogmatic religion that continuously evolves, and therefore many ancient practises have either been abandoned or amended to such an extent that they are barely recognisable today, in many cases only the merest vestige of old practices remain. Sometimes a ritual has in fact been so completely lost that no more than a symbol remains.

The triangle, for example used combined with a pentacle beneath, is universally identified as a symbol of the third degree in Witchcraft now, but this is a completely new innovation having evolved in modern Wicca since 1951. I am fully aware that purists could argue against this, for one has only to search alchemical treatises or ancient books on magic, such as the *Clavicle of Solomon*, and the like, to find a precedent, but here we are essentially referring to the higher realms of Ritual Magic - not Wicca.

Pentacles, triangles, and hexagons etc have though been used in Masonic ritual since the inception of the first Masonic lodge, but if you delve back a little further, you will find a whole series of sigils that go back into the aeons of time and which were not always recorded, or written down. In fact, much knowledge was memorised, and this included secret signs. A written document if found, could take you on a short walk to the gallows.

There are though exceptions to the rule. My own feelings are that this old sign of the triangle by itself for example, correctly aligned, is a remnant of the old initiatory rites of admission to the Craft, and has little bearing on modern initiation rituals as we know them, particularly with its heavy emphasis on Masonic practises, which of course date way back in 1717 when the first Masonic lodge was founded, and which in its turn, was based on ancient Witchcraft practises. To Witches the three points of the triangle represent the triple aspect of the Goddess, to wit - Maiden, Mother, and Crone. To a Mason it has a different interpretation, yet they both come from the identical source.

One has only to study what was known of Wiccan practises at the turn of the 17th century into the 18th to realise that Masonic ritual was based on these self-same Pagan practises gathered from contemporary sources of the time. So when Gerald Broussec Gardner rewrote the near forgotten remnants of the Hand of Rite, or Hand of Write, and came up with the Wiccan 'Book of Shadows; then either vertantly, or inadvertently, he was restarting an old Wiccan tradition after a gap of over 200 years.

What goes around comes around, as they say, and with both Witchcraft rites and Masonic practice there is a distinct parallel. These I can verify as both a Witch and an initiated Freemason. The oaths taken at both Masonic and Wiccan initiations and subsequent elevations have a great deal in common as far as certain instruments of the Craft are concerned, such as the sword. I will go no further than this, for my oath taken at my Masonic initiation still holds, despite the fact that I am a lapsed member of this illustrious brotherhood; much of Masonry has a distinct resemblance to ancient Witchcraft - including the secrecy and oaths.

If we throw our minds back to 1717, that year saw a great renaissance taking place in Britain, very similar to the spiritual revolution that transpired in Britain after 1951 when the final shackles of religious freedom were removed with the abolishing of the Witchcraft Act. That self-same year, saw two major events that would subsequently have positive repercussions over 200 years later in the 20th century.

The two events I refer to, are the revival of Druidism and the establishing of the great Masonic Temple. Coincidence? I think not for this was the dawning of a new age of spirituality, as the burning days were now far behind us, and a new enlightenment came to the fore.

Druidism had little to go on to resuscitate the order, except Roman writings in the main, for the whole cult of the Druids was wiped out when the genocide of an entire culture took place with the invasion of Mona (now the Isle of Anglesey) when Suetonius Paulinus led his legions to the fray with murder in his heart and a determination to exterminate the Druidical order once and for all. The Druids were the spiritual leaders of Britannia at the time and heavily influenced the Celtic culture and politics of the land. The crimes levelled against them were many, and hypocritical. Long before the Boudiccan revolt in AD 61 the island had provided sanctuary to the rebel leaders on the run from the Roman heel. Iceni, Coritani, Catavaulani and Belgae fled there and were protected. There is however no doubt, that Druids and their agents were acting as a fifth column throughout the length and breadth of the British Isles, urging rebellion, and insurrection.

Most of what is known about the Druids is largely due to Roman writers of the period, and is contradictory. After the Roman conquest of England they wrote of the rebelliousness of the indigenous tribes here and guerrilla warfare still being waged by them against the invaders. The Silures (Welsh) were particularly troublesome, continuously harassing the Romans and then retreating into the Silurian hills - but the Druids - no! The Romans recorded that they had bent the knee and submitted to Roman rule, they paid their taxes, and gave their tithes as demanded, Roman chroniclers had nothing but praise for them for years - then overnight a whole propaganda machine swung into action against them. This is strange when you reflect on not only the Roman writings, but other facts recorded at the time, for although most of the written works of the Druids were destroyed by the rampaging Roman hordes, enough records have been passed down verbally as to the basics of this ancient religion that existed alongside ours and based on similar worship.

If we examine the Gaullist records of Druidism you find that they are an absolute parallel to the Celtic/Britannic practices. For example a Xtian in Germany follows exactly the same path as a Xtian in Egypt shall we say, he might be a Lutheran, and the Egyptian a Coptic, but they use the same holy book, the Bible (The exception being the Catholics who ignore everything). All the early Roman records are exactly the same as those known in Gaul (France).

Julius Caesar for example attended great gatherings in France in the area where the city Chartres now stands, where they heard grievances, dealt justice, exchanged ideas, and recorded old lore. He actually writes that '*They teach to the young all those things that they worship, of how the Sun and Moon revolve in the firmament, The worship of the old Gods, and to pay reverence to them, paying emphasis on the power and majesty of them and who were often referred to as 'The Immortal Shining Ones'*.

Their knowledge was immense, and they taught sciences so advanced that even today we marvel at their knowledge of the lunar heavens and astronomy, as the construction of Stonehenge shows (notwithstanding the fact that English Heritage who own the site vigorously dispute that it ever had anything to do with the Druids).

They believed in re-incarnation the same as we do, and just for the record so did the early Xtian church, changing their minds and declaring such a belief a heresy in 553 AD at the Church Council of Constantinople. Life after life, was then changed to Life everlasting - subtle! What was taught on Monday then became a capital offence on Tuesday, but then that's Xtianity all over. Another factor is that Druids worshipped all things in nature, from stones, and animals, to nature Gods. The only black spot I could find that did contradict this was the occasional animal sacrifice, usually when they performed augury (foretelling the future).

What triggered this 'volte face' we will never know, but from then on Druids are recorded as performing vile rites, both animal and human sacrifices, and worshipping a deity called Andraste who demanded sacrifice. No crime was too horrible to be levelled against them, but these are Roman writings, and is it not fact that the victor writes history? Historically though, there is evidence that any Roman caught by them during the rebellion was, delivered up to Andraste in sacred groves, devoid of any tlc!

Tacitus wrote explicitly of a confrontation with Druids on Mona in the final battle and marvelled at the ferocity of them, considering they were not a warrior cult, but it was on their womenfolk he dwelt most in his writings, before whom even the stoutest Roman quailed. Whatever the truth may be, one thing is a certainty, and that is that overnight, the Druids were completely and utterly estranged from the invaders, the truce was off. And a new Romano/Celtic war was on.

When John Toland revived the Druid Order in 1717 he had essentially to look back on all occult and esoteric works known at the time in order to lay the base foundations of Druidism. One must remember that memories of old Witchcraft practises were still fresh in the minds of people at that time, and clearly this arcane knowledge could be adapted to the new order, after all Wicca and Druidism ran a close parallel years before, and side by side, they had both faced extinction over the years. Both of these highly religious orders could be called the 'Old Religion' in their own right.

Next, he had to refer to the old Roman writings prior to the planned genocide of the Druids, for ultimately genocide it was. Paulus Suetonius over a long sustained campaign slaughtered them all on Mona, their headquarters, (now Anglesey) massacring men, women and children indiscriminately. Druidism as a cult was dead. Despite dreadful losses at the hands of the Iceni queen Boudicca (Boadicea) and with his army diminished, he stationed several legions on Mona over the next few years to destroy every tree on the Island, The sacred groves where the Goddess Andraste was worshipped were felled, and eventually Mona was left a desert.

The works of both Dio Cassius and the Roman historian Tacitus were undoubtedly consulted, together with earlier writings about old Witchcraft practises as well as surviving Druidical records, sparse though these were, but the Druids had entered the 18th century anew! Interestingly, that self-same year the very first Masonic lodge was formed, and many newly initiated Druids flocked to become Freemasons as well. Freemasons equally eagerly sought to enter the new Druid Order. From 1717 onwards there was a new renaissance in the wind, much the same as was to be repeated in 1951 when the hated Witchcraft Act was repealed.

With the influx of Druids they brought with them the wind of change, and their own revived practices. Quite independently of those who sought to create a new mystical order. When the foundations and mysteries of Freemasonry were laid, they had already started to absorb old Pagano/Wiccan rites into the order, plus a small amount of ceremonial magic, these then were to be the basis of Freemasonry. Clement of Alexandria wrote that Hermes, a leading scientist of his day had written two treatises on music, that were incorporated into mystery schools that were all the rage at the time, it was these self-same mystery schools together with Pagan rites still existing, that later became the first Masonic Temple.

A rub, a polish, and some new ideas, throw in a little snob value to make it an exclusive club, invite a selection of Jewish scholars to expound the foundations of Solomonic Magic and Mysticism, plus Cabalistic practise and open it up to business-men whose lives were lacking in spirituality - result - Wicca in an amended form had survived the days of the hempen rope, and was now ensconced legally in both Druidism and Masonry.

For reasons best be known to them the Temple of Solomon, and its construction and destruction was to feature heavily in the revised rituals within the first years of its formation. This was henceforth to be the new path of Masonry, but the Wiccan foundations would be a strong thread running through it. The Old Ways were thriving once more!

Over 200 years later Gardner would call upon the knowledge he had acquired as a Freemason, and use it as a basis for a contemporary Witchcraft revival. What goes around comes around, and thus Masonic ritual, in being introduced into the new Wiccan movement, had called up old Wiccan practises that had been preserved in the new Masonic Order. The old ways had never ever really died out over the years as we saw when those in hiding came out into the light and rejoiced at their newly won freedom in 1951. Masonry had inadvertently kept alive many of the old Wiccan practices, all it needed after 1951 was a hand to guide them.

Druids - Mona - and the Romans

It is a matter of deep regret and sorrow that much of the ancient practises of the Druids has been lost to history destroyed in an almost unparalleled genocide, their background, such as is known, is important to us, as much of what is recorded of their beliefs may well have fashioned or influenced ancient Witchcraft beliefs and practises, or equally vice-versa. What we do know is often contradictory, obtuse, and heavily reliant on ancient writings with particular emphasis on old Roman records, and the likes of Julius Caesar, Tacitus and Dio Cassio.

From my own studies of this period I would prefer to concentrate on the positive aspects of the Druids that are known to be true, and to look askance at some of the Roman writings about them - for does not the victor rewrite history according to their own outlook? This is particularly so with all Roman writings whose records are heavily biased in their own favour. I am going to analyse and cross reference many of these aspects in this and the following chapters.

It is a strange fact that the earliest writings of the Romans about the Druids show a strong affinity with the Old Religion, and the worship of the Earth Mother and Goddess Deities. Also there is not one single negative report about them after the first few years following the Roman conquest of a large portion of Great Britain. No, they are good guys they report, they have (albeit reluctantly) accepted Roman rule, they bend the knee to the new occupiers, and most importantly of all they pay their taxes and tithes to great Caesar.

Roman observers speak of how they worshipped the Sun and Moon, and we know the populace identified with the Sun and Moon also, and that the Sun was the God Force and the Moon was the Goddess, usually depicted as Gold being symbolic of the Sun and Silver as reminiscent of the Goddess.

There is not one single negative report about them, all is harmony, the Romans leave them alone as long as they keep the peace, obey the laws, and pay their taxes, and in their turn the Druids leave the Romans alone. Rome despite all its aggressiveness and subjugation was extremely tolerant of the religion of those they conquered, usually simply adding a statuette of the local God or Goddess into a niche in their temple.

Julius Caesar was certainly not opposed to either the Druids nor their religious practices, and that is clearly shown with his conquest of Gaul (France). His benevolence to them is evident, but all things come to an end and I believe that this started in Gaul much the same as it did in England with the building of Romanesque temples on sacred Pagan and Druid sites.

In Britain the rot set in with the Roman love of water and they soon started the acquisition of sacred Celtic springs, spas, and sacred wells, which were of spiritual significance to the Celtic religion. Local resentment grew into outright hostility as the religion was violated, and all the statues of the Celtic Gods and Goddesses placed within the Roman Temples to placate them were of no avail.

Analysis of Britain's religions with particular analysis on the Celtic aspect shows a distinct link between Witchcraft – or to be more correct – wise craft as it was formerly known and Druidism. Once more we are largely in the dark with regard to the exact practices of both of these, and they are most certainly not one of the same, but followed a similar pattern of sun and moon worship identified by both entities as a God and Goddess together with a close alliance with everything in nature.

So let us examine the roots in Druidism. Caesar was impressed by his initial contact with them to find that Jupiter, so sacred to the Romans was worshipped by the Druids and mentions that the Greek and Roman Gods also featured in their worship such as Apollo, Mars and Mercury, again suggesting that the Gallic religion established the Druid religion here and founded their own independent mystery schools.

Many writers even suggest that the Atlantean civilisation had a distinct influence on both the Old Religion and Druidism for they both embraced both sun and moon worship and this once more was part of the Atlantean cult. One thing is certain, and that is a very powerful celebration of the mysteries was performed annually that embraced elements of both Greek and Egyptian practices; such as the fabled Elysian rites and mysteries which were performed, plus the rites of Isis and Osiris. Once again showing that there was never a single God or Goddess, but always an anachronism between male and female in interpretation, these practices were later to be displaced by Xtianity that was hell-bent on establishing, with the aid of Paul and Peter, a macho, masculine orientated religion to be forced on the Pagan populace worldwide regardless.

One notes that December 25th was sacred to the Sun God and the alleged birth of the Xtian God was superimposed on this date under the Xtian edict of replacement theology, and again the Sun God was resurrected in a period of the year in what we now call Easter based on the ancient ceremonies of Eostre. It is another example of how these traditions were annexed by Xtianity. A theory supported by Artemidorus who speaks of the worship of Ceres and Persephone on an island off the coast of Britain. Surely then this must be the Island of Mona that was the centre of the Druid Cult in Britain and which in turn was the scene of the mass genocide of its indigenous population under the Roman General Suetonius Paulinus. Incidentally, there is no mention anywhere in all the Roman writings of Andraste being worshipped there as is mentioned in the Roman epistles. The other alternative is the Isle of Man, which had strong Druidical links but all the indications point to the island of Anglesey.

Another rite that was prescribed by them was the initiation. Again it shows a startling similarity with the Old Religion. The candidate would be bound and placed in complete darkness with perhaps the only light coming from a single candle. Both in Druidical and Wiccan initiation, the potential initiate would be left alone in stygian darkness for hours on end, to meditate, and to be at one with the night and the spirits of the departed - a practice that has passed into obscurity over the centuries to all except a small cluster of hereditary Witches. Even now it has been known to happen, whereby a new initiate would be tied to a tree in a woodland or forest and left alone to be at one with nature and their own thoughts. So in this the 21st century this old practise has managed to survive despite having reached near extinction

On this note may I add that the one within the Coven known as The Watcher – always a man, and in days of yore, a trained warrior as well, would be to hand with both sword and spear to drive away any predators that would be attracted to the helpless initiate together with flint and tinder to make a fire. Bear in mind that England had wolves and bears in those days, like America has now – perhaps a practice better not to be resuscitated in America!

The same thing happened here in Britain when Augustus landed on these shores bringing with him the Xtian gospel, accepted at first as a strange new religion the first churches were built on sacred sites here, but this had a far-reaching and far more sinister purpose. The idea was to lure the local offspring into the Church and catch them while young. St Augustine's philosophy was that if they entered the Church in order to stand on their sacred site eventually the origins would fades into obscurity and the memory of what had been there would eventually vanish - and it worked, As the older generation died off the children came to accept the Church as having always been there in living memory and so invidiously they became converted and the Old Religion started to die out.

Initially they built the churches to represent Pagan symbols with the emphasis on fertility so sacred to the old way, and this design is perpetrated to this day with new churches although the origins may have been forgotten long ago. The doorways were constructed to represent the vulva of a woman, and the spire was a phallic symbol, truly Pagan! The churches were carefully divided into two distinct sections designed so that the Old Religion and Xtianity could worship in their own beliefs side by side, so much so that Xtianity in those early days was referred to as the 'new' religion.

This worked fine for many years, particularly as Xtianity became a snob religion associated with the upper classes and nobility while at ground roots level the peasantry worshipped the Gods of Nature still. I will show the outcome of this at the end of the druidical chapter, but in the meantime show how the Roman pattern of attempted conversion ran a close parallel.

Then some forty five years later there is a complete 'volte face'- the whole of the country is simmering with resentment at the harshness of the Roman yoke on their necks, the Druids are reported as the spiritual leaders of a growing rebellion, and overnight the Roman propaganda machine swings into action libelling them as perpetrating vile practices, indulging in inhuman sacrifices of people, and every vice imaginable! Somewhat strange after extensive writings for the preceding 47 years praising them.

The fact of the matter is that they did clearly identify with the Old Religion that was universally practised by the populace, but at the same time were secular, maintaining what I see as a religion within a religion. Once Rome accused them of plotting subversion the Roman General Suetonius Paulinus was dispatched to their headquarters on the Island of Mona

(Anglesey) with orders to suppress them and crush any insurrection against Roman rule, which the Romans did with vigour. He mustered the fourteenth and twentieth legions and set of to put all resistance to the sword. Druidical resistance was so fierce that the Romans palled against their fury, particularly that of their women.

Tacitus wrote at the time of the ferocity of the resistance they encountered before which the highly-trained Roman forces paled at first, and had to be urged on by the centurions to confront them. Just as the Celts' women were as feared as their men folk, so were the Druids' women an equally fearsome sight for as the Druids attacked, their women dressed in fearsome attire did execrate dreadful curses upon them.

In the conquest of the Celtic nation here the Romans made frequent comments on the fact that unlike Rome, Celtic male society placed women on the same social level as themselves. The worship of the Goddess as Queen of the Earth being the dominant factor, which had in turn led to immolation of womanhood as a whole. Women under the Celts and the Old Religion could own and inherit land, sit in council with the tribal elders and become chieftains and leaders in their own right.

A classic example of this is the great Queen Boudicca (Boadicea) who took over leadership of the Iceni after the death of her husband Prasutagus and in AD 51 was instrumental in drawing away the legions busily committing genocide against the Druids on Mona, forcing Suetonius Paulinus to abandon his policy of extermination and march east to confront her.

Boudicca was a queen in her own right and as such united resistance in a mighty rebellion against the oppressive Roman occupiers. Regretfully she was ultimately defeated after a succession of mighty victories against Caesar during which she slaughtered some 80% of the Roman army and burned three of the four major Roman towns existing in the east together with the entire population. Namely Camulodunum, now Colchester, Londinium, now London and Verulanium, now St Albans. Her fury was legendary and her hatred of the brutality and suppression of Rome not without reason. Prior to the rebellion the chauvinistic Romans refused to acknowledge her as a queen and when she rebelled they had her flogged and as a final indignity had her teenage daughters gang raped before her eyes. Her rebellion granted a respite to the siege of the Druids on Mona but after the collapse of the revolt in AD 61 Suetonius returned to Mona and over several years succeeded in slaughtering them in their entirety.

Notwithstanding this he ordered the complete and utter destruction of the island to eradicate all trace of the Druid culture and religion. The legions spent years cutting down the sacred groves and eventually every tree on the Island was felled. Never before in history has such a destruction been wrought on such a massive scale, it took years to complete. Romans were notorious for sacking and levelling towns to their very foundations in a matter of weeks, but the entire island of Mona (Anglesey as we know it today.) was completely and utterly destroyed, and all traces of the Druids reduced to ashes.

There is a strange and very sad event that followed here, for following its destruction some 2,000 years were to pass until in the 1900s a farmer's plough uncovered a stele with undecipherable writing on it, and it was taken to a local Catholic priest who was also a scholar. He translated the inscription and together with the farmer returned to the field where he excavated some further 48 steles. The news of the discovery was commented upon in the local press and eventually came to the attention of the British Museum who swiftly descended upon what was regarded as one of the most remarkable archaeological discoveries in years and which in turn they earnestly believed could at long last shed some light on the Druidical beliefs and their affiliation with the Old Religion,

The priest, forewarned of the coming of the researchers, and in view of what the tablets contained, which he described as 'Pagan, and an affront to Xtianity', set about destroying them over the weekend with a sledge hammer so that the esoteric knowledge they contained would never be released. The powdered fragments he threw from a nearby bridge into a fast-flowing river. Subsequent excavation of the site I understand yielded up a single tablet which is now in the British Museum. It is described as unique and would from what it contained have thrown a completely new light on the original religions of this country and the interweaving of Druidism and the Old Religion as such, but has been lost forever.

So what do we know of the Druids? What can we analyse from the scant records existing? No one is sure as to how the word Druid originated, and it could well have come from Ireland where Druidism was strongly entrenched, the Irish word *Drui* meaning 'men of the trees' I think that the fact that the Gallic Druids who had strong affiliations with Britain were called *Druidh* is a far more likely source however. This word in the language of Gaul is interpreted as Sorcerer or Wise One. It is almost certain also that Druidism was introduced into this country via Gaul and it is to France that we must repair to try to track down what information exists.

We know from the *Encyclopaedia Britannica* that old records show they were experts in medicine and herbalists, the same as their Old Religion counterparts were. Also, like the wise women and wise men of the villages, they understood and loved all things in nature. They understood natural theology, and were experts in geography and natural sciences, but the greatest attribute that has been passed down through history from them is their accomplishments in astrology.

Stonehenge, one of the outstanding monuments ever to have been constructed, has been attributed to them, and there does not seem much doubt from its positioning that it was a major, albeit primitive observatory in its heyday.

Eliphas Levi the famous transcendentalist wrote. "That they were Priests and Physicians who cured by the use of magnetic forces, and by the 'charging' of amulets. Modern-day Druids from the orders I referred to earlier always dress in white, though from contemporary reports it appears that green was the predominant colour amongst the hierophants while the priesthood wore robes of brilliant green.

Again, a parallel between Druidism and the old Wiccan ways of the Old Religion is the mutual belief in reincarnation and the transmigration of the soul force. From the worship of both sun and moon, we find that the female element in the form of the Moon Goddess prevails, as was the lore of the Witches of old. Pagans, Wiccans and Druids used the cross as a magical symbol to represent the four seasons and this is a further example of the Church's doctrine of replacement theology, by the usurping of the cross as a Xtian symbol notwithstanding the fact that crucifixion was carried out on a stake and not on a cross as is popularly thought. This cross though was an even sided or Celtic style cross, as we know it today.

The pentacle or five pointed star was a sacred symbol together with the 'U' or horseshoe shape. The four points of the original cross represented the elements of Earth, Air, Fire, and Water, while the five-pointed star had three differentiations. On the one hand – and most important of all, it was the sign of the Goddess in the 'Star Goddess' position. The pentacle was always displayed with a single tip up, representing the head of the Goddess, the two parallel 'arms' were her limbs, and the two splayed base sections were the legs, a symbol of sexual fecundity. The five points were also representative of the five paths of wisdom, a Wiccan secret that is taught at the third degree, and cannot be disclosed here, plus they also stood for the five elements, a slight contradiction as technically spirit is not an element as such.

Druidical worship of nature spirits emphasised the form of wood spirits in the form of dryads in particular. In fact there is a school of thought that the word Druid could also have been originated from the word "dryad".

Stonehenge? Caesar mentions the worship of Mercury by the Druids who he states as being worshipped beneath great stone blocks – this could well be Stonehenge? Another reference mentions Mercury being worshipped beneath a great stone cube.

"Their temples wherein the sacred fire was preserved were generally situate on eminences and in dense groves of oak, and assumed various forms – circular, because a circle was the emblem of the universe; oval, in allusion to the mundane egg, from which issued, according to the traditions of many nations, the universe, or, according to others, our first parents; serpentine, because a serpent was the symbol of Hu, the Druidic Osiris; cruciform, because a cross is an emblem of regeneration; or winged, to represent the motion of the Divine Spirit."

I have referred to crucifixion earlier, as being performed on a stake as against the cross, which has emerged as a popular fiction. Very rarely was this carried out on a cross and because of the expense, special dispensation would have been sought from the authorities or the condemning court for a cross to be used. This myth of the cross has been perpetuated through various writings, rewriting and editing of the Bible over 1400 years - basically ending with the 'perfect Bible', the King James version currently in use.

Wiccan Ways, Old Ways and Weddings

Some covens over the years adopted some rather strange ideas with regard to what should take place prior to a newcomer's initiation. Most of these seem to have been imported when the French weavers came over; bringing with them some decidedly odd ideas that had evolved on the continent. Before we condemn these, what are referred to as 'ordeals', we have to realise that covens on the continent had to be far more resolute than covens here as the persecutions in France, Spain, and Germany in particular, reached a height of ferocity, triggered by the Inquisition that was unknown here. One can only conclude that these ordeals that were inflicted on new initiates was to test their resoluteness in such uncertain times.

I have found that some covens do still practise some of these old original ceremonies, when at one stage they had all but died out, but in actual fact they seem to be on the increase, almost as a protest at the New Age fervour that is sweeping the USA, and here also, which trying to bring Wicca into the 21st century in a new ultra-modernistic enactment of the Old Religion. This new trend is looked upon aghast by Gardnerian and Traditionalist Witches alike and is absolutely anathema to those of hereditary stock. For what these 'neo' Pagans are forgetting is that the Old Religion is just that, the OLD Religion, but of England.

Some of the rituals from the misty past that were known as the 'ordeal', are still practised in some covens, and do leave a little bit to be desired; and while we ourselves long ago decided to abandon the practise in full, we do allow it occasionally in an amended form. The most that some ever do to a candidate once they have been selected is to leave them tied to a tree for a period of the night (a warm one may I add) to meditate and commune with nature before they face the ordeal of initiation.

Watchers appointed by the coven will keep a vigilant watch throughout, and the coven itself will be nearby enjoying hot coffee and sandwiches should they be needed. This ordeal is as far as modern covens go nowadays but years ago it was a completely different picture. After the initiate had been alone for about two hours blindfolded, they would return and imitate animal sounds. This was to test the courage of the one that they anticipated joining them, but must have been a harrowing ordeal.

Following this the initiate was freed and given sustenance, but one bond around the waist would be left in place, they were then led joyously to the initiation site, clapping and laughing to where the 'birth' would be symbolically re-enacted. This could be enacted by the initiate simply crawling through a tunnel into the open at the beginning, but once there the main ceremony began. And it is this method which is the origin of the 'triangle (as well as the symbolism of maiden, mother, and crone). The triangle also represents the 'v' shape of the pubic area and once more is identified with fertility.'

The rite did have a number of variations that differed on the continent to here, but one thing they had in common was that the rite was performed sky clad (nude) and that both sexes had to crawl through the legs of the High Priestess at the climax of the ritual. In some ceremonies all the women formed a crocodile and with their legs apart, the initiate had to crawl through them, the fecundity of this is obvious, a nude line up of women of all ages in age order with their open legs forming a triangle became the vaginal passage and at the end the initiate had the waist cord cut to symbolise the severing of the umbilical cord.

At this point the initiate was ceremonially bathed exactly the same as a new-born baby would be, usually in a sacred spring or stream. In some ceremonies this would have been an essential element for there are records worldwide that depict the initiate being covered in animal blood prior to the rite, while others suggest a substance such as red ochre or 'Dragons blood' (Dragon's blood for the record is jewellers' rouge) was used to smear the body. This then is the origin of the fertility symbol of the triangle just as the pentacle is the symbol of the skyclad Goddess, and is why it is essential that the pentacle in all rituals is positioned correctly.

Although this book does not detail ceremonies I will however point out a factor to those who wear a pentacle, or have one in their home, and that is never to display it upside down, a terrible innovation that has crept in accidentally through a publication by a well-known practitioner of the Craft whereby the pentacle was published upside down and has been copied by some new age Pagans. I go into more details on this in a separate chapter that follows this entitled 'Turning the Goddess on her Head'. The pentacle is a star in shape and the outline of it when observed must essentially be humanoid, and that is of a figure of the Goddess in the 'Star Goddess' position with the top point being the head the two side arms being of course the arms and the bottom appendages, forming a triangle – again the fertility aspect, showing the Goddess standing with legs apart. The High Priestess takes up this posture when she adopts the Star Goddess position, that is legs wide apart and arms held out to form a pentacle.

If the pentacle is reversed it becomes a sign of evil and bad luck will befall the wearer for it will be associated with the Goat of Mendes, and a depiction of evil, often identified with the Xtian Satan. Although Witches do not believe in Satan as such, identifying him as a Xtian invention rather than a genuine entity, it does not belie the fact that it is the reverse of the Goddess as a symbol of good, and therefore depicts the darkness of the left hand path and evil.

I do not mean that bad luck will necessarily befall the wearer, but what he or she is wearing will certainly cast dark images around them, and leave them open to malignant and dark forces, who will be attracted to them. It is sheer folly to tempt fate and lose the protection of the Old Ones. This again is a deadly trend among many new age advocates which is more a symbol of rebellion against society as against a genuine love of the Old Gods of the past and is to be deplored.

Sometimes I am asked as to which is the correct way to wear a pentacle ring and I can only give the tradition that we were brought up in, and that was to wear the ring so that you always saw the head of the Goddess with the body stretching outwards; so an observer seeing your hand before them, would see the Goddess in the correct position.

Some practitioners prefer to be able to look down and see the Goddess looking up at them, and probably are happy to see this as a sign of her smiling protectively up at them - so be it, but this is only on the finger and a ring, never as a neck ornament or brooch should it be upside down. The rule as far as the silver cladagh ring is quite emphatic, this is the silver ring whose origins lie in Old Ireland and was centred in the village of Cladagh and essentially must be made of gold, by tradition it is handed down from the mother to her eldest daughter, the Irish tradition is identical to our own, except traditionally ours must be silver, but the rules are the same, and that is the heart must be seen in full to those who observe it, when the Witch looks down upon it, they will see the top of the heart with the point stretching outwards.

Rebirth into the new way of life is once more part of both ancient and modern religion, and in Xtianity many are what are called 'born again' Xtians. The entire concept which is symbolised by rebirth is that all the sins of your previous years right up to your new conversion are behind you completely and utterly.

To a Xtian you are literally newly born, and pure as a new born baby, now ready to start a new Xtian life anew devoid of all the sins of the past. A very fine concept indeed if it was practised. In theory a murderer having 'seen the light' so to speak could be reborn and become a respected member of the community, as could thieves, rapists, and all sinners. Outwardly by this Xtian theorem Adolph Hitler himself could be forgiven and pardoned if he truly repented and accepted the Xtian ritual of rebirth. So the old AH is dead and a new reformed AH is ready to take his place in society. Ugh! Well I found a little crack in this 'reborn' syndrome; for even as a Witch I have a substantial number of Xtian friends who are devout and sincere in their beliefs.

Well one friend of mine who was not a practising Xtian at the time, sadly had to divorce a somewhat errant and rather promiscuous wife after putting up with her infidelities for years on end. It culminated with her running away with an itinerant and leaving him with a number of debts. To cut a long story short, a divorce followed and in the depths of depression he 'found' religion. He was converted to the Xtian faith and became a 'born again Xtian' with the old life wiped out and a new one looming, his unhappy past behind him - in theory.

Some two years later, and well after his divorce he met a Xtian girl from the self-same group of evangelists and a marriage was arranged. Delightedly they informed their minister of their intentions to marry – and were promptly refused! No, they were informed quite curtly, he had been married and divorced and no way could he be married in church. In vain he argued that the very concept of being reborn was to wipe out the past completely and utterly, so why was the past an obstacle now?

Well it appears that in being 'reborn' there are exceptions to the rule, murderers, genocide, adulterers, even harlots and mobsters could be forgiven, including Genghis Khan and Attila the Hun - the Scourge of God - if they repented. Notwithstanding the fact that countless millions died through their ravages and that they both kept a vast court of concubines, the fact was they had never married, but divorce, ah, now that was a far more serious sin.

Thoroughly disillusioned the couple left the church and I am pleased to say became Pagans. After accepting their conversion was genuine they were duly initiated, and came the great day that they were handfasted. They have been devout and loyal followers of the Old Religion ever since. The Church's loss was our gain, and soon he and his bride will enter the third degree and start their own coven together.

Another old custom I will record here, being as we are on the subject of weddings, is the wedding ring itself. The symbolisation of the rings being placed upon each other's fingers is clearly a remnant of the old Pagan fertility rite where the placing of rings was an act of consummation, the male finger representing a phallus and the ring the female yoni.

What has passed into history once more and is near forgotten is that the wedding ring was of pure iron. It appears that gold only entered the equation after the near extinction of Pagan practice, and that Xtians wanted to show their wealth and substituted gold. When you look at all the trappings of a wedding today costing thousands of pounds, and the bride all adorned in white – bride being a remnant of the Goddess Bride, then you realise how Mammon has entered into the Church. A far cry from when the newly-weds jumped a fertility fire, or their union was celebrated by the local blacksmith who had made their rings of iron to order and married them across his anvil. Remember smiths were considered magical people, and smithying was a magical trade. When faced with the exorbitant costs of marrying today then small wonder that so many still flee to the old smithy at Gretna Green.

Again near-forgotten was the ritual of the leaf as a symbol of consummation,. There are two rituals near identical in fact, one is that just before the ring was placed on the bride's finger a leaf would be placed in front of it and the bridegroom therefore had to push his finger through the leaf and into the ring as a symbol of braking the hymen. The other ritual was near identical and the bride offered her husband-to-be a leaf in the palm of her hand and again the groom had to penetrate it with his finger.

The superstitions associated with weddings are legion but one that goes back into the realms of time is that of the sweep - no wedding once upon a time would be complete without a sweep being invited. I would love to know the origins of this dishevelled and grimy figure dropping fragments of soot wherever he went to the pristine and glistening purity of the bride in her white raiment. We know that the very word 'bride' has its origins in the Goddess Bride (pronounced bree-day) a virginal Goddess associated with purity, but the sweep?

My own conclusion is that it is a remnant of the 'man in black' the coven summoner of old referred to in a separate chapter. He was a guardian of the coven and was always on hand to protect the High Priestess who represented the Goddess. My guess is that this is a vestige of the old ways and the sweep has become a symbol of that self-same guardianship. When you consider that many sweeps take a black cat along with them as well as part of the proceedings then the occult association becomes stronger.

This association with black and the sweep goes even further when we find old traditions being passed down from father to son and mother to daughter when a sweep would be invited to be the first to cross the threshold within seconds quite often of midnight being struck on New Year's Eve; for legend says he is the harbinger of luck and disperser of evil for the coming year.

In olden days (remember the sweep could not be everywhere at once) people would often tremble at the prospect of a red-headed man or woman being the first to cross the threshold and thus bring bad luck with them in the coming year. So much so that children would be told to look out for who was coming to the house so that a redhead would not be the first to enter, and they would keep their fingers crossed and hope that if a dark-haired man was not the first to enter on New Year's Day, then at least let it be someone with brown hair. A superstition that evolved from this was that a piece of coal (black!) could be used as a substitute - strange. In Ireland, which abounds with red-headed men and women, there are a variety of superstitions where a red-haired woman could find herself barred - and feelings could run high!

We do know the origins of carrying one's bride over the door-step, one of which is that it was considered unlucky for the future of the marriage if the bride trod on the step, to ensure this did not happen accidentally the groom would carry his newly wedded wife over the threshold. Oh and by the way it was essential that they start off on the right path, for it was decreed that the groom must enter with his right foot foremost.

Birth-Marriage-Death, the natural sequence of life, but another old custom that seems to have disappeared over the last 50 years - probably with the rise in petty crime; is that of leaving every window and the front and back door wide-open as the funeral cortege left the house, and would remain so until the owner returned. This old custom was designed to make sure the deceased's spirit had left the premises and would not be trapped inside as its mortal shell was interred, it was essential to avoid the wraith of the dead person becoming earthbound.

In all the years of my youth I have never ever heard of a house being burgled while the funeral was taking place. (A sad reflection on today's society when this would provide an ideal opportunity for a drug-addled lout to pillage the house.) This custom seems to have been particularly prevalent in villages while in towns all the curtains in the house would be drawn the night before the funeral and not reopened until they returned from the interment. If the deceased was lying in state either in a closed or open coffin inside the house then the curtains of that room would remain closed throughout and remained so until the relatives returned.

But that was yesterday.

Besom, Brooms and Public Weighings

Besom brooms and public weighings - this is Eastern Europe in the 21st Century.

In 1993 my filmmaking took me to Russia, and while there I could not resist investigating as to whether, alongside Xtianity, Paganism too, had been suppressed by the all-powerful Communist regime over the onerous years it had been in power, and had crushed anything that did not conform to the party line. Or had it managed to survive?

Surprisingly I found that not only had Paganism survived, but was in fact flourishing! My only regret was that I did not have the time to spare to travel to the areas where it was strongest. Strangely enough, Moscow was a hotbed of a new renaissance, as were Nijniy, Novgorod, and Viatka; but as I was resident in Moscow at the time my enquiries were essentially centred there, although the most Pagan area that came up in convers-ation again, and again was the province of Viatka!

I never had time to attend a ritual while I was there, but I found that the modus operandii was vastly different to our concept which is now so closely aligned with Gardnerian style rituals, plus the fact that there was a very distinct overlap with many of our ways, with the longest day rituals in June, which I will explain later. One thing came over loud and clear, and that is Russian 'Witchcraft' or their own form of Paganism is much more closely allied to the land than ours is currently.

As I have said in previous chapters, it is a sad fact that here in Britain we have lost so much lore and ritual over the centuries, but the sheer vastness of that enormous country has resulted in vast enclaves of people and communities being cut off from civilisation, and the all pervasive incursions of the Russian Orthodox Church.

Here in the sprawling forests and scattered villages their isolation has meant that the old ways had survived. Provided they sent their percentage of produce to the communist collectives at regular intervals the commissars had little interest as to what they got up to. As long as they delivered unto Caesar, what was Caesar's, then Caesar left them alone. In the Russian tongue the word Paganism is literally translated as 'Peoples Faith' and the quaint rituals of the peasants who found delight in dancing in the forests and over- imbibing vodka were nor regarded as menacing the State, after all what Russian did not get drunk under their oppressive rule.

In Moscow itself these 'country ways' are being avidly sought and practised as they attempt to revive everything from old folk dances and customs to primitive beliefs. To the townspeople as a whole though, this renaissance is regarded as 'an antique old national belief'. In researching old customs I found a strange contradiction with regard to rites that were performed on the longest day i.e. the Summer Solstice. The longest day falls on June 21st the same as here, obviously, but the great Solstice celebration is held on June the 23rd and is known as the Feast or Night of Ivan Kupala, this is extremely prevalent in the Viatka area of Russia. Whole villages leave 'en masse' for the shelter of the forests to perform these old rites and worship the Old Gods. The sheer diversity of this huge country shows how the Old Ways have been preserved and have evolved independently.

As far as I can make out the 23rd is regarded as a more potent day as folklore says that nature reaches its zenith on that date. They say that flora will bloom at midnight when their rituals are performed, that at midnight a fern plant will blossom, and any man or woman who manages to pick it during this brief period will become all-powerful for the coming year. As a Magi and an omnipotent being, he will be able to see treasure underground! He will be able to master the tongues and sounds of all wild animals and birds; he will also be able to speak to trees. I found this old custom both beautiful and refreshing.

One custom there, that is identical to ours, is the gathering of morning dew, their's being collected up in small phials at the break of dawn on the 24th as against our covens gathering up this magical fluid on the 22nd after the midnight celebrations, and, as here, this is followed by a dawn ritual. Like us they believe that this elixir will keep them young, beautiful, and healthy. How I wish this was true, but this was believed aeons ago here and is an integral part of our past. Note however, that this fluid is used in specific rituals to this day.

In Russia at the break of dawn on the 23rd of June the village maidens collect plants and flowers and weave these into intricate patterns not unlike our corn dollies. Wormwood is entwined within these as a protection against evil spirits which are believed to be exceptionally dangerous that night. Wiccan custom here feels that the consecration of the sacred circle is adequate protection in itself and there is no need for individuals to be consecrated as we do, such as with the bestowing of a 'gifu' to each covener.

Much of the rituals performed run a close parallel to the European traditions of lighting and jumping bonfires in purification rites, but they are dedicated to Ivan Kupala. I was told by a Russian who had returned from Serbia that Witchcraft was still rife in the rural areas in particular, but that Witches were still feared and avoided, this was to a point of near hysteria, but at least we now know it has survived and later I will try to find out more about their rituals. I found no evidence of persecution though, if someone was suspected of being a witch.

Regretfully this inherent fear is so deeply imbedded that men are petrified that they may inadvertently marry a Witch, for these creatures can appear as beautiful and submissive wives, but subliminally may turn out to be a Witch. They seem to associate a new bride who they take to bed with some awe, fearing that she might be a vampire and they will awake the next morning to find themselves utterly drained of blood, and a beatific smile on the face of their bride!

So deeply ingrained is this fear that historians from the Novi Sad University have delved into ancient records held in the deeps of their crumbling cellars to revive a Witch test - and remember that this is in this the 21st century and is really believed, and all this is happening, even as I write. After months of research they found an ancient ritual that could determine if a woman was a witch or not, by weighing her with, and without a broomstick - true! In no time at all, they had set up a Witch testing centre at Djundjerski Castle in the town of Kulpin.

Initially, we are informed, if the story is to be believed, that the Witch testing centre was a 'tongue in cheek' attraction, initially for foreign visitors and tourists to see the re-enactment of this age-old ritual. But overnight they were inundated with hundreds of enquiries from would-be bridegrooms, fearful that their potential brides could turn out to be Witches, and were willing to pay for them to be tested. Now I gather there is a regular procession of brides accompanied by their husbands-to - be, for the public testing before attested witnesses.

The girls are first weighed in public, and the weight read, and announced to the crowd (could be embarrassing even at that stage, although a well-padded Russian gal is considered highly desirable). Next they are given an ordinary run-of-the-mill broomstick identical to the besom broom of the Middle Ages - and still sold in garden centres to this day, (in fact no Halloween party would be complete without one). Now, with the broomstick between her legs, the bride-to-be is weighed a second time and the new reading is then read out aloud. In theory their weight should be fractionally more, although with the primitive scales (they use a pendulum scales of justice style machine), usually used for weighing sacks of potatoes and the like are not accurate to within a few ounces I am sure.

If the bride-to-be weighs more at the second weighing then she is declared not to be a Witch and given a certificate to this effect to display to all the villagers back home. The legend says that if they weigh the same at the second weighing, then they are being supported by the broomstick - a sure sign that they are in league with the infernal one. I have been told that superstitious bridegrooms have demanded, and paid for, a second weighing to be absolutely sure!

What started out as the revival of an ancient custom to attract visitors dramatically backfired as old countryside fears rose to the fore. So much so that many visitors from surrounding countries have brought their spouses and intended spouses along to be weighed just in case, and as a result the certificates are now printed in many languages, if I win the lottery I am going to take my mother in law's ashes there just to prove a point.

In Russia they pay particular attention to water rituals concentrating on consecrating the all-holy liquid which is taken to the sacred site in quantity and taken home afterwards to be used for rituals throughout the year. I have yet to find out who Ivan Kupala was, or is. My time in Russia was far too short and I was working and had no transport. My Russian was extremely limited, and I found it a complex language, I spent five years in Czechoslovakia and found that tongue comparatively easy, but through my interpreter I found out that *Kupala* is the Russian word for 'swimming' or 'to wash', and is based on the word *Cupat* meaning water purification. There are far more complex rituals that take place on the other Sabbats, and water seems to dominate many of them.

We must remember that holy wells and springs were a primary point of veneration to our ancestors, and were a target for the

Xtian invaders who sequestered them. Even the Xtian 'Holy Water' is based on us, and has been usurped by them, for we used to consecrate spring water and use it in ritual long before them - and still do. One thing I mention out of interest is that no Xtian clergymen are ever taught how to consecrate water, nor what is used, strange but for some reason it is not part of their curriculum. What is common knowledge to all initiated Witches is still unknown to the Church I guess this is one secret we still have.

NB A debate ensued amongst clergymen in mid 2003 when they debated this very issue and each one admitted he or she had never been taught how to make Holy Water. It was quite hilarious as each expounded his own method of consecrating it, and it varied from the wild to the wacky, with one stating he simply poured it from a tap and used it; while another said he muttered a verbal blessing over it.

Most said they blessed it in their own way usually by making the sign of the cross over the chalice; one even said he dipped a holy wafer in it and then used it - no wonder their exorcisms rarely work! I must give the top prize to the ecclesiastic who smiled and said "I must admit I was never taught either, in fact when I asked the bishop how it was done he just ignored me - so I just pour it into a kettle and boil the hell out of it! Amen!

Witchcraft - the Roots of Witchcraft and Its Impact on the USA

America - Land of the Free! Here within this vast continent the old Pagan religion of Great Britain and most of Europe has been reborn with a vengeance. Year after year more and more denizens of the USA throw off the cloying shackles of Xtianity to rejoice in a newfound freedom as they revert to nature and the worship of the great Earth Mother. From California to Kentucky, Oregon to Arizona, and from New Mexico to New England, a New Age is sweeping America. Everywhere the Goddess is returning to her ancient roots as womanhood, suppressed by the Xtian doctrine for centuries comes back into her own as the Eternal Earth Mother with her cohort the Lord Cernunnos by her side.

Wonderful America! Now dedicated to the old ways is a forerunner of a new Pagan renaissance that is sweeping the civilised world. Sincere in its new beliefs. Devout in its worship, and blindly loyal in its love of the Goddess it is the heralding of a new age that Huxley could only have dreamed of when he envisaged the future of mankind - erroneously may I add!

But sadly, Oh America, over the years the majority of you have lost your roots in the process. Accept or reject as you wish but let us hope that this book will bring you back to the basics of the Old Religion and its ancient Pagan practises practised for thousands of years - a religion as old as time itself and whose basic simplicity was its great attraction to the masses with the worship of a God and Goddess as the Sun and the Moon.

I have sat in the sweat lodges of the Navaho, and walked with the Hopi and I have learned to respect the basic simplicity of their beliefs. Start here America and look to your own indigenous roots, and to your own indigenous people who worshipped the Sun and Moon and only took from nature the basics of what they required. The North American native worshipped everything that moved on the face of the Earth, and saw magic in the still of the desert, in rocks and in trees, and in the all life-giving runs of water and well, they lived close to and with Nature.

As the new renaissance sweeps the country, Wicca has degenerated into a mega-dollar industry. Everywhere New Age shops are springing up with a wonderful assortment of paraphernalia and artefacts to help get the wannabe Witch started. Within its walls they can procure everything required to start on the bottom rung of the ladder that they hope will lead them to supreme Witchdom, if you have the money you can acquire power. Shelves displaying a vast variety of statuettes, from Isis to Astarte bewilder the newcomer as he or she wavers from old Egypt to the Thessalonian Witches in deciding what path they should take.

Books on every subject imaginable cover miles of shelving as they offer a tantalising range of subjects that can, and do, range from Tantricism to Telepathy. Here within the pages of these epistles freely on sale the potential Witch can find everything required to be a lone practitioner - known as a hedge Witch in Great Britain, or how to form your own coven (frightful thought!) or even cast a spell completely and utterly devoid of training.

Illustrated will be definitions and descriptions of every artefact you will need for your altar to get started. You will also need an almanac to ensure you conduct your newly-found rituals at the correct moon times, be able to study its phases, and learn to differentiate moon meanings according to the seasons, from this you can find what moons dominate and influence the Wiccan equinoxes and Sabbats.

So dear reader with your credit card in your hand you can buy everything required for the mastering of the ancient art. You will emerge from the shop with a beautiful silver chalice, suitably ornamented of course, and you can even get your potential Witch name engraved on it (Lord of the Rings chalices seem to be very much the 'in' thing nowadays). Next, a highly polished brass or copper pentacle (you can get them in solid gold I hear) plus of course the absolutely essential wand without which no self-respecting Witch would be without - Oh these by the way can come in either crystal or silver and the head of which (according to price of course) will contain a rare crystal or have a mounted gem stone. Perhaps you would like your birthstone inserted for instance?

Next stop is to acquire a suitable blade for your Athame, a white handled knife, and a sword - again your local occult shop will supply you with all of these with a guarantee that these blades have never shed blood or been involved in violence, what they do not do is tell you how to occultically cleanse and purify a blade just in case and thus remove any negative vibrations it may contain, and finally an altar cloth.

The book will instruct you to obtain a thurible for solid or gum incense, together with a good supply of charcoal, plus a second one duly perforated for stick incense. Do not forget a good depiction of the God and Goddess to stand on the altar, Pan, Cernunnos, and even Baphomet are easy to come by, but there seems to be a dearth of western-style Goddesses so you will probably have to settle for Isis, or an eastern one. Greece seems to be the favourite place to obtain the Gods and Goddesses of Olympus, which are favourites, but they do appear to be scarce in Texas.

Reverting to your book you will find you require three candlesticks for the altar plus four for the quarters of the circle, and by the way you can now obtain full-sized circles in heavy cloth or plastic beautifully illustrated with the words of power in Runic, Theban, Futhorc, or even in Passing the River script, not forgetting Hebrew of course, together with the Zodiacal signs thrown in.

Yes, this is American Wicca in the 21st century, where instant DIY Witchcraft can be obtained overnight as the suppliers of occult paraphernalia strive to part you from your dollars and sell you old religion. Many athames come already engraved with the 'secret' symbols as do the traditional white-handled knives, in fact anything and everything is for sale.

Next find a group of aficionados to found your coven, in all probability you will have to purchase another book to learn how to do this. So let us presume you have 12 people, after all you MUST have the magical 13 including yourself - the book says so, (although history has never demanded a specific number) and to be politically correct and also to conform to tradition you should have balanced the numbers and have picked 6 men and 6 women with a High Priestess to rule over all. (Could this really be politically correct if you are outnumbered fellows?)

The first thing of course is who is going to be HPSS? If the one founding the coven is of course a woman then logically the mantle of power will fall around thy shoulders, after all it is you who have paid for everything. If you are a man then you will have to choose a lady who is willing to take up the mantle. I feel I should warn that once you do so she will immediately be your boss, and you must obey her. Sorry fellows but that's the law, so choose someone who is not very dominant, preferably subservient and is not a woman's libber, and who will obey your slightest wish for an occasional box of chocolates - well you can try, but without a strong Priestess at the helm you are doomed! On a serious note the High Priestess must have knowledge, must be firm and gentle too, she has to represent the Goddess in all her forms remember - but here we are talking 'real' covens' not book-based or correspondence course ones.

Right! Now we now have everything to start up and become what is known in Yankee land as a 'bootstrapper' i.e., a self-taught, self-initiated Witch, and who will now run a bootstrapping coven devoid of roots or any form of heritage to be conducted according to what your particular book dictates.

If the new Witch has chosen carefully and knows a little bit about Witchcraft or has at least a modicum of knowledge then he or she may well have chosen wisely and selected from titles that do give a fair and accurate picture of Witchcraft. Recommended reading is of course authors such as Gerald Broussec Gardener, Doreen Valiente, Janet and Stewart Farrar etc. At least with such books as these the coven will be following a reasonably correct path, but without an experienced and fully initiated Witch at the helm it will be the blind leading the blind as they falter and grope their way through rituals. The secret they will have to learn from an experienced High Priest or High Priestess is the intonation of the words to raise power, for unless this can be mastered then all is lost at the very start.

There is an old maxim of the Craft that runs "In Herbis, Verbis, and Lapidibus, Magna Vis Est" translated "In Herbs, Words, and Stones doth lay a Great Power", this can also be interpreted as "In Herbs, Words and Stones doth lie the Power" but from the beginning you are taught the intonation of words that are the secret of all magic - Verbis is the operational word here.

The greatest danger to these bootstrappers (your word my American friends - not mine - In fact I had never heard the expression until I conducted a lecture tour of the USA in 2003 through the courtesy of Levanah Shell Bdolack of the American- based Clearsight organisation) is what if they get hold of some nebulous book on so-called Witchcraft that has about as much in common with the Old Religion as Xtianity has with voodoo.

In my travels in the USA I was frankly staggered at the amount of spurious material on sale, and moreover what was being bought, a trend that has already crept into Britain as our bookshelves become polluted with so-called New Age sentiments, usually, the same as I found in America, sects and schisms that allegedly came over from hereditary covens (they are always 'Hereditary') from Latvia, Croatia, Russia and Timbuktu, plus Italian Stregas originating in every state in South America. Traditions may I add that no one within these countries have ever heard of and of which there are no historical records whatsoever.

Some of the genuine ones have come mainly from central Europe, France, Germany, Sweden, Norway, Denmark, and Spain etc where years of persecution, far more terrible than anything we in England experienced drove the indigenous Pagans underground and only now are they starting to emerge again. These people can tell of ancient practises that are authentic and deserve to be read. Regretfully I can offer no criteria whereby you can judge them, except to say that if they run a close parallel to English practises then there is a fair chance of them being genuine.

On a historical note I find Iceland is predominately Pagan, and what is the equivalent of the Old Religion is the centre of religious practice there. Xtianity has been making inroads for centuries but the old ways are still strong and holding their own - in fact the Wiccan laws are recognised and upheld by the government.

To quote a case in point I delved through a series of newspapers kindly sent to me and was surprised to find a matrimonial case listed and reported upon. It seems a British sailor had sailed into port one day and in a whirlwind romance had spent his fourteen day furlough serenading his heart's choice in the form of a young maiden who reciprocally fell in love with him. Her parents were not happy when he proposed marriage as they were both practitioners of the old religion, and unlike our modern counterparts who insist on free choice at the age of 18 their beloved daughter had been brought up in the Wiccan faith. The end result was that the local High Priest and

Priestess, albeit reluctantly, but convinced of the couple's love for each other conducted a handfasting and registered it with the local authority. The Icelandic government recognised this as a legal marriage.

The parents were convinced that it was infatuation but as the saying goes the daughter was over 18 and a woman in her own right. Well it turned out that the sailor who had sailed right into port sailed right out again and when sued by his wife for maintenance argued - long distance - that he was a Xtian, and claimed the marriage was not valid in law - British law - absolutely correct, but this malcontent had been handfasted in Iceland and Icelandic law ruled.

Woe betide him if ever he set foot in Iceland again. I do not know the ultimate outcome but presume that under what was old British tradition, another practice that has fallen into disuse may I add, the handfasting vows would have been renewed at the end of a year and a day and the souls would then religiously be entwined for eternity. It would therefore have been possible to break this 'marriage' as they had not remained together for a year and a day.

Pagans accepted trial marriages for the above period and this gave the couple a good chance to discover their compatibility to each other during this period. Contraception was extremely effective at the time and they could ensure that no child would emerge from the union, some of the remedies I have discovered that were used are frightful, but they worked.

Another blight that has gained momentum in Britain and America as well is the glut of so-called tarot readers, in Britain. They infest the psychic fairs in droves each and every one of them touting their wares and varying their fees and vying with each other to attract the ever-avid populace anxious to learn their fate and future - if you do not like what you hear from one then simply go on to the next until you hear what you want to! Those who tell the unwary what they feel they want to hear swiftly gain a name as being good readers to the detriment of quite often the genuine. Such is the growth of these so-called masters of the art of divination that in England they predominate the psychic fairs to such an extent that they are more like tarot reader gatherings.

In America I did not find a single occult shop that did not have a cubicle or cubicles available with the shop's own resident reader, not that there are not shops devoid of them, but certainly in California I did not see a single one. Tarot is the curse of the new age. They attract a procession of hopefuls into the shops and once having completed their findings and had their future divined, wend their way into the shop itself and spend more dollars.

The problem again is the amateur who buys one of the dreaded books and starts to study tarot, often devoid of any spirituality or psychic awareness, they spend a few days - often less - 'studying' and I use the word loosely, and cap in hand set themselves up as a reader. Sorry, of course you can study tarot and eventually become expert but you will never reach the heights of one who is born with an instinctive psychic awareness as were many true Romanies of old, sadly a dying race. They study each card and attempt to differentiate the meaning of each card and its divinatory meaning, try to distinguish between the Minor Arcana and the Major Arcana, and the end result when these two divinatory packs are mixed is an amalgam of them both, as against individual readings, and often the readers do not know that the major and minor roles are reversed in importance in a reading, quite contrary to the names outwardly.

I have watched tarot dealers in England carefully at these gatherings often in the company of people whose skills in tarot are formidable, and seen them look at me in sorrow when we have watched the amateur shuffling and incorrect laying out of the cards and the newly-read dealer attempt to give a 'book' reading.

So America you are not entirely alone, the rot has set in here in Great Britain, and England in particular. It is another example of the degenerate path into which the old Pagan ways are falling.

The fact is that world-wide the old ways are fading. And the roots of what we affectionately call the Old Religion are being eroded despite an upsurge in numbers. Fortunately in both America and England there is still a hard core and backbone of the Craft where the old ways are faithfully adhered to and old traditions faithfully observed. I was gratified when I searched myriads of Pagans/Wiccans to find so many devout and sincere followers of the true old ways, but was equally amazed at the sects and schisms running websites and organisations alongside them.

To take just one example I tracked a number of so-called 'Gothic' covens and made tentative overtures to them to test the water. Their response had very little in common with fellow groups of real Witches in the USA, but seemed more intent on exhibitionism than Craft which they simply used as a veneer for their activities. When I challenged them in a spirit of goodwill they turned out to be wonderful and lovely people and stated that it was trendy to be Gothic. Fine, but trendiness is not part and parcel of the Craft.

With the rebirth of Wicca after the repeal of the infamous Witchcraft Act in 1951, the new followers such as Gerald Gardner laid the foundations for the revival, and in their turn his devotees spread a new and balanced system of Witchcraft that 'blew away the cobwebs' so to speak and brought Wicca into the 20th century. Gerald became the father of modern Witchcraft, just as Doreen Valiente became the mother of the Craft, right to the end of her life she held the old ways together and faithfully kept sacred the true principles of Gardnerianism and all he taught.

Doreen was an old Witch of an old and dying generation. All the writings and papers that Gerald created over the years came to her and were preserved for prosperity and upon her death she bequeathed them to John Belham Payne who ran the Centre for Pagan studies at Maresfield in Sussex. One of my most precious possessions is Doreen's pentacle of the third degree; which came to me after she passed to the Summerlands. It was a great honour. I am so afraid of losing it that I only wear it for rituals with the coven at home.

Audrey received two beautiful pewter owls that once adorned Doreen's mantelpiece. Audrey, Doreen knew, loves owls and had taken the name Athene at her initiation as a Gardnerian. Athene's emblem was an owl. The pair are prominently displayed at our home for all to see now.

Here within an old barn a beautiful temple was created and all her artefacts were on view to the myriads that flocked to see them and to the wonder of the covens that came and held the sacred rituals there keeping to the roots of all that Gerald Gardener had taught.

Here within its daub and wattle walls Sabbats were held, initiations and elevations took place, and many a time its interior echoed to the sound of merriment and laughter as handfastings took place. As my wife Audrey and I approached our golden wedding we too were handfasted there to irrevocably join us in the lives to come, our only regret after a lifetime in the Craft was that we had not been handfasted earlier.

The Temple became a scene from the past as I donned mediaeval armour for this great occasion, and my lady Audrey wore an equally beautiful mediaeval dress. Here after close-on fifty years of happy marriage before the great altar displaying both Gerald's and Doreen's artefacts and with the original book of shadows on display we affirmed our love for each other and were joined as one by Tanith who had been my High Priestess for years. I would like to add a note at this point that over the years Audrey was bringing up our five children, three girls and two boys. Deirdre, Martin, Karen. Vanessa and Wayne and felt that she could not devote the time to taking on the mantle of being High Priestess despite being well qualified to do so,

Audrey initially was a different tradition to me and was initiated by Tom Penfold, a leading Sussex Gardnerian Witch, who ran a large coven in Hove with his wife Mabs. Tom was also a leading Mason and Grand Master of his lodge as well as a serving police officer, Mabs held a high position at the Law Courts at the Strand in London. They were Gardnerians as of old and were initiated by Rae Bone who was a High Priestess of Gardner's.

Initially the old covens remained underground as they had for centuries and refused to accept the new renaissance, declaring that Gardner has breached the code of silence and was betraying the sacred oaths he had taken at his initiation. Occasionally one would emerge and guardedly speak to the press who were forever clamouring for news of witches' covens, but the vast majority remained incognito.

We ourselves, the Order of Artemis, did not really come into the 20th century until the late 70s. At that point we realised that Gardner had done Paganism a great favour by instigating the revival, and although we did not agree with the fact that Witchcraft was now within the province of all to join, we swiftly saw that it was leading to a revival of all things green and was a positive step forward for those fighting for conservation issues, nearly all the conservationists were Pagan though not necessarily Wiccan.

Looking back now in retrospect we realise that with diminishing churchgoers Xtianity was in decline and that Paganism was going up. A survey some years ago declared that there was now estimated to be in excess of one million Pagans in Great Britain counting Witches, Druids, and fellow travellers who supported all green issues. A survey by the government two years ago demanded in its questionnaire that one's religion had to be declared, another example of the despotic dictatorship we have had to endure under the Blair regime.

E-mails flew back and forth for weeks between Pagan groups as we protested and large numbers stated outright that they were Witches, while others simply put Pagan etc. Unlike America we do not have official recognition of Wicca as a religion here and we saw this as an opportunity to be recognised officially, as British law states that a religious movement may be recognised as a religion if more than 40,000 people are its followers, no problem here as we know of 43,000 practitioners alone in England and a survey of sister groups enveloping Druids etc hit the 1,000,000 mark. Eagerly we awaited the results of the survey but when we asked for figures we were informed they were not currently available. They did state that those who proclaimed themselves Xtians were down in numbers from the previous survey some five years before from 8,000,000 to 5,000,000.

There were basically two camps now, Gardnerians who dominated the scene and were the fastest growing group versus the old hereditary and solo witches. Numerous other groups had sprung up in this period and made a small impact on the scene, such as the Alexandrians, a group founded by one Alex Sanders who claimed to have been initiated by his grandmother by way of a ritual that not one single hereditary Witch had ever heard of. He obtained a Book of Shadows apparently from a Gardnerian and promptly rewrote it for his followers. He became popularly known as 'rent a witch' as, forever the showman, he delighted the press for years with what were quite often bizarre antics but after he failed to raise a demon on stage as he had promised an audience invited to an old cinema, his star faded overnight.

What he would have done if a demon had appeared goodness only knows, as Witchcraft has no connection with such practises whatsoever, this being merely a mediaeval conception beloved by authors such as Dennis Wheatley and other writers of occult fiction. Alexandrian covens are still to be found but many of his original followers graduated eventually to the Gardnerian persuasion and absorbed themselves in his teachings.

Many eminent Gardnerian authors such as the Farrars, and eminent followers such as the Lindfields were originally Alexandrians. I met Alex on a number of occasions in Sussex but found we were not compatible though we remained friends. My personal opinion has always been that the real power was vested in his wife Maxine, a truly dedicated Witch, and extremely expert.

It was at this point in 1976 we decided to adapt and come into the modern world ourselves. Much of the old ways that were still preserved was what we called the 'Hand of Write' or 'Hand of Rite'. Quite clearly what the New Forest coven had imbued to Gardner and upon which he had based his newly fabricated Book of Shadows, was an amalgam of ancient Witchcraft lore skillfully intertwined with Masonic ritual.

Now there is a strange parody here for many have accused Gardener of fabricating his Book of Shadows and claim it is clearly fraudulent as so much freemasonry is obviously incorporated into it, but consider the following facts when we traverse history.

The early 1700s saw an upsurge in spiritual enlightenment as we came out of the dark days and everywhere at the time groups sprang up eager in the study of esoteric knowledge. In 1717 there were two highly memorable events that were to have an effect on 20th century witchcraft in years to come I believe.

In that self -same year one John Toland resurrected, albeit from scanty records, a new Druid order which he called the 'The Druid Order', and who came to be known by the far more popular name of the 'Stonehenge Druids' because of this ancient stone circle in Wiltshire they used for their rituals.

On a historical note incidentally there is no record of the Henge having ever been used by Druids despite the popular belief that that it was a Druid stronghold, in fact English Heritage who now own the site emphatically deny for reasons best beknown to themselves that Stonehenge has any connection whatsoever with Druidism. My own belief that is also shared with many is that as Druidism was undoubtedly rife in the area then it would be most surprising if they had not used it.

Also in 1717 when we saw the rebirth of Druidism, a new esoteric group sprang up called Freemasons, and we saw the emergence of the Masonic Grand Lodge. These two momentous events became intertwined for many Masons were Druids and many Druids also became Masons by affirming their belief in a supreme entity that could be identified with God,- a specific demand to such belief being a perquisite of admittance.

When the first Masonic charters were being written how much, one must ask, was invented and written into Masonic practise outside of the old testament and Masonic emphasis on Solomon's temple? Such information was readily available of course but as far as the initiation into masonry is concerned how much of old Wiccan initiation rites was formulated into masonry? Old records show a startling resemblance to ancient Witchcraft rituals in broad outline, so were these initiation rites copied and revised to form the roots of masonry? I personally believe so. And also by a quirk of fate to re-emerge 180 years later when these old Witchcraft rituals were written inadvertently and without pre-knowledge of their origins into the new so-called Book of Shadows now combined with the New Forest coven's remnants of the Book of Rite, even though much of this had undoubtedly been passed down verbally over the years.

The early 1700s also saw an upsurge in far more open practises of Witchcraft for although the formidable Witchcraft Act was still in force, discretion still had to be exercised as we still saw Witchcraft trials at the end of the 1700s albeit that the penalties were no longer so severe and rarely enforced.

It is a matter of record that 1930 saw a major Witchcraft trial in Britain occur with the trial of R. H. Naylor and the infamous Helen Duncan prosecution in the 1940s for prophecy. This trial which ended in her imprisonment was the subject of much condemnation by the people and press of the day and even brought the Prime Minister Winston Churchill out to comment that in the 20th century such a trial was a farce and not worthy of a civilised country. But I will go into these trials later in the book.

Puppy Papers! - A Modern Abomination

I have met wonderful and sincere people who came to me on my USA tour seeking old and esoteric knowledge and supporting their authenticity by producing diplomas and certificates from covens, universities, and colleges to show that they were bona fide practitioners and qualified Witches.

I have seen PhDs in Witchcraft and doctorates in ritual magic; also I have seen websites where for a handful of dollars they will enrol you or even create an authentic-looking illuminated document or certificate from a non-existent college to order. These will show you are anything from a lawyer to a dentist. Doctorates are issued en mass - especially to doctors of divinity and philosophy, and I swear there are more reverends in one state within the USA than the whole of the unholy Church of Rome.

Diplomas! Certificates! Doctorates in Witchcraft to show you have been trained as a Witch and are now fully qualified. How long are these courses? One year, two years, three? What can you possibly learn in even three years? You would remain at second degree in a genuine coven for at least two of them, and that would only be if you made second at the end of a year and a day after your initiation - again, rare. Also what is buzzing around in my mind is who authorised them to pass these people as 'qualified'? With the exception of one who I know was initiated as a first degree and thereafter started teaching via post, undoubtedly aided by books of spells and ritual so he would have only limited know-ledge.

What is the background of these examiners who issue these diplomas so haphazardly? What is more important is when these poor people approach covens for example when say they visit England and find that a paper qualification is not acceptable to allow them to join in a particular event, except the Summer Solstice, when all are welcomed into the circle - then what do they think? Does it dawn upon them that their background and roots are spurious and regretful as it is, they cannot be accepted, and most of these from the nation that invented the dreaded puppy papers?

What then can one do when a genuine and avid seeker of the Old Ways seeks hidden knowledge but whose roots are suspect? I have had people come to England from both the USA and Canada to seek re-initiation and who have been unhappy with their initiation via mail order for example. Then they meet a real coven, only to be told that traditionalists insist on a year and a day during which they candidate must prove themselves as having the right temperament and outlook to be trained as a Witch.

Make no mistake, for one thing that cannot be denied is the complete and utter sincerity of 95% of the people I met, the biggest problem I found was when asked a question from a member of an audience that bordered even remotely on what I would consider a secret of the Craft i.e. a ritual or practice that is restricted to the initiated. I found I could not answer him or her as not only did I not know their background or roots, but also the fact that amongst the audience there were a large number of people who had come to listen.

For the record this is essentially a love of Nature, animals, and all things green, plus a wish to serve the Old Gods. I have had two candidates who were so keen that they obtained temporary residence here and trained with the coven and ultimately each eventually went through full initiation rites as a Witch of the first degree, and then requested what they called 'puppy papers' to return home with, stating that without them they would never be accepted into the Craft community in the USA.

Puppy Papers!!!!! What the *@^#+&* are puppy papers? What diabolical politically correct nincompoop invented this idea may I ask, without which you are not a bona fide witch in the USA? Oh - and they MUST be Gardnerian to boot, no other sort of Witches exist in their blinkered eyes.

Never mind if some old crone in the backwoods of Witch country in rural Cornwall in Southern England initiates you into the mysteries; an old woman with the knowledge of centuries running in her Witch blood whereby you emerge as a new Witch from one the most ancient covens in the United Kingdom - Oh no! - This is no good at all. If she ain't a Gardnerian and probably may never even have heard of him, 'an her granddaddy won't be able to help as he cannot even read or write - joking I may be, but the peasant and Witch of yesteryear could often neither read nor write and the knowledge was passed down verbally, also very practical as the ebullient Witch finders could never discover any documentation whatsoever to accuse a suspected Witch.

O.K., so you still want puppy papers? Well I am quite sure if you visit one of the sites I have mentioned above they could create an authentic forgery to order, simply tell them what you want and point them in the right direction. Tell them that Gerald was your uncle, and that old Dorothy Clutterbuck was your great, great grandma, who founded 48 covens in the New Forest, and that furthermore she was a direct descendant of Merlin the Magician! Give them a week or so and eventually a beautifully illuminated scroll will be produced confirming you as a Master of Magic, a Gardnerian, and having a degree in raising old Beelzebub to order; for another $10 I expect you could have it embossed in 9 carat gold.

Do you honestly believe that if a Witch was on trial in the 17th century that the case would be thrown out of court when the defence counsel argued (if they could get someone to defend them that is) "Your Honour, I declare this woman to be innocent as an extensive search of her property by the Witch finder general has failed to find any evidence whatsoever of the statutory puppy papers proof absolute sir that she is a Witch, they never part with them, they can't be accepted by old Lucifer without them you know"?

Judge studies papers in front of him.

Defence counsel continues. "She claims the cauldron is for cooking, the traditional blunt athame, so-called, is used to spread her butter, the broomstick is simply for sweeping the floor, and the alleged wand is actually an oversized toothpick - and the black cat - well that's just a pet!

Judge "No puppy papers you say? Hmm the rest is circumstantial - case dismissed"

On a serious note did old Dotty have papers to show her background and training? - Did she in turn swear a suitable affidavit to give Gerald a licence to instigate the new renaissance? I think not. I cast my mind back to some of the most famous Witches I have known and very often worked with, Mabs and Tom Penfold for example were two leading Gardnerians who were brought into the Craft by Rae Bone, who in turn was one of Gerald B. Gardner's High Priestesses, and they in turn also initiated my wife Audrey as a Gardnerian, reciprocally I and my Priestess brought them into Artemis as Traditionalists and they insisted that I also was initiated by them as a Gardnerian years later.

Did Rae Bone give them these dreaded puppy papers? No. Did they give a single one of the myriads they brought into the Old Religion a set of 'puppy papers? Did Rae Bone ever receive them from Gardner or dear Gerald from Dorothy? No! That is not the way of Witchdom, The mother of modern Witchcraft who was a friend of mine for years was Doreen Valiente a High Priestess of Gerald B. Gardner and the one to whom he bequeathed his Book of Shadows and a vast collection of artefacts. Doreen and I, together with her last High Priest John

Belham Payne, discussed the issue of the trend for puppy papers and it was greeted by all of us with both laughter and ridicule, and this from the acknowledged grand matron of magic herself, and whose fame is ever as great as Gerald's. Doreen Valiente is the mother of modern Witchcraft and the nearest she may ever have had to puppy papers was probably a post card from Gerald from Singapore, which would at least prove he did know her.

I have never, over a span of 50 years, and with well over 100 covens springing from my loins been approached by a single person from any of those covens, founded by the Order of Artemis, and who have hived over the years ever been asked to authenticate their heritage! And these stretch from the USA to Australia. They would consider it an affront if any of them were challenged, and they are worldwide, why o' why is this something particular to America?

In England we stand proud of our heritage, and lament for those of our ancestors who died upholding their faith. My wife Audrey was a Kemp, and a direct descendant of Ursula, or to be historically correct Ursley Kemp the Witch of St Osyth who was hanged in 1582, and whose body was rediscovered and put on exhibition in 1921 by the workmen who discovered her grave during road widening. The rotting coffin was put in a decrepit garden shed, complete with the rivetted Ursley to view at 2 pence a time. Poor Nan Kemp, another ancestor of Audrey's, was hanged at Lewes and her grave is at the road junction by the hostelry the 'Jugg Arms'. I wrote at length about them in my book '*The Last Bastion*'.

Most of the old Witches who were the cornerstones of the Wiccan revival in the 1950's are long dead and gone. The old Storrington coven, and its sister the Bramber coven, are gone. The Willingdon and Seaford coven are also gone, extinct by the end of the last century. Many new ones have filled the gaps they left behind, many of whom sprang in turn from their loins. The Craft is strong, but we have lost so much from their demise. We never even thought of asking them to write out some puppy papers for us before they went on to the Summerland - perish the thought.

Myles C. one of our Witches has passed to the Summerlands many a moon past now; and a Xtian zealot in his family took it upon themselves to destroy all the ancient documents and artefacts he owned and gave him a Xtian burial to boot. Can you imagine what the consequences of their malign action could have been if members of his coven in turn were asked to authenticate their roots? And his relatives had discovered these puppy papers and destroyed them? Overnight every member, of any group he had founded after having hived, would be disenfranchised overnight. It so happens Myles came from my coven, and in his turn had probably nothing other than a few letters that had passed between us, if he had kept them that is.

In another incident I myself only learned of the passing of one of my old compatriots from the Storrington coven long after she had passed away. She died alone and with no known relatives and all her possessions were sold to a local dealer who cleared her flat. I spent weeks scouring the local bric-a-brac shops in search of her cauldrons, statuettes, swords etc, but to no avail; my only success was the recovery in an antique and bric-a- brac shop, called Aladdin's Cave in nearby Ashington, of an ancient wooden carving of the foliate God in the form of Cernunnos of hers. This was unique for I knew it had a false back where spells were kept. It now rests proudly by my fireplace, and one day will be bequeathed to the Witchcraft Museum at Boscastle in Cornwall. The point is not that none of these old Witches had one iota of proof of their ancient heritage, nor had their fathers and grandmothers before them. When I think of the vast amount of wonderful material she had acquired over the years that was now lost, presumably for ever, I find it heart breaking. I can only hope that at least some of it fell into sympathetic or even Pagan hands.

Senua A New Goddess for the Future

Selene of the Moon, the Supreme Goddess Demeter, Isis, Astarte, Cerridwen and the very British Goddess Bride, whose purity gave us the name for virgin brides are well-known to all Pagans. But over the years the main focus of worship has been on Goddesses that we have inherited over the centuries from both those who traded with us, and those that came to invade. They all had one thing in common, and that was they introduced us to Goddesses from as far away as Egypt, and the Middle East, when both Greeks and Romans brought a whole pantheon of Gods and Goddesses in their wake. The Nordic invaders brought us a more aggressive variety of Gods in particular, such as Odin, and Thor, and all of these were eagerly absorbed into the British culture.

We are a little thin on the ground as to local Goddesses, and the Romans did us no favours with their recordings of the Druids and their favourite top of the hit parade with Andraste. Only the Romans said all those nasty things about her, guess that was because the dear old Druids did offer up lots of prayers and invocations to her before battle, and the Romans did get quite a pasting initially. So much so that Suetonius Paulinus left them alone for a few years and went off to do battle with an upstart Iceni Queen called Boudicca, who had been burning her bra and singing 'Rule Britannia.'

Come to think of it she gave the Romans quite a pasting as well, winning every single battle until the last, thereby losing the war, she really should have had a man to help her. Many years were to pass before Suetonius, suitably reinforced, returned to do battle and wipe Andraste off the map, and according to Tacitus the Roman army was petrified when they were confronted by the Druid's women with mistletoe in their hair (not an invitation to a quick kiss incidentally) who insinuated that they were going to wear the Roman men's manhoods as necklaces. Only massive Roman forces eventually took the day, and then afterwards they decided to give Andraste a really bad press in the Roman 'News of the World'.

Well in 2003, some 1600 yeas later we Brits have found a new Goddess that we did not even know existed - Senua! It was a team of archaeologists who excavated her shrine in Hertfordshire and were amazed to find they had unearthed not only a previously unknown Goddess, but from the votive offerings also discovered, a highly successful one as well. Their analysis is that she probably goes far farther back in history than was first thought, and was probably a much older Celtic Goddess who had been adopted by the Romans. If the Romans found the local British had something really going for them with their libations to her, then whatever they could do, Rome could do better.

They probably saw the villagers offering cakes and apples, and simple gifts of trinkets, but Romans could do better, and get even better results by offering gold and jewels and 'Romanising' her. To their minds they undoubtedly associated this completely British deity with their own Minerva, for here in cold and wet England was a warm and welcoming Goddess representing womanhood and wisdom.

Certainly, from what they found buried this would appear to be the case, for gold and gems do not perish, but the simplistic offerings of the Celts would have been long gone. 26 pieces of gold were recovered with the silver statuette and copious amounts of jewels and beads (the beads though could well have been Celtic) inscribed plaques, and ivory cameos, The inscribed plaques are particularly interesting for they are all praising the Goddess for her help, and accordingly the populace are rewarding her with expensive gifts as a thank you. Silver plaques, and badges abounded, together with brooches and cloak clasps in gold. A silver plinth was found nearby upon which the figurine once stood with the name Senua engraved upon it. The name is further substantiated by the libations to 'the Goddess Senua, found alongside her. These in many instances were inscribed by benefactors with names such as Cariata, Lucilius, and Servandus. The inscription from this Servandus read 'Servandus Hispani willingly fulfilled his vow to the Goddess Senua'. For months archaeologists attempted to decipher the corroded offerings and it was only when these ancient artefacts were X-rayed that the Goddess's name was revealed. I eagerly await the first photos which will be released shortly of her, but she is described as badly corroded, 15 cm high, wearing a robe that bared her left shoulder and the same arm supporting a fold of material. Her hair is parted in the centre, culminating in a bun at the back.

How little these Romans knew that the Gods do not seek wondrous gifts but are far more appreciative of a portion of an apple, or corn cake, plus a libation of wine into the ground, materials that in their turn nourish Mother Earth. This is what Paganism is all about, simple sacrifices of food and drink to acknowledge their gratitude, but Britain was under the Roman heel.

Water was always a holy element to our forbears, and there is evidence that the shrine was adjacent to a spring, now dried up. This may well be the reason that the shrine was abandoned, or perhaps the hoard was buried during some invasion, and the shrine destroyed. Only the crumbling remains know the truth and this is locked forever in its broken stones. But we have a new Goddess - Senua, and she is 100% British. I trust it will not be too long before a newly hived group will call themselves 'The Coven of Senua' - may they thrive and honour her name, and remember the old ways with their libations to her to enrich the earth as of old.

So mote it be.

The Legend of the Witches' Farthing

Its origins, background and history

In avoiding publishing secret and specific ritual in this book, I realise that it is going to be read by both practising Witches, and many who are interested in the old ways. Our Wiccan history has many fascinating facets, and much of the lore of yesteryear has had an impact on our modern society. Many medical cures were known to the village wise woman, and subsequently have been absorbed into modern medicine. This could be something as simple as the old Witch giving you willow leaves to chew on, and suck the juice out of as a cure for a migraine or headache.

We now know that willow leaves are rich in salicylic acid, known as aspirin, so an old Witches' cure has passed down over the centuries to become a common commodity today, alongside digitalis and many other cures, but one little-known fact that has influenced the history of this country and driven politicians to vie for power is a simple little coin that has passed away in the age of decimalisation.

I have therefore decided to include in the book a chapter on what is known as the Witches' farthing, and how the actual creation of a Witches' farthing as a talisman came about. Only a farthing that has been created by a Witch is authentic, and can only be created within Magic Circle. Only the initiated, and possibly some Hedge Witches, who may also have the knowledge, would be able to perform the ritual. But initially I will dwell on the Witches' farthing itself as a talisman, and how this came about.

As a talisman as such the magic farthing has passed into history, its power now legendary, and its curative powers awesome if it is created correctly. By tradition, and there are many legends associated with it, when it is presented to someone who is ill, or afflicted, it must be wrapped in silver and given to him or her on a full or new moon, this is done in the presence of the Witch, his or herself. The recipient must unwrap it in front of them.

The coin will have been consecrated on a waxing or waning moon, depending on whether the coin is intended to banish a sickness or disease, or aid the recovery of a patient by strengthening him or her. A waning moon will charge the coin to diminish, such as shrinking a tumour, and a waxing moon will recharge the patient's batteries and give them energy to recover.

Another almost identical tradition is exactly the same as above, except that the farthing is sandwiched inbetween two either larger silver coins when it is presented, or between two coins of similar size. These would usually be a pair of' groats', solid silver four penny pieces; or a pair of 'joeys', silver three penny pieces. Afterwards the silver coins could be spent on nutritious food, but the Witch's farthing would be kept in a 'placket' – cloth or soft leather drawstring bag and secreted away.

These farthings are much sought after to the present day since their creation in 1613. The older the coin, the more potent its powers. In fact to obtain one at all is no easy task as they are retained by not only those fortunate enough to own one but by their families for generations afterwards. Witches also presented them in the dreaded burning and hanging days to those who aided them, and to sympathisers and friends.

There is strangely enough no heavy ritual involved in the creating of such a talisman and the ceremony has not to my knowledge altered one iota over the centuries, and Witches to this day still create them out of as old a coin as they can obtain. Those with the Queen's head on them are the most favoured coins, as this is symbolic of the feminine element and identified with the Goddess. Most of those used today are of Queen Anne, or more modern coins such as the young Victoria.

New coins of course were selected in the very early days, as they were regarded as being uncontaminated, having never been involved in usury and the like, even so they were always regarded as contaminated originally in view of the reason that they were minted on the orders of the paranoid, Witch-hating, King James as I will explain in another paragraph. The coin is brought into the cast Circle on the end of a ritual sword, athame, or white-handled ritual knife and laid reverently upon the altar. The High Priest and High Priestess firstly exorcise it so as to banish any evil associations it may have had. Then it is ceremonially washed in natural spring water or if possible in water from a holy well. Most Witches in England usually have a bottle or two in reserve, usually taken from the Chalice Well at Glastonbury or similar, or from a pure stream.

Next the coin is dried, blessed and consecrated in front of the whole coven. (It is incidentally traditional to create these talismans in sets of four.) Once dry they are placed in a plachet, sometimes called a placket, as described earlier, sometimes a special purse is made by the coven of a specific scarlet material if they are for healing, and royal blue if they are to be endowed with power. They are then left there on the altar until the next new moon and full moon. On the night in question they will be taken out at eventide and left in the open to absorb new beginnings from the New Moon, then replaced in the plachet at dawn the following morning for approximately fourteen days, until the Full Moon; then the process is repeated.

At the next Esbat or Sabbat, if the Moon is right, they are blessed once more by the High Priest and High Priestess, and then by the maid of the coven or a virgin; thus giving them the benefit of a triple blessing in total. Sometimes this ceremony is conducted on a full or waxing moon if an Esbat or Sabbat does not fall on an appropriate date, the exception being Candlemass.

The four coins are now placed deosil in the four corners of the circle at the four cardinal points of the compass, and noted, as to which are North, East, South, and West, the northern coin being attributed with extra special powers. Next four white, green or blue candles are placed on top of the coins (Each one is usually placed in the bottom of a candle holder) once in place a taper is lit from the centre altar candle, and they are ritually lit. At this point the Lords of the Watch Towers are invoked. The rest of the rituals as planned, and then proceed, until the time comes for the Agape, but the candles must burn down completely before the ceremony can end.

At this point the four farthings are gathered up and ceremonially placed back in the plachet, (although sometimes this can be a small box), but should really be a purse as described. A note is made prior to the inscribing as to which farthing was the northern one in particular, and this is marked separately. Covens in the olden days would keep one set of four to use on the four great Sabbats, and create further sets to present individually to those whom the coven chose to honour. Over the years this once again seems to have been another old custom that has virtually died the death and faded away. Artemis has maintained this tradition whenever we have been able to secure four farthings. A 'stockpile' of four is always to hand, and two of the very oldest ones are imbedded in the great cascading candles, which have grown huge over a period of fifty years and cannot be moved.

The coins are now ready for inscribing, and on the next full Moon they are removed from the plachet and inscribed with an invoking pentagram cut into the metal, sometimes other sigils are added, particularly to the northern farthing. Until I recorded this the last High Priestess outside of ourselves known to have kept this ancient ritual alive was one Glyndon, known to Witches as our Lady Glyndon. She died sometime between 1960 and 1970, and if any reader has any news of her coven, or knew her, I would be most grateful to archive all the information I can gather on her.

After her passing to the Summerlands her plachet was ceremonially opened in the presence of four covens, and the High Priestesses of the attendant covens were each presented with a coin in her memory. I would fondly imagine that they now nestle under the central Goddess candle on the altars of those same four covens. Those coins, dated between 1613 to about 1750 that were given away by Witches over the years to their benefactors are now highly prized collectors' items and change hands for mega money, but this is sad, for to us they are priceless.

In fact there is almost a black-market in them in the Houses of Parliament where to any aspiring politician it is a 'must have' if he or she is to succeed and reach any degree of eminence in politics. It is said that many a British Prime Minister carried a coin on their person and never, ever, showed it. They are regarded as family heirlooms and in politics in particular, are handed down from father to son.

Well, how, you may ask, did all this originate? The full story when told is stranger than fiction. First let us turn the clock back to 1613 when the very first coin was struck, and thus found its way into the English currency. Like so much of our history its roots lay in a famous, or should I say infamous trial that took place in Berwick some 23 years beforehand, in 1590 to be exact. It was the trial of the Berwick Witches that precipitated the paranoid and highly Xtian King James to embark upon the most ferocious persecution of our people, after what was frankly a pretence of a trial, and where the evidence in one instance, rested upon eggshells found in one of the houses of the accused. Eggshells!!! Yes, apparently these devilish Witches were using them to sail around the king's ships in order to sink them - and raising storms in the process to boot. It seems incredulous to us in this the 21st century, but the Berwick Witches went to the gallows on this evidence.

James, the bigot, never sat comfortable on his throne after that, for was ever fearful that the cold dead hands of the Witches he had so cruelly misused would stretch out from the grave and seek retribution. He felt that all he could do would be to reduce their power by creating a coin so small its value could buy a Witch's soul. He summoned his treasurers and told them of his grand plan, and instructed them to create 'a coin so small that it shall be but a quarter of a penny, that it might be used to buy the soul of a Witch'. Not exactly the going rate for one's soul according to my knowledge of the subject, the last I heard was that old Nick was offering forty years of happiness in exchange for it, now let's be honest, that is more like it.

Just imagine forty whole years of wine women and song, (or men if you're a woman and are so inclined) exquisite wines, fast cars, a beautiful house, holidays abroad, never having to work, - well its certainly tempting - but a farthing? - I ask you. He certainly slated us, and even wrote a whole discourse against us in 1597 in his classic *Demonology*, not counting his revision of the Bible à la James. (Men only - no women of note) but I digress. It was this wayward king who found a reference in the Bible to 'the wisest person in the known world, a woman known as the 'Wise Woman of Endor' and it was written that such was her wisdom that kings and emperors would travel far and wide to lay their crowns at her feet to seek her guidance, her CV must have been very impressive, Endor was quite a few weeks journey away in those days.

A woman! So clever? It could not be His Majesty decided, if she was so clever then logically she was in league with the infernal one, and it was him that was guiding her. Out came the charcoal and a sheet of parchment, and a quick revision ensued. He would expose this recalcitrant female for what she was. Result - a completely revised new edition of the Holy Book where all references to the woman were expurgated or revised - in the new version, known and used to this day as the King James Version, she became the 'Witch of Endor' and allegedly corrupted King Saul who sought her advice.

James it seems was paranoid about the fair sex, and decided to continue his editing of the Bible to edit all references to women where they were shown in a positive light, and depict them as essentially bad. After all the Old Testament did say that women were the source of all evil, and it was Adam's second wife Eve who started the whole discourse by talking to the serpent in the Garden of Eden and enjoying a Cox's Orange Pippin in the process. I guess he was unable to chop down all the apple trees to stop it happening again.

So the Royal Mint went into overdrive on the King's instruction and cast this new coin in their thousands, and promptly valued them at four to a penny. It did not take long for them to be nicknamed 'little Witches' or the Witches' farthing knowing the King had had it struck as an affront to the Witches. To his chagrin the Witches did not take it as an affront to them at all, but adapted the coin to the Craft of the Wise, bad move James.

The farthing thereafter was given away by Witches along with spells, herbs, and a whole variety of cures. In no time at all it was reputed to hold special powers. Old chronicles tell of travellers who possessed it miraculously avoiding bandits, or being saved in the nick of time (if you'll pardon the expression). Others who possessed it attracted wealth and fame to themselves, and often obtained high position, probably why it was, and is so avidly sought by politicians. Outside of this, luck and good fortune was reputed to befall any who possessed it, and it was also attributed with being able to ward off the evil eye and cure the sick.

Overnight a legend was born. A Witches' farthing bound onto a wart would cause it to shrink and vanish within days, while one worn in the right shoe would ward off accidents. Those who suffered severe headaches and migraine would borrow one and place it on their forehead as a cure, and if it were carried in a purse then money would be attracted to it. Its powers became legend and within the space of a few years King James' mighty rebuke to the powers of Witchdom would backfire, the coin so small that it would buy a Witch's soul was now a much-desired item, with this in your purse it would never be stolen, and the owner would never be cheated. Pity that James never got himself one!

In the 1850s Nanny Morgan a famous Shropshire Witch was renowned for her famous farthings, yet overnight they became just a part of history, at the date of writing this, I only know of four covens who possess them, and none who still create them according to ancient ritual outside of ourselves, and we have probably created no more than a dozen in a span of fifty years or more. In concluding the legend of the famous Witches' farthing, I feel we should end on a historical note.

In 1864 a 'placket' of coins was discovered in a house owned by an Olive Molland, (some chronicles refer to an Olive Malland) and she was immediately arrested on a charge of Witchcraft and sent for trial. The result was a forgone conclusion in the weight of the evidence against her, to wit, the sole evidence against her was simply a packet of farthings that had been found during a search of her house. For this crime she paid with her life on the three-legged mare so the records say, for the unenlightened, a three-legged mare was a triangular gallows where three people could be hanged at the same time, there is a fine example at the back of a restaurant in York, still there in 2006.

When the coins were first minted they were bright and burnished and shone like gold, and the Royal Mint in their infinite wisdom thought they could be mistaken for half sovereigns so in 1897 the farthing was darkened to avoid confusion, even this event did not pass unnoticed by the Witches who claimed they had cast a spell to achieve their darkening in a final act of retribution, and as a memorial to those who had died in the burning days, and the persecutions of yesteryear.

Sabbats, Fairies and Old Pagan Ways

Some fairies are closely associated with Witches and they have long been known to intermingle, the legends and myths here are endless, so I will just give those associated with the great sabbats and festivals. Let us start with the first major event to start the year; next to Hallowmas probably the main sabbat of the year is Candlemass.

Many covens may not necessarily agree with us, but we were taught that Candlemass and Hallowmas were the most important, and the ceremonies we conduct on those days are long and varied as the old fertility rites are enacted. It is Candlemass, when we always initiated all new Witches, and used to conduct the Great Rite and Hallowmas when the Great Rite was performed as a reaffirmation of new life.

The ritual in the form of Imbolc commences on February 1st, and climaxes the following day February 2nd. The old date for this sabbat was February 16th, and was referred to as Oimelc. Essentially a Fire Festival, it followed on from the old Skill fest, which was held on January 15th and 16th, the original Celtic Spring festival of Imbolc or Oimelc. It was dedicated to what they called the White Goddess, identified as Bride or Bridget. The word Imbolc literally translated means 'In the belly' and heralds the forthcoming birth of springtime.

The whole earth is pregnant with new life at this time of year as bulbs strain to reach the sun, seeds germinate after the winter, frogs and toads take their first faltering steps into sunlight from underground chambers and the fairies emerge from their hideouts. This rebirth was universally acknowledged by the people who would remove newly-laid eggs while still warm from under the ducks and hens and bury them into the womb of the earth mother. Here they would be allowed to remain buried for the passing of three whole days and nights and then dug up to symbolise rebirth. Often they were then hardboiled, and many a game was played with them, varying from throwing them in the air and catching them on your forehead in what was called 'nutcracker man' the secret was to get them to land wide end on where the egg sac is and break at this point so as to remain standing upright, to what has evolved as an egg and spoon race, to painting eggs.

The village people who rallied to watch these rites enacted marvelled at the sheer spectacle of it, when they would all light candles and form a great circle of light around the priests conducting the rituals. To them it was 'The Feast of the Waxing Light as they simulated the passing of winter and welcomed the coming light that would climax on the 21st of June with the longest day. To them this Day of Days was the traditional 'Feast of Pan' as well, and was dedicated to purification, The Lord of Death and Resurrection, the giver of new life in the reincarnatory cycle, hence why the Great Rite was performed.

The White Goddess Bridget was an equal partner to Pan in these rites and would personally perform the rite of the Feast of the Flame, there is evidence of bunches of dandelions being carried by the performers and not infrequently a newly born lamb would be carried above the High Priest's head for all to see, as he circumambulated the circle; then gently it would be returned to its mother. Next the High Priestess, skyclad with all the women devoid of raiment would now dance around the Magic Circle covered with nothing more than woad, waving willow wands in honour of the Crone, while the youngest girls would lay gifts to the Goddess at the Altar.

Over the years The Goddess in the form of Cerridwen entered the equation, and it is usual nowadays for these Goddesses, virtually one and the same as far as the rituals were concerned, to be honoured; but remember that February 2nd - our

Candlemass was also known as Brigid's Day, (not spelt with the 'd' at the time - and sometimes recorded as Brighid, with an 'h').

Now in one of these Celtic rituals the Goddess Brighid would appear as a fairy according to folklore, not that this happened in the circle, but on the perimeter. It is widely reported in old tales that at the moment of her manifestation she would fly around the circle, remember that fairies were accepted as naturally as you and I accept the reality of butterflies as part of the scene. Then in the form of a fairy she would chase away the Hag of Winter. The Celts noted that the fairies were not seen during snow etc, and by tradition it was said that at Oimelc they would venture out from their subterranean chambers to welcome the coming of the warmer days.

When we were in Ireland we visited New Grange where the locals swore that on each full moon a troop of sepulchral horsemen could be seen entering the chamber, and that at Imbolc the fairies who lived inside used to exit and mix with humans.

The next festival, to take them in order is the Spring Equinox which falls on March 21st.and is the celebration of fertility for man, woman, and animals. It was sacred to the Druids and known as Alban Eiler. To the Saxons it was equally sacred and was called Ostara. Technically the true vernal equinox commences on March 20th and lasted for three days culminating on the 23rd, this in turn laid the groundwork for the festival of Vermas which took place ten days afterward - March 21st and was celebrated on March 31st. To the masses it was referred to as 'Hearth day' and again was associated with the great festival of light. This period was sacred to Eostar, Eostre, Persephone, and Demeter and marked the balance of night and day. The Great Rite was a celebration of latent fertility in both male and female energies, and was celebrated in intricate fertility rituals; it was a time for the mating of bird's, animals - and us.

It was reported that the fairies had started to become more active as well, for although they had reappeared in February, apparently they would unhesitantly return beneath the old burial mounds with each cold snap. As soon as the sun came out they could be observed bathing in the streams and ponds. Our ancestors, who always left out little tributes of food and drink for the faerie folk, would leave double the amount at Ostara from the great feast that was held on this day. If you neglected to do this there would be no help forthcoming from them until the next Ostara.

There is a slight confusion of records here for another account states that if you neglected the fairies during the feast and did not leave them the little titbits they expected, then you would have to double the amount due to them at the Summer Solstice in June. Traditionally you would afford them gifts of honey, a great favourite of fairy folk I gather, plus cream and milk, and freshly churned creamy butter, though strangely enough, no one ever reports seeing a fat fairy!

The next Sabbat is the great Fire Festival that was known as Bealteine or Roodmas, sometimes called Rudemas or Bealltain, and which over the centuries has come down to us as our beloved Beltane. It would start on May Eve and continue in celebrations all the following day with a quickening of joyful celebration that was symbolised by a beautiful virgin girl who would represent the Goddess of Spring. In this form she would appear as the Goddess of the Witches, the first of the revered trio of maiden, mother, and crone. She would be chosen by popular consent and had to be young and beautiful. From the moment this honour was bestowed upon her, great prestige was afforded her. She would be revered throughout the celebrations. A great feast was prepared for her to celebrate the coming up of the Sun from the South, then at a signal the traditional Beltane fires would be lit and within minutes could be seen blazing from hilltop to hilltop as the entire populace celebrated the Goddess in the form of Freya, Holda, Held, Hilde, or Goda. But the dominant Goddess who exuded carnal delight and pleasure was Frigg or Frigga, she whose name has passed into antiquity as a representation of sheer unbridled sex.

Once more on this day that represented fertility the Great Rite would be performed. Beltane is the third festival, and during this celebration it was expected that the manifestation of the forces of spring would be apparent and the growth of plants and crops would speed up. The bonfire ashes would be traditionally scattered on the fields once cool, and each villager would grab a handful of the phosphate-rich wood ash to scatter on their garden.

This wonderful Fire ritual was also dedicated to the male Gods in the form of Boab. Once this day was called 'Boabsday' as against the Beltane that we identify with now, it was also known as 'Boabstime.' This period was essentially identified with fire and heat as a welcoming to the Sun God Boal or Bel. Many old customs were enacted this day, one was a ritual which sadly once more has fallen into near obscurity, it was that on the day of the May Day celebrations tradition decreed that you should search for a Witch stone to take back and tie to your gate to ensure luck for the coming 12 months. Again this is a ritual still fervently practised by Artemis; my gate has more Witch stones than I can count. Farmers would also follow this custom and gather up a number of these 'hag' stones as they called them, (for the record never less than three or nine), and by eventide they would be tied to the farm gate at the setting of the sun.

Fairies, it is recorded, loved to watch these rites and were very active by now, it is said that they were fascinated and peered from the undergrowth at the villagers dancing around the Maypole when it was erected in the fields. Only later did it come to be erected on the village greens. It was said that those youngsters who fell asleep beneath a hawthorn would wake up in fairyland.

If we go back to the Arthurian legends we find that Guinevere was supposed to be of fairy origin and that on May Day she would gather in the magically endowed hawthorn flowers. In Wales she was called Blodeuwedd and they say she was made of compressed flowers gathered by fairies, from this flowery form she eventually evolved into a white owl. It is a fact that many of the old Gods and Goddesses and old nature spirits were said to have taken fairy form, and Puck the ever-smiling one was said to have taken the form of Hob.

June the 21st was the day when the summoner called all the covens together in the days before the Xtians came. The day when the populace gathered to watch, observe, and join in the sacred ceremonies, and marvel as the gathered covens whirled deosil in an ever increasing frenzy as they summoned up the power and the villagers in their hundreds would dance in an ever increasing circle, performing the circle dance or the spiral dance, for yes this was the Summer Solstice when the uninitiated could watch and even join in the universal Sabbat - and it was on this day it is said, that the Fairies grew to human height, and joined in the festivities. Well that is what the legend says, but let us look at the Solstice itself.

Firstly it is the longest day of the year, and signals the start of the decrease of daylight as we start to approach autumn, and eventually winter, and is known as Midsummer's Day. Outside of the Witches who observe the 21st as the true Sabbat time, there are many calendars that would, and do belie this, and place Midsummer's day on the 24th of June. But in the Northern hemisphere the correct date is as we traditionally observe and is the 21st, while the solstice period when the sun passes through this transcendent period, is from the 20th to the 23rd.

It is the Alban Hefin of the Druids, who worshipped the Sun God on this day, and we can still see the re-enactment of as much of the old rites as can be resurrected, for they are regularly performed by modern Druidic societies within the confines of the great megaliths of Stonehenge in Wiltshire. On another note I would like to say that the myriads of the great unwashed, who on the pseudo pretence of allying themselves with Paganism and the Druids, descend onto the stones on this day without even a smattering of knowledge of our Pagan roots; do so without a vestige of respect for the ancient rites that are about to be unfolded.

By tradition this is a day of love and joy when everyone came together to honour the Old Ones. Within their groves the people would summon the Sun God, the Lord of Light, for on this day his power was at its mightiest. This was a rite that they would perform once again between July the 19th and 20th in praise of the old rites that heralded 'Sunfest' as this period was known, although the Sun God's powers would be greatly diminished. This day though, the Summer Solstice, is the day of the shortest night, and longest day, and is sacred to both God and Goddess and they would be worshipped in the form of Heartha, Vesta. Rhea, Artemis, Calliste, Callistra, and Arianrhod. They would all celebrate love, marriage, and life itself.

The fairies both loved and lamented on this day as the hours of sunlight they loved to revel in would steadily diminish, and it was now a slow progression of time before they would have to retire to beneath the ancient tumuli as the North Wind began to sweep in. It was said that you could always tell which of the populace were the human incarnations of the faerie folk, for they were always those closest to the balefire basking in its warmth.

Old legends say that on the Solstice the faerie folk would swing from sheer happiness, to deep depression for on the one hand they loved the celebrations and warmth, while becoming embittered in the knowledge that they had already had the best of the summer days, culminating in this the longest day of all. As a result everyone present would be on their guard against tricks the fairies would play on them.

They said that Puck and Loki would be rampant, and Loki's tricks would be the most feared. Another way you could tell who were fairies, and who were not, was by listening to the music emanating from the little groups they formed. The fairies' music was the sweetest they had ever heard, ethereal and haunting, and it was said that once you had heard fairy music it would ring in your ears forever. Certainly true from the experience of my wife and myself in Ireland one day.

I must admit as bewildered as I am, at the phenomena we experienced, those haunting refrains I heard, I will never forget to my dying day. While on the subject I mention 'en passant' that we once had another similar experience, but this time at my home in England. We had celebrated the 'Rite of Pan' that night, and had followed it up with a traditional agape. For 24 hours after the ritual, the house echoed to the haunting melody of the Pan Pipes.

Lugnassadh, or Lughmas, is the 4th festival and has come down to us as Lammas. Once more there is an overlap from July the 31st through to August the 1st. As its very name suggests it is a Sabbat dedicated to the God Lugh, but equally it is dedicated to Habondia, the Goddess of Plenty, but Ceres also dominated on this day, and it is to her that we owe the name Cereal. Kore was also important to the Sabbat on this day. This festival is a celebration of the coming of autumn, and the great Agape that follows is the feast of a bountiful harvest. Lugh is identified as a God of fire and light.

The entire coven gathers this day to perform rites for material supply, and in olden times the Great Rite would be enacted once more. The Xtians took this old Pagan rite and transformed it into what has become their Harvest festival. They have even copied the beautiful ritual which is 100% Pagan and that is what we call the 'offering of the first fruits' when every covenor would bring fruit and vegetables at the foot of the Altar and later during the love feast would partake of a variety of the fruits.

This was one particular Sabbat when the Rite of Old Allan was meticulously preformed. The following morning the coven would take all these offerings of vegetables and the remaining fruit and distribute it to the poor and needy. Another Goddess that is venerated this month is the beautiful Goddess Diana, the period of 12th to 13th of August, is known to Witches as Diana's Day. Also the weekend following Lammas was sacred to the fairy Goddess and they would incorporate the Friday as well.

With the fading away of summer we come into the Autumn Equinox that traditionally falls on September the 21st, although the true equinox ranges from September 20th through to the 23rd. This day is a celebration of thanksgiving for the blessings of the year, it was at this Sabbat that both Witches and villagers, together with all country folk, would honour the Old Gods and give thanks for food, shelter, and clothing.

The Sabbat ranged high on magical levels for the very atmosphere would be charged with magic as both sexes emitted tremendous energy fields, but the energies of both sexes would be balanced against each other that day, as in unison they bade farewell to the Sun God. This day the great Goddess Demeter ruled supreme and the covens would choose a mother to represent her.

One old custom that has fallen into disuse and which we never want to see revived is that of the Xtian 'all saints' day'. To all Pagans this is a flaunting of the degradation of everything we held sacred of the old ways. The Xtians do of course still celebrate All Saints' Day but really have no idea of its origins or how it came about; for this dreadful day was a celebration of their dreaded replacement theology whereby they had superimposed their doctrine on all the days that were revered by the Pagan populace.

It was a celebration for the destruction of our old holy shrines and altars that both peasant and Witch revered, a rejoicing of the annexation of our sacred sites, and a celebration of all they had stolen and usurped from us; whether it be by readapting our customs and presenting them as Xtian ones such as adapting holy water, used by Pagan priests. It was a day years ago when they would seek out a Pagan site and destroy it. This could vary from the filling in of sacred wells to digging channels, and diverting sacred streams. (As a point of interest they have never learned how to sanctify water, and the technique is still not taught at their theological colleges, but I have dwelt on this in another chapter - Amen!) They took our beautiful 'cakes and wine' ceremony and turned it into a form of ritualised cannibalism in the form of the Eucharist at communion where they believe the bread turns into human flesh and the red wine becomes human blood. A symbolism that would make any self-respecting Pagan throw up their hands in horror!

They celebrate the success of a mighty propaganda campaign which suppressed womanhood, adapted many of our customs and rewrote them to suit Xtian Theology, including such facts that when they found they could not eliminate or eradicate the old Pagan Gods, then the cry was "then let's canonise them" so the great unwashed would now bow the knee to the old Gods, in the form of Xtian Saints. The idea was that within a few decades the coming generations would have forgotten the origins and become Xtians - and it worked. Yes! This was the day that was a celebration of the crushing of all we held holy and the superimposition of the newly arrived saints to replace the old Gods and Goddesses we loved.

The result of this was the eradicating of the Druidic Alban Elfed, the banishing of 'Herfest' of the Sun God and our lady Demeter, and the emergence of the Virgin Mary in her place. It was on this day that both the hours of the night and the day were also equal, to identify with the male and female energies that became anathema to the new religion.

Anything that had the slightest resemblance to masculinity or veered towards feminism in particular suggested subliminal sex, and the union of the Sun God with Demeter at the traditional Alban Elfed made them throw up their hands in horror. It was replaced by the image of the Virgin both symbolically and factually.

Today we have returned in force.

The Real Pagan Roots of the USA

So now in 2006 we are in a dilemma, on the one hand we see the re-establishment of the God and Goddess worldwide, an upsurge in all things green, the ecological and conservation groups growing in strength, but most important of all the acceptance of Witches and Pagans being part of the community. There is tacit acceptance now of the fact that we are not Satanists, and that the Lord Cernunnos is not the Devil invented by Xtians, and we do not go around violating virgins, eating babies and kissing Satan's bottom every Sabbat. That is indeed progress, fantastic! But despite all this we are depicted in cartoons, film, television, and most importantly, children's books. This is where the first roots of prejudice starts, by sowing the idea of the evil Witch in young susceptible minds.

If we were any other religious minority there would be an international outcry of religious persecution, and political correctness, that damn awful, all-embracing culture that offends all persuasions with its patronising outlook, for once would be justified in coming to our rescue. So where are you PC Brigade? Why do you not take up a worthy cause for once? We are all losing our roots as new rituals and practises are introduced as if they were ancient, on an almost monthly basis, as each new book appears on the market.

It is this very fact that prevents so much knowledge being passed on. Hereditary Witches and old established covens are now ever more cautious as to whom is admitted and trained, lest they break their oath and leave the coven, taking with them the inner secrets of the Craft, only to find subsequently that it has appeared in a book. In England the clock has been turned back to 1951 when so many were wary of disclosing themselves, but like us eventually did so, many to regret it and now in 2006 have 'gone to ground' again.

Notwithstanding this, a wonderful resurgence of colourful Pagan gatherings such as the fabulous Green Man festival held annually at Hastings in Sussex continues to show the growing strength of conventual Paganism. Here within the giant castle walls, Pagans, Witches. Druids, morris dancers, and a host of assorted neo-Pagans gather in countless thousands annually. Everyone without exception, bearing a green face in honour of the old Gods, and of the Jack (Jack o' the Green) in particular. Joyously he is carried round the streets, where the entire town turns out to honour him.

The townspeople place garlands on their gates, and green branches where the Jack will pass, 20 foot high statues of the God and Goddess are carried in the procession as well as figures from history, and avid followers comb the streets in search of any unwary passer-by, with a pot of green greasepaint to daub the face of any one who has not been greened; all this in a great spirit of fun, to which nobody takes objection, in fact it is considered lucky to be bushwhacked and 'greened' and unlucky to have a clean face!

Here, on the hilltop, where the old castle stands you will see at the 'end point' of the procession this vast Pagan gathering, eating, drinking, and making merry as in days of yore. This is indeed true Wicca and Paganism at its very best, thousands and thousands of Pagans descend here from all over the country to celebrate, and there has never been a single incident over the years of drunkenness or riotous behaviour in all the years it has been held.

In fact I wrote an article some two years ago for the local press on this gathering under the heading. "And not a policeman to be seen" and it is true, there has never been sight of a blue uniformed 'bobby' as we affectionately call our police at the castle site since the very first festival.

Curious that the local law never bothered to monitor the event, I interviewed two uniformed officers as to why and what their attitude was. Smiling, they replied "Well they're all Pagans, aren't they, we never get trouble with Pagans, we only patrol the streets to keep the way clear for their procession". "We have never been called to any disturbance with them ever since it started." To this the second one added "We did have to keep an eye on Xtian fundamentalist groups at the beginning some years ago, when they demonstrated against the gathering, but over the years their numbers grew less and less as they never got any reaction from the revellers - except good humour, and now they never bother to turn up at all.

I have been invited to similar type gatherings in Florida, and would dearly have liked to have attended to compare them. I understand that much of the north American native culture has been absorbed, and that certain groups follow much of the teachings and philosophy of the red man. This can essentially only be good news, for the indigenous peoples of America followed the sun and moon and both worshipped and identified with all things in nature.

I have stayed with both the Hopi and the Navaho and learned much from them but found that unless you were completely and utterly accepted by them then they would reveal but little of their old ways. They are to America what the old Hereditary Witches are to England, they look at the new renaissance somewhat askance, on the one hand welcoming the upsurge in Paganism and understanding, and at the same time drawing back at the commercialisation that has followed in its wake with the utilities that are now on sale by them. They have been forced, reluctantly may I add, to enter this world of commerce as well, they are usually impoverished, living on the sterile barren lands, they have been driven onto over the last two centuries: as they were forced onto reservations that were outwardly of no value to the settlers. Their poverty in many cases is abject, and a disgrace to such a mighty nation as America.

It is this reason, and I am certain that it is for this reason alone, that each reservation has to rely on the gawkers and the curious who visit them to sample their way of life and see what an 'Indian' is. One thing I learned was that these native Americans detest being referred to as Indians! This was a misnomer created by Christopher Columbus who, upon landing on the shores of America, thought that he was in India and mistakenly in his notes referred to the first natives he met as Indians - which they are not. For them to have become a tourist attraction must be like living in an aquarium for the entire world to stare at. Well let us clarify this point - Indians they are not - they are North American Natives, Indians come from India and it was only the arrival of the very first explorers who arrived on the shores of the American continent who mistakenly thought they had landed in India and it was they who referred to the first natives they met as 'Indians' - regretfully the myth started and countless movies since have indelibly etched this noble race with the title of 'red' Indian.

Circumstances have forced them to eke out a living selling 'native' wares such as dream catchers, native dolls and necklaces to the tourists who are tolerated; they are not loved though, for there is little reason as to why they should love the white man. To these proud Pagan people, they represent the white race who robbed them of their lands and their Heritage. Fortunately with the upsurge of human rights riding parallel to the upsurge of the old religion they are better protected now and whenever there has been a decree to steal - and that is the operative word - steal further lands from them then the might of the press and television highlights the injustice and usually a public outcry ensues. For this they are grateful, were it not for the power of the free press and the advent of television their plight would never have been highlighted and brought to the attention of the world.

Until you have 'talked the talk', and far more importantly 'walked the walk' with the red man, only then will you realise the proud and spiritual nature of them with their inherent love of nature. Until you have walked among them an outsider would never understand.

I have been privileged to sit in a sweat lodge and commune with the otherworld with the Navaho, the ceremony being conducted by a shaman known as 'Eight Horses'. There, with my host, Levanah Shell Bdolack, and my wife Audrey we left the world outside and entered into an ethereal realm that passed all too soon. Until you have experienced this spiritual cleansing you have never lived.

To hear the ancient chants as the shaman invokes the Navaho totems in the form of Great Eagle, to hear him call upon Buffalo the great provider, and to invoke Bear - and call upon the wisdom of the Coyote to enter the lodge, and to step outside and refresh your body beneath a warm sun as you pour the all-refreshing elixir of life from a nearby stream over you, and wash away the last traces of the sweat and the impurities you have discarded in this spiritual cleansing.

This is a practise that has followed us over here, and a wonderful one it is. Many a coven I know will erect a sweat lodge in the native American style and savour the cleansing rituals with their own invocations; but to sit with the Navaho and hear words that have echoed down a thousand years from our mentor there, the wonderful Navaho brave who enjoyed the name Eight Horses was a unique experience and one I will never forget,

Why, you may ask, in this day and age with human rights dominating civilised society, (in theory) should their rocky sand-strewn and infertile land now be wanted? The answer is of course resources such as minerals that were not known to have been there when they were forced onto this wilderness and eventually granted rights to what was a barren wilderness! How little at the time could they have foreseen that one day great riches would be found beneath its surface. The main factor that has more than once precipitated conflict with the powers that be, has been oil, and latterly I have heard uranium too.

When I stayed with the Navaho in 2003 there was an on-going fight with the government attempting to sequester a large open tract of desert that had always been Navaho land and still was, and desert it might be and as far as they were concerned desert it well may remain for it is theirs, full stop.

They were offered a goodly and not unfair price to sell but were adamant on a matter of principle that they would retreat no further, they were offered blandishments and bribes to part with this dusty outwardly useless piece of desert but they would not yield. In desperation they were offered land twice the acreage in exchange but still refused. When I left they had been told that special legislation would be passed to enable the authorities to compulsory purchase the land.

It was with much fondness we left the Navaho and went on to the proud Hopi, a nation that resides in high mountains, and boasts the tradition that they were never conquered by the white man. We were greeted with apathy that bordered on outright hostility; we were white and clearly not wanted.

A hired guide showed us a few sights and gave a dialogue on their history, and their persecution, and showed us to a rock face where, over a hundred years beforehand, they had hurled the Jesuit priests from, after a Hopi girl had been raped by them. All the tribesmen and women ignored us, then one asked what were the pentacles that Levanah, Audrey, and I wore, we explained that we were of the old ways and worshippers of the Earth and Earth Mother. The effect was miraculous, within minutes we were welcomed everywhere, told of the old ways, asked into their houses, and offered refreshments and hospitality. One would have had to be there to see such a 'volte face'.

When we left they brought out presents to us, Audrey was presented with a Hopi Katsina doll, as was Levanah and the tribesmen placed a beautiful necklace of blue beads around my neck. It was a wonderful meeting of fellow humans, and fellow Pagans, and made me realise as a Witch how much we had in common with the red man, and had suffered the self-same persecutions thousands of miles apart.

Witchcraft and Xtianity

There is a misnomer that has been perpetuated since time immemorial that Witches are anti-Xtian, and I would like to put this to rest once and for all. Throughout history the established churches of all denominations have relentlessly persecuted us in the name of the one they call their saviour. This prejudice has lead to the most barbaric persecution known, not only to ourselves, but Jews and any other Xtians who they felt were weaker, or any who dared challenge any fundamental teaching of the Catholic Church in particular. They would brook neither discussion or debate, their rule was completely autocratic. If the Pope said the earth was flat - then it was flat.

This could include the most eminent scholars of their day, plus eminent Xtian theologians who expounded simplistic theorems against the Church's established teaching; and could range from arguments that the earth was not flat, to daring to uphold the rights of women. The stake was their destiny for daring to veer from the teachings laid down. Joan of Arc died as a heretic (later branded a Witch) because she said God talked to her, this to them was reason enough to put her to death, their God did not talk to the motley masses and the great unwashed, only to the ordained priests - Amen.

No, the word of the Church was absolute and Catholicism once more led the way in depravity. Xtianity has given us little reason to exactly be enamoured of their teachings, for when they ruled supreme they committed genocide on an unparalleled scale against Witches, Jews, Albigensians, Walbigensians Aztec, Inca, and Maya etc, to name just a few, the latter more in their quest for gold and riches than the saving of Pagan souls. I base any onslaught I make against them on one single sentence found in their own holy book called the Bible upon which their faith stands or falls - and which they would do well to remember, and that is - quote - "By their deeds shall ye Judge them" - I rest my case.

Why then do I say we have nothing against the Xtian creed as such? Well the answer is quite simple for the original teachings of Christ, their most holy man, runs a close parallel to our own teachings of 'An' ye harm none'. His teachings were of peace, love, and forgiveness, and his way of life displayed this in all his glorious works. He was a great Magus who could perform miracles, the same way as we cast spells, and like us he concentrated on healing the sick and afflicted. His messages rang out loud and clear throughout the known world, and that was of peace on earth, a sentiment that we Witches heartily endorse.

He was a master within a magical thirteen members, a mystical figure that all Witches know can raise power, (Note, not that thirteen is the limit but where possible should be the minimum number present), and these will form the inner circle of the dance when the power is raised. If more than 13 are present which there invariably are at coven meetings nowadays, then by tradition the highest degrees i.e. those of the 2nd and 3rd degree will form the inner circle where the main power will be concentrated, and immediately set about raising the cone of power; while the others will form the outer circle and circumambulate as directed or if insufficient numbers become guardians of the quarters, as the rite is performed.

The group of disciples, associates with Jesus, depicts to us a full coven, the Coven of Christ, and this has all the trappings associated with it,-with the exception of the imbalance of the sexes present, but we have to remember that in his day it was a male dominated society and was the norm. It would have been near impossible to raise great power though in an all male coven, the Goddess element would be an essential ingredient.

As Witches, and I feel certain that I speak for the majority, we completely endorse Dan Brown's theory that the clean-faced figure to the right of him is a woman, to wit Mary Magdalene. Occultly it makes sense; there are many other pointers as well. In their own holy book, for example there is a reference to Mary Magdalene washing his feet. Judaic law is quite explicit on this issue, only a married woman may do this, and only for her husband.

The evidence grows stronger therefore to show the female element in their Messiah's life, and that she was in fact married to Jesus. The way the Church has denigrated woman over the years is an abomination, and once more is contrary to his teachings. In the case of his wife Mary Magdalene (the foot washing is enough to convince me of this) the Church has gone out of its way to condemn her, even going as far as to paint her as a fallen woman, harlot, and prostitute. There is absolutely not the slightest historical account of this, or any record existing whatsoever, to bear this out, once more this is an affront by the Church to denigrate and subjugate all womanhood, and they have the effrontery to slander one of the most sacred symbols of femininity in Christendom and their own faith.

Once more we see the Church going out of its way to vilify Mary for no other reason than that as a woman, she is a threat to the male-dominated chauvinistic Church, so she must go, or be denigrated. Suddenly the story of her being a prostitute is entered into the equation - and sticks. Once a woman has been given a bad press it is exceedingly difficult to get rid of. No, Jesus, their Messiah and his doctrine had to belong to the Church 100%, to use and twist as they the Church decreed! There was no room for a woman in his life, so wherever possible as many references that showed her in a good light must be expunged.

He taught us to love our enemies, and Witches try to emulate this with their doctrine of love, albeit we do tend to devote our greatest love to the Earth Mother and Nature in all her forms, for the green of the fields and forests are our sacred church, the roof of our cathedral is a canopy of blue sky, or a green leafy bower. We have no need of stone buildings and elaborate architecture. There is a beautiful little poem often to be found engraved on stoneware sold in garden centres that sums up the Wiccan outlook absolutely, it runs as follows.

The Kiss of the Sun for Pardon
The Song of the Birds for Mirth
One is nearer God's heart in a Garden
Than anywhere else on Earth.

That little poem above sums up all that is Pagan, not for us the sumptuous and magnificent cathedrals erected to an unknown God who never manifests as our Goddess does, but a woodland glade, or the sheer and utter simplicity of the tranquillity of ones own garden. Beautiful words that are dear to Wiccan hearts.

Christ knew that 13 was the magical figure in nature, there are 13 months in the year, not 12 as is generally accepted for technically they should be 28 days each as is decreed by the 13 full moons that there are in a year. Hence, the reason as to why the Zodiac has now been increased by one, to make 13.

Both scientists and astrologers now acknowledge thirteen cycles or lunar months should be the established format now; and in view of these conclusions have added a 13th Zodiacal sign, that of Arachne, the Spider, to the astrological charts. Technically those astrologers who run a daily forecast chart in the national dailies should re divide the signs and take 2-3 days off each to regulate the pattern, the result of course will be that those who were on the cusp will find that they have now entered into a different sign, Scorpios will become Sagittarians, and Pisceans will become Aries etc.

In his turn Jesus was persecuted for being a radical and as we all know, paid the supreme penalty, then after allegedly surviving the cross, a fact we believe, he is lost to history. There is a vast amount of evidence to show that after this terrible ordeal he survived and made his way to Kashmir, and lived a long life there. Nearly 400 years later the gospels started to be written mainly based on scant and hearsay evidence, and like Chinese whispers a new legend surrounding the death or disappearance of this most extraordinary man came to the fore, legends that bore little resemblance to the man himself or what he preached.

This by itself would not have been too bad, had they stuck to the cast-iron principles he had laid down in his teachings, but oh no, they were hijacked by the churches of the day at the instigation of both Paul and Peter's scant records at the time. Paul had never met him, but Peter had. Between them they wrested the only authentic records that existed from the one man who knew the truth and who could have told all, and that was Jesus' brother James, and as a result they were lost forever and replaced by the theology of the misogynistic Paul.

At this stage all the purist teachings of Christ seem to disappear like snow in the early morning sun. At the hands of the new mammon based Xtian hierarchy, blind dogma creeps into the equation that has little if any resemblance to the Holy man's teachings. And it is from this point onwards that one of the mightiest religions the world has ever seen sets out to convert all and sundry at the point of the sword with the cry of "convert or die". Oh dear Jesu, if you had only been around to see what this new faith has done in thy holy name.

From then onwards the rot had set in and institutions made vast fortunes on the strength of the persecutions whether it be by Xtian zealots returning with plunder from the crusades, or the gold of the Incas, Maya and Aztecs. Great cathedrals were built on these proceeds, including a vast city within a city in the heart of Rome now known as the Vatican. The Christ man who is known to have thrown the money lenders out of the temple in one of his rare fits of chagrin, could never have dreamed of the countless millions that would one day be spent erecting vast complexes to him paid for by the blood of millions slain by hell-fire evangelists who still exist to this day, and would do so again given the chance.

In Italy, in 1952 I was shocked to see one of the poorest villages that ever existed in what was the 20th century. Open sewers ran down a deep gutter to the side of the road. It was, virtually an open cess pit swarming with myriads of flies. Many houses were semi derelict, or in poor condition, the roads had massive potholes, everywhere it reeked of poverty. This region, admittedly, was still reeling from the consequences of the Second World War that had decimated the countryside.

As I wandered into the village square I was astounded to see an ornate church in the centre, well-kept and in pristine condition. While I was drinking a glass of the local wine in a run-down taverna later that day, I saw a Catholic priest collecting money from all and sundry, and it was noticeable that none refused him, he seemed to be regarded with a degree of reverence that I felt bordered on fear. Later I discovered that a beautiful and heavy solid gold crucifix adorned the altar, and that it had been paid for by the villagers' contributions since the war.

What astounded me was that the priest was now collecting for the price of a magnificent ruby that had been reserved, and which was destined to be put in the centre of the magnificent solid gold cross that ornamented the altar of this church. Here before me I was witnessing a collection for just one single artefact in the church, that would have paid for fresh water to be piped, and a mains pipe for the sewage, but no, a ruby was considered more important. Is it little wonder that the main converts to our Pagan faith are Catholics?

One convert we had, I will never forget to my dying day. It was late evening when I received a phone call one day, outwardly purporting to be from a nun at the local convent, stating she wished to leave the order, and had heard we held open meetings to which non Wiccans could attend to discuss the Craft prior to applying to join, after a probationary period of the traditional year and a day.

A little unsure, I said she could attend our next meeting, although in my heart I was not at all sure she was genuine. I checked the telephone number out she had called from and yes, it was the convent's number she had referred to. To our utter surprise, on the day she turned up in all her glory - full robes and wimple! She was 100% genuine and henceforth attended all our meetings on a regular basis, discreetly removing the onyx and silver crucifix that swung from her waist and slipping it into the folds of her robe whenever she arrived.

Occasionally on a winter's night I would drive her back to the convent and wait as she let herself in by a lychgate. With the nights darkening, it was not always possible to run everybody home, you can imagine our astonishment when at the very next meeting we held, she turned up on a motorbike with 'L' plates, and with full leathers on! Yes, she did eventually became a Witch, although sadly, in an almost all-female Dianic group, a legacy I felt from all the years she had been cloistered with women only.

We had many an interesting debate with regard to the ongoing furore within the Xtian ranks over the ordination of women priests that was splitting their ranks, and I gathered it was a hotly debated subject within the convent walls. The powers that be continuously argued that the priesthood was an exclus-ively male domain, and that there was no such thing as a woman priest and they would resist their ordination with all fervour. We all knew what the real fears were though, of course in one way they were right, there are no such things as women priests! For once a woman was ordained, - she became a Priestess!!! - Not a Priest, and that was essentially Pagan, and that clearly was their real fear - Priestesses within the Church!

While they were vilifying women, they were also building up the image of their messiah to make him more palatable to their potential converts. A gigantic Xtian PR machine now swung into action to present the new image, a feat that would be praiseworthy even in this the modern technological age. The earliest description of Jesus portrayed him as a slender man, with a distinctive stoop, fine aquiline features, clean shaven, rare for his day, and with a receding hairline, he was slightly built which may have helped him to survive the crucifixion. 300 years on the depictions show him as a handsome, bearded young man with a strong face.

A slightly-built man such as Jesus would have a far better chance of surviving being crucified, body weight being an essential factor to the terrible drag encountered. It would therefore be logical to be able to present his wounds three days later as wounds to the feet and hands are not fatal. In lectures I am often asked about the spear thrust into his side whereby quote 'blood and water issued forth'. Well for a starter dead bodies do not bleed, and the traditional way of checking for life was to plunge the tip of the spear into the thigh where the sciatic nerve is, not a very big target as it is a single nerve running down the thigh, and very sensitive as anybody who has ever had a 'dead leg' will know.

Even the crucifixion itself only entered Xtian mythology years after the event, crucifixion was performed on a stake with arms across the head and secured by a single nail - two in all with the crossed feet, the early records in Greek refer to it as a *Stauros* (Stake) it was over 300 years later that it became a cross. This is borne out by the book devoted to the subject entitled '*The Non Christian Cross*' which investigates the subject matter in depth. The author writes, "There is not a single sentence in any of the writings forming the New Testament which in the original Greek, bears even indirect evidence to the effect that the *Stauros* (Stake) used in the case of Jesus was other than an ordinary Stauros". Penultimately he adds; "The Romans usually used a tree, the cross was introduced after Christ's death by converted Pagans who were allowed to incorporate previous Pagan symbols into Xtian worship. In this case it was the Celtic, even-sided cross that was a Pagan symbol alongside the pentacle (star), circle and triangle.

Xtians have embraced and absorbed much of Paganism into their rites, usually to make the new ways of Xtianity all the more attractive to the peasants and country folk in those days. The bread and wine rituals are based on our cakes and wine ceremony, when we baked little moon crescent cakes and distributed them to the worshippers, their agape is the same as ours as well.

We use holy water in our rituals and this is 100% a Pagan custom based on the water from holy springs and wells, this again has been snaffled by the church. The peasants would gather herbs and sweet-smelling woods together with pine resin as incense for meetings; again this was swiftly taken up by Xtians and became an integral part of their ceremonies. A Catholic mass is almost 100% Pagan except for the deity and the Virgin Mary replacing the Goddess of Nature. Devoid of the dogma of course.

If Xtians really had learned to practice what they preached; and spread the word as their Messiah intended with his doctrine of love, then it could have conquered the world, and we could never have achieved the comeback after our near extermination that we have. But avarice, greed and power have corrupted the teachings of the Holy one we all revered, until modern day Xtianity bears little resemblance to the creed their saviour preached.

One must also remember most importantly that it was man that wrote the Bible, not Jesus, he had no part in it whats-oever - guess he never even got to editing it, but when you analyse its contents you quickly realise how out of step its contents are with civilised behaviour and thinking. We all know Xtians do not practise what they preach, but when you read the Bible-with emphasis on the Old Testament, one can only say 'thank goodness they do not, if we did we would all end up in court. Let me treat you to just a few little extracts starting with Exodus 22. "Thou shalt not suffer a Witch to live".

Wow! That is a really good starter - a law advocating murder for anyone out of step with their thinking. This incidentally under the old Witchcraft Act encompasses anyone fortune telling, soothsaying, making predictions or even offering to heal. Tarot cards from which our modern playing cards were derived were considered instruments of the Devil and could swiftly precipitate you into becoming toast, so to speak. As the commandments also state, 'Thou shalt not kill', then anyone obeying the one law of slaying anyone even remotely connected with the occult, essentially violates the other - strange book this bible. I wonder who executes the executioner.

In Wicca although we do not technically need images of our sacred God and Goddess in order to worship them, as we have no dogma, most of us like to have a representation of our deities on our altars. This is the beauty and flexibility of the Craft as we obey the law of 'do as thou wilt-provided ye harm none'. The Xtian doctrine is quite the reverse and states 'Thou shalt not worship any graven image' and also 'Thou shalt not have any God but me'.

Roman Catholicism (why is it nearly always them?) seems to violate every rule in their sacred book, their churches and cathedrals are full of 'graven images' including all the disciples, Mary Magdalene, the Virgin Mary, and Jesus as well. Not only do they worship them, but talk and pray to them in addition. (Wasn't there some rule about 'communicating with the dead and spiritualism being outlawed?) Oh no - not another burning offence. Regarding the 'no other God but me' I find a triple deity aspect within Xtianity with the 'Father, Son and Holy Ghost' in my simple arithmetic I make that three Gods in all.

In the 1940s a man narrowly escaped jail when he advertised a book under a box number offering a salacious review of murder, genocide, incest, rape, buggery, sodomy, and adultery and every form of sexual deviationism known to man and woman. This erotica also recorded mass genocides, slaughter and torture. Eagerly the gullible public sent off their postal orders. (No-one sent cheques, as they did not want it to be known to the bank - or their wives - that they were purchasing such pornographic material). When the discreet brown paper parcel arrived they were surprised to find a brand new copy of the Holy Bible within. A few stalwarts screamed fraud, but as the miscreant pointed out somewhat 'tongue in cheek' it was all there, quoting 15 detailed accounts of incest alone within its pages. A somewhat bemused Judge listened intently to an extract of a wife who had offended God being punished for chastising her husband (Woman's Lib was not around at the time). His crime? Exposing his genitals in public. Result? Wife punished - and husband's behaviour upheld! Excuse me, but are we on the same planet? If you don't believe me see Samuel - Old Testament.

Rape abounded throughout the Bible, he argued, with one case alone recorded of a man raping his own sister, and again in Samuel an elder of the tribe is recorded giving a public performance of his sexual prowess by making libidinous love to ten of his father's wives in succession, to the cheers of a crowd of leering spectators. Result - case dismissed, as 'no case to answer'. The punters the Judge ruled got everything they expected, and much, much, more, as well as a salutary lesson. The more I read, the more hilarious the good book became. I remember admonishing my daughters, one of whom was taking a somewhat dangerous evangelical twist in her life, that the Bible quite specifically allowed me 'to sell into slavery' any daughter who dare to disagree with daddy! Result one good girl and utter disillusionment with the Church at such a doctrine. Read Exodus 21.7 I said.

If one obeyed the Bible literally, and there were times remember when its contents were obeyed to the letter of the law, then we would all be in mega trouble. Leviticus strictly forbids any man to shave and then implements this by forbidding you to trim your beard as well, Leviticus 19.27.

Butchers would suffer major setbacks in revenue as it is illegal (most of these incidentally are upon pain of death) to eat any part of an animal that chews the cud, so cows and bullocks are out, or of any that have cloven hooves, (so exit venison etc) and you must not eat pork, rabbit, hare etc. Even touching leather made out of pigskin renders you unclean. Can you imagine walking the streets like lepers for the rest of your life, ringing a bell and calling out 'Unclean, unclean - I touched my wife's handbag!

According to Leviticus 15 I must keep well away from my wife when she is in her 'period of uncleanliness'. She loves the idea and says I should have to do all the cooking etc for both of us one week a month while she watches TV. Funny that bit as she still goes to the shops unchallenged. I think I'm being conned, I mean, she's not even a Xtian.

I really am getting somewhat confused by all these dictats in the Old Testament, particularly one which dictates how far one can go from their bed without washing their hands; it fails to say whether this should be before or after, so for the sake of the argument I will presume after. The problem is distance. Now if both my wife and I have to get up in the night for a call of nature, then handwashing is an essential to both of us, but why should I have to wash my hands to close a window but if my wife shuts it she does not? The answer is measurement according to the Bible so tonight I will change sides in bed and if she is over 10 paces away from the window or door she can wash her hands.

I recently received an e-mail from the USA quoting somewhat 'tongue in cheek' an extract from Leviticus 25.44 stating that all Xtians were allowed both male and female slaves 'provided they were purchased from neighbouring states' stating that he had been told that he could legally buy Mexicans according to God's Law, but could not purchase Canadians and asking the question why? - as Canada was technically a neighbouring state! Just for the record Leviticus 25.44 was used as justification for the slave trade, it being permitted and lawful in the Bible.

According to Leviticus hell-fire looms for me if I plant two different crops in the same field (Leviticus19.1) as well as both my wife and I stand condemned to eternal torment for having garments made out of two different types of thread. I told her not to buy that wool and cotton jumper!

You are even allowed to slay your neighbour if he violates the Sabbath by doing any work, Leviticus 35.2 including offering up burnt offerings on the wrong day. Me? I'm not even allowed a bonfire according to the local council. Does anyone really wonder why the Xtian numbers continue to decline and Pagan numbers increase? There is so much love in our ways, love of nature, love of all that is green, love of the environment and love of animals. Can you imagine a Pagan killing an animal and burning it as an offering to a deity, no way.

If Xtianity ruled I would technically be afraid to walk the streets in my smart three-piece suit. Why? Because I could be stoned on the spot as it has no fringes on the borders and blue ribbons as demanded (See Numbers 25, verse 38). I could go on and on, so please excuse me for poking a little fun at Xtians, after all they have done far worse to us.

We Pagans revere the Xtian Messiah and all he stood for, it is the myths that have grown up around him, and over which he had no control, that is our argument. I do not believe he ever intended to create a religion based on his doctrine, it was not his way. No it is the Church that has desecrated all he stood for and debased his holy teachings.

So remember our creed is one of love whereby all Witches take an oath to help, and to heal, and to preserve nature. We were, and still are, the original conservationists, and the Xtian Church has nothing to fear from us except as they grow ever weaker, we grow steadily in strength. The Old Ways are returning as of old, and this time there will be no retreat. We are here to stay, the old Gods have returned. The Goddess heralds the mornings calling to her consort alongside the dawn chorus of the birds, and the Horned God stalks the woodlands as of old. The Age of Aquarius has arrived, and it will be an age of enlightenment.

So Mote it be.

Crucifixion - Myth and Legend and the Mystical Thirteen

The facts are that the crucifixion of the Xtian Messiah and all the legends now so closely associated with the Xtian religion were not put together until well over 400 years after this infamous event. The writings with regard to the 'modus operandii' - re carrying out crucifixions are numerous and well recorded including the cost to the local authorities who at the end of the day would have to pick up the bill via the tax payer in the form of a local rate. If a felon had to die so be it, and if it was numerous felons, then the cost would escalate. Why use two bulwarks of wood they would have asked, and the cost of nails to perform the grisly task was highly prohibitive as well.

A blacksmith could work all day smelting iron ore and casting nails and would be lucky to achieve a dozen or so together with his other work. No, the chronicles are quite clear here that all crucifixions were to be carried out on permanently sited stakes on high ground for all to see and whereby the squeamish could circumnavigate the hill if they wished.

The victim was nailed to this stake from a movable platform while still horizontal and the arms folded above his head and thus secured there by a single nail through both wrists, it was customary to penetrate one wrist prior to being lifted onto the stake to make the executioner's task easier, whereby he now only had to penetrate one limb. So once again a popular fallacy has crept in with regard even to this and the popular conception of nailing through the hands is once more a misnomer.

Once in position, and now hanging by his wrists, the next part was easy the i.e. the securing of the feet, again by a single nail through the ankles, these being the strongest part and thus ensuring that the nails would not tear out through the flesh. The same was the 'raison d'etre' as to why the palms of the hand could not be used as it was just a matter of time before the sagging deadweight of the body would cause the hands to tear away and the body fall down. Once more the instructions were quite clear on this matter; the unfortunate was to be secured firmly by the wrists, again proved by archaeological excavations.

Once performed the opposite side of the stake would be used for the next victim, a matter of economy. This way a single stake could be used as a double crucifixion, plus only four nails were required as against eight, a considerable saving, and the powers-that-be saved on the cost of a further upright and two cross bars – and labour. Also, as a deterrent, one body would always be on view from any direction.

The best historical recording of this and costing lay with ancient Roman records, when the authorities were faced with mass executions by crucifying the prisoners from the famous slaves' revolt under Spartacus when thousands of insurgents who had been captured were displayed along the Appian way leading into the city of Rome. Even the citizens were appalled at this mass execution, but mainly from the stench of the hanging victims permeating the city and the hordes of flies it engendered which could have precipitated a pestilence.

Most historians now accept that the Xtian Messiah was crucified on a stake, and a number of religions such as Jehovah's Witnesses publish and accept these findings. Another anomaly also arises from this, and that is does crucifixion kill swiftly? And the answer is a definite no, what usually happened depended on the seriousness of the crime and this determined in turn how long the victim suffered there. A straightforward execution would normally be for anything from sunrise to sunset, approximately 12 hours, or the passing of a day, with the victim executed by the breaking of the legs with an iron bar at dusk. This 'mercy' was at the discretion of the sentencing courts as to how much the miscreant suffered.

The answer is that this barbarous means of execution was in fact an exquisite form of torture to prolong the period of suffering prior to formal execution, for as long as the sufferer could raise himself on his feet, (an agonising process that further contributed to his agony) then he could draw breath. This could last for days on end and many executioners vied with each other as to how long they could keep a victim alive who had been awarded the most supreme punishment 'To hang on the stake until you die'. When this occurred the executioner's assistants would be instructed to give the victims wine, or water on a sponge at the end of a long pole two or three times a day as sustenance.

This was no act of kindness, no not a bit of it, as it served a double purpose, on the one hand the victim's life and suffering was prolonged plus the fact that the drink offered was on a sponge which the sufferer sucked to quell his thirst, was the supreme insult and final degradation to the dying man. All Roman soldiers were issued with a sponge at the end of a stick to clean themselves with after attending a vital daily ablution in the common mass toilets. If the executioner wanted to be particularly spiteful after giving the victim water he would substitute vinegar and salt.

This myth of crucifixion was to save the lives of a number of Rabbis in World War 2. One incident that proves the fallacy of this was after the town of Kiev fell to German forces in the Russian campaign. After the Wehrmacht had taken the town the SS set about rounding up any Jews they could find and crucified five Rabbis to their Synagogue doors.

When Russian forces counter-attacked three days later they retook a large part of the city and were astounded to find that four of the Rabbis had survived their ordeal and had actually fallen down as the nails had torn through the palms of their hands. The unfortunate fifth one, who was in his eighties, had not survived the ordeal and had died from shock and loss of blood; further proof that this method was not lethal until the final moment when mercifully the legs were broken and the person was unable to raise himself to ease the pain in his hands. At this stage the body slumped forward, the diaphragm contracted and in minutes the person suffocated to death, being now unable to draw breath. It is a recorded fact that the Messiah's legs were not broken and that he was taken down after what was a comparatively short period of suffering, outwardly dead, in a trance, remember we accept him as a great magus, or even unconscious, to be spirited away and presumably resuscitated. It therefore comes as no surprise then to hear of him being able to display his wounds days later and announce he had cheated death. Why his legs were not broken will forever be a mystery and continue to throw doubt on this momentous event that was to change history, and have such impact on the world thereafter.

Many Xtians will outwardly accept that there is room for doubt there, but counter their argument with the fact that a Roman soldier did ascertain death by plunging a spear into his side, a forgery of which has circulated ever since and became known as the Spear of Longinus! Again this does not hold water when closely examined. Firstly they state that the wound would have been fatal in itself, and secondly it was reported that blood and water did come forth.

So once more let us examine the facts, the standard and extremely inaccurate method to establish total death was by the simple expedient of jabbing a spear into the thigh where the sciatic nerve ran, this highly sensitive (and narrow) nerve would immediately cause a living body to twitch if you were lucky enough to find the right spot. I am sure that in our childhood days we have all suffered the indignity of a 'dead leg' administered by a recalcitrant companion and know the effect it can have.

So even if the soldier was able to find the right spot then an injury to the thigh even if he missed the area would not be fatal, but a superficial injury, Add to this the fact that it is recorded that 'blood and water did come forth, let us then accept this then at face value. Dead bodies do not bleed - only living ones. Roman soldiery were notoriously haphazard with prisoners and would have just gone through the basic examination of a dead body, usually being more interested in receiving a payment from the deceased's relatives for safe delivery of the body.

I have added this chapter, as it is upon this erroneous happening that Xtianity was founded. From the teachings of a compassionate albeit revolutionary man who preached love and forgiveness to all people, a religion of 'He' but the Genocides that have been perpetrated in His holy name by those who have usurped His teachings and which led to the creation of the holy Roman catholic Church and ultimately its infernal and heartless inquisition which still exists as I reported in detail in my book '*The Last Bastion*' by Zambezi publishing.

Can you imagine the man who in a fit of exasperation threw the moneylenders out of the Temple would have stood by and dumbly watched as some poor accused and stark naked woman would have a red hot iron applied to her breast and been told 'Ease your suffering and confess' adding 'in the name of the Lord'. No way - he would have gone spare to see what was being perpetrated in His name years later. Even many Xtians today will shake their heads sadly and say 'The only Xtian there ever was died on the Cross'.

How did this all come about you ask? Well at the beginning we referred to the fact that the New Testament of the Xtians' holy book, the Bible, was commenced being written some 400 years after the event, when memories of the occasion were already sketchy and beginning to fade, and myth was already entering the frame. Apparently 12 of the 13 disciples wrote accounts of what they saw, but history has lost these. Four hundred years later four were 'found; allegedly written by Matthew, Mark, Luke, and John. One does not have to be a genius to see the startling similarity between these chronicles. If four different people gave four different statements to the police regarding a road accident they had witnessed firsthand you would find you had four completely and utterly differently versions ranging from the colour and the makes of the car to which direction they were travelling. Strange is it not that the first four books in the New Testament are almost identical as if they had been written by the same person?

One major exclusion from the full Bible, as an example, is that the whole of the apocrypha has been excised as if it had never existed and books from famous female prophets have all been excluded. The reason for this is pretty clear - women! The Xtian doctrine is highly patriarchal, and there is no place for women, unless you count women being put in their place, covering their heads in church, especially Catholic women.

So out goes approximately one third of the book before the sanitising even begins. We see the Old Testament with Genesis altered, we see Exodus altered to suit their purpose in the suppression of all aspects of feminism. Particularly if you study St Peter's diatribes as well as the edicts of St Paul. Let us take just a few samples, although I could write an entire book on this subject alone

The original writings of Genesis were essentially centred on the first Man and Women created by God and placed in the Garden of Eden. To wit Adam and Lilith, no dear reader you have not read wrong - Adam and *Lilith*! Eve was his second wife and did not come along until a considerable time later.

We know the parable of the Xtian God taking of 'earth and of clay' and creating man ' quote 'in his own image' the story goes on to say that' he was 'good in the sight of God' now comes the rub. Quote - *'Then did he take of earth and of clay and make woman in like image* - wow - and she was good in the sight of

God; and so they were left alone to be fruitful and multiply, which Lilith did with remarkable frequency but regretfully only producing daughters.

This did not seem to worry God unduly at the time, but he obviously had some secret agenda, such is the inscrutability of the Almighty. Well it seems he liked to pop in for the odd chat and to see how his new creation was getting on, after all he had had a pretty busy for six days creating heaven and earth not to mention all the firmaments. The fat went in the fire when Lilith, sweet girl, mentioned en passant a remark regarding her partner Adam. Oh dear, it seems the offending word was Partner' Apparently God angrily retorted that "I did not make thee to be Adam's partner, thou art not his equal!!! Me? Personally I just adore women who can fight their corner and argue from logic as against emotion. Sweetly she replied "I was made of clay and of earth as was Adam, therefore I am his equal".

Poor Lilith - wrong move, pack your bags and go sayeth the Lord, well the actual wording if you want to be exact was '*And he cast her and all her daughters out into the lands of Canaan and Nod, to walk in the wilderness forever* (Make a note of the Canaan and Nod bit as it is very important later!). This did not go down with Adam at all well, he'd quite got used to being a family man and she kept the bed warm as well, The negative side was that she was a bit of a women's libber but you can't have everything can you?

It was not long before the Almighty came round again, only to find a somewhat unhappy and lonely Adam pining for his wife. Well the charitable side of God rose to the fore and he decided that if Lilith had learned her lesson and would toe the line, well he'd give her a second chance. At this point I must go back to old records, as there is somewhat of a contradiction here. One report states '*That God in his infinite wisdom did send forth seven angels unto Lilith with the message "Be dutiful and return to thy husband"*' other documents state it was nine angels, while another states it was three, so let us just say that he sent a number of angels forth.

Lilith seems to have agreed to a truce and came back - outwardly suitably subdued, a duly chastened girl (not really though, we all know how cunning women are). God was over the moon so to speak, told her to behave herself and do as she was told and all would be forgiven - let bygones be has-beens so to speak. Well our girly smiled sweetly once more and God was happy, after all he was the boss. Beaming with beatitude he announced that as a reward our Lilith would now give birth to a boy, and he commanded he be named Shibboleth. So all is now well.

Nine months later, at a guess, little Shibboleth enters into the Garden of Eden and all is well - until God drops in for a chat and to see how everything is. History does not state what happened except that God had a little dig to the effect that he is supposed to have said "O Woman, thou who brings forth child in pain and in suffering, while man suffers not, do you still claim to be the equal of man?" Sorry God, this time wrong move on your part, after all you must have invented post natal depression, you did make everything after all.

Snap! Up comes Lilith spoiling for a fight, bringing up the old earth and clay argument, and the next thing we know is she's back in the wilderness (Canaan and Nod - watch this space) with her newly-born baby. Well God realises she did have a point, after all he DID make her out of the same material as Adam, so he decides to have another go and get it right this time. He puts Adam, so the Bible says, into a deep sleep, and while he slept he took his third rib and created Eve from it, Woman model mark 2. Improved version. Dutiful, subservient, and obedient. Looking back I think he must have got the blueprints upside down. It seems that harmony was now established and Lilith was history, but let us examine this episode further. Eve only had sons, two in all we are told, named Cain and Abel, The Bible says that Cain slew Abel and he in turn is banished to Canaan, where, wait for it, he found himself a wife.

Why, I am forced to ask, do Xtians not ask such logical questions as - "Hold on Reverent, here are only three people in the whole world - to wit, Adam Eve, and Cain – so where did this wife come from?" Strangely this question is never asked but everything in their good book has (to coin a phrase) to be taken as 'gospel', and not queried. We all know the entire story is fable but if the Bible had not been amended, and Lilith cut out of it, then the story would make sense as Lilith and all her daughters were out there in the wilderness just waiting to be discovered by a virile young man.

Many fables could well have been based on fact, even if highly exaggerated and embellished over the years and the scribes who wrote the Old Testament were not averse to filching stories from other religions and amending them so as to be attributed to their Saviour. A typical example of yet another form of replacement therapy is the Bible story of the feeding of the 5,000 with 3 loaves and 5 fishes. Nearly every old religion has this story attributed to their own deity.

In China the story is told of a great mass of many thousands in the desert who are starving and all there is to feed these hordes are 7 rice cakes and 3 flour cakes, Then miraculously, after their preacher inspires them, they are all fed as nearly all who were present had secreted food about themselves and were now shamed into producing it; such was his eloquence. Take the same story, make it 5,000 souls and alter the food to what your own culture would eat, and make it your miracle.

When James decided to do his own edit on the holy book (there were two major edits over a period of 200 years - namely 1408 and 1611) he found to his surprise the story of the great King Saul seeking out a wondrous woman of great and infinite wisdom who lived in a far off land called Endor. It was said that such was her wisdom that great kings, princes, and emperors travelled miles to consult her and did lay their crowns at her feet. Gee - some gal!

All this did was to incense King James and inspire him to take out his blue pencil and rewrite the whole chapter. The effrontery of it, he mused, to dare to put a clever woman into the good book. What could he do? No way could this be allowed. Next thing you know is that they will be back on this 'I am equal' lark, Well we cut that Lilith female out eventually, damn revolutionary, don't know how God could have made such a mistake. Well, she was just a prototype after all, what impertinence, if we allow this 'wise woman' bit to stay in goodness only knows where it could lead, damn creatures will be asking for the vote next.

Well with a stroke of sheer genius he realised that he would have to accept the fact that she had more brain cells than was permitted, so how come she was so damn clever? Got it, it's quite clear that this is part of the plot by the Infernal One who has trebled her allocation, Old Horny just had to be involved somewhere. So out with the blue pencil once more and write in 'Witch'. Saul did a naughty and sought out the 'Witch of Endor'. In addition to this constant editing, and there are many, but one thing prevails and that is they were all exclusively aimed at the suppression of the fair sex and the furtherance of the patriarchal cult.

Not only was the great Xtian propaganda machine brought in to quell all resistance but the innovation of original sin now entered the equation. Eve must have been a bit of a raver as well, and she clearly was a bit of a temptress on the side, after all who listened to the serpent? And who took the first bite out of the apple, yes it was her. No. Original Sin is an 'in' thing for every sermon. That'll teach them.

Well the new Bible suffered appalling cuts as we now know, but the worst thing that happened was constant misinterpretation as this work was translated from Hebrew to Aramaic, then

Greek, then Latin and eventually English, these misnomers were to lead to the near genocide of our people and the near extinction of Paganism,

All this came about by one single sentence, containing the word *kaskagh* meaning a poisoner. It commenced its life in Exodus XX11 stating "Thou shalt not suffer a kaskagh (Poisoner) to live" This was in the original Hebrew text, it was initially just a simple slip of the pen, we presume that altered *kaskagh* to *kasagh*, it also appeared in other translations as *Kuf* and *Kafshin* and also as *Kufshin* etc. From here a single letter altered the meaning to sorcerer, and eventually to Witch. Take as an example the omission of the letter 'l' would turn world into word.

It came about that the infamous Kramer and Sprenger, two vile and infamous Dominican monks used this extract to commence the persecution of all alleged Witches, while their demented and deranged minds feverishly wrote in lurid paragraphs into their foul book *'The Malleus Malleficarum'* that became known as the 'Hammer of the Witches'.

Using the decree of Exodus that Thou shalt not suffer a Witch to live' these suppressed sexual perverts advocated the stripping of women and the shaving off of all their body hair so that they could examine 'their most secret parts' as they searched for any protrusion, teat, or pimple from which their master Satan could suck. The end result was the hideous deaths throughout Europe of over 18,000,000 souls of which the infamous Inquisition held mass burnings that included any suspected innocent or not with the cry that one should not hold back from the burning of innocents, including babes and children as well, stating 'God will know his own'.

If ever you wonder in this the 21st century as to why so many are turning away from Xtianity, then the answer is look at their record, even their own Holy book states 'By their deeds shall ye judge them'.

One of the tenets of Witch and Pagan alike is the belief in re-incarnation, now regarded as a heresy by the Church, yet strangely enough this was actually taught by the Church itself right up to 553 AD. In that year they convened the Church council of Constantinople who unanimously decided that this idea of life after life after life, each incarnation leading to the betterment of both soul and body was not exactly helping them to attract converts to the Xtian faith, The end result was quite a clever one, simply alter it slightly to life everlasting and God would give everybody a short cut to eternal life, or life ever-lasting by the simple act of conversion. In 553 AD this became law and it became a heresy to believe what they had preached for the previous 553 years.

Well we have devoted a few pages to various elements of Xtianity and how it had such a profound impact on us; so let us end this chapter on a somewhat humorous and historical note. Those of us who know the Pagan path know of the secret degrees, signs, and elevations as we progress to the supreme accolade of the third degree, which of course I cannot show here. It is not exactly a secret that high-ranking Witches wear a traditional garter above the left knee as a mark of their rank, another old custom that like so many others is sadly dying out. It is a matter of record that these varied as to what secret signs and sigils were engraved or embossed upon them (Sorry but you will have to be imitated to find out exactly what) but I can disclose that they were by tradition made out of green leather or snakeskin. It is also a fact that many people of very high rank still adhered to the Old Faith, while many were still sympathetic to it, including many Royals as I mentioned but did not name in *The Last Bastion*. In fact it is said that the Round Tower at Windsor Castle in Berkshire was constructed to enable a group of eminent Witches to be able to worship in secret, under the benevolent eye of the king at the time.

The Round Tower is supposed to have been the scene of the famous incident when King Edward 111 was dancing with the beautiful Countess of Salisbury when the horrified onlookers saw a green garter slip down to her ankle from her left leg in the middle of a pirouette, thus proclaiming for all to see that she was a high ranking follower of the Old Religion. Such a public proclamation could lead to her being tried and executed as a Witch if it became known outside of those present. Highly unlikely that any present would have betrayed her, but there were servants and minions present in attendance, and they would talk. Edward did not hesitate, swiftly he picked the offending garter up and placed it on his own leg for all to see. It was a multi-factored gesture that contained a number of elements, on the one hand the gesture placed the Countess of Salisbury under his immediate protection, but most significantly it proclaimed him as being in the position of being the God Incarnate to all Pagans.

The incident did not end there as the wheels were immediately put into motion to form a new order that would put the final nail in the coffin of any potential accusers. With alacrity he announced a completely new Royal Order to be known henceforth as 'The Order of the Garter' to be formed of 12 knights of the realm to serve him, and a further 12 to serve the Prince of Wales - two covens of 13! The symbol of this authority was the right to wear an embroidered garter high on the left leg, of which the five-pointed star, the pentacle, was prominently displayed. It was about this time that it became known as the 'Goblins' cross'.

The King's mantle itself was embroidered with 168 'stars' while if you count the one on the garter, a quite deliberate gesture, it made 169 in all. 13 covens of 13.

No-one would have dared challenge such authority. Where there is a will there is a way.

Part of the Witch Rune runs as follows and I will record it here as part of the analysis of this mystical number.

The mystery of the mystical 13.

“Thirteen silver moons in a year are.
Thirteen is the Covens array.
Thirteen times at Esbat make merry
For each Golden year and a day
For the power was passed down through the ages
Each time between woman and man
Each century onto the other
‘Ere time and the ages began

So runs part of the mystical Witch rune, that fascinating parody that illuminates so much of the ancient ways of the Witch and is contained in those enchanting words. Thirteen is a dominant factor in the circle of life, as is green, yet this figure and colour have become associated with misfortune. On Friday the 13th triskologists fearfully lock themselves indoors fearing to venture out, and many a person will not travel on that feared date. Meanwhile the Witches treat this day as a jamboree, and if by chance an Esbat, Sabbat, new or full moon fall on that particular day it is a cause of much rejoicing. Friday - named after Frigga the Goddess of love, the eternal Venus of halcyon days is revered and honoured in all fertility Sabbats, and so much the better if perchance it falls on the thirteenth.

It is one of the most natural cycles in nature and civilization after civilization has worshipped and acknowledged it. A year is thirteen cycles of 28 days; a fertile woman pays her tribute to the moon Goddess thirteen times a year; there are thirteen major planets that circle the Earth including our own, now that science has recognised the existence of Arachne.

I would like to bring a little-known fact to your attention with regard to this number, let us take a symbol that is known world wide - The Great Seal of the United States of America, symbolised by a bald eagle holding a clutch of arrows. On closer examination the following is revealed:

1 There are 13 stars or pentacles on the seal.
2 There are 13 stripes.
3 There are 13 letters in the motto.
4 There are 13 Laurel Leaves.
5 There are 13 Arrows.
6 There are 13 clouds in the Glory.
7 There are 13 berries on the Branch.
8 There are 13 feathers in the left wing of the great Eagle.
9 There are 13 feathers in the right wing of the great Eagle.
10 There are 13 feathers in the tail.
11 There are 39 (3 times 13) letters in all including letters in "The Coat of Arms of the United States of America"

And 13 times 13 items above comes to 169, a magical figure that is all powerful being 13 times 13!

Surely it is not coincidence then that this figure has occurred so often even in the American coat of arms, or perhaps I should say their Great Seal. It is a mystical number. The superstition seems to have arisen over the fact that the Xtian God had 12 apostles, which together with himself made a full coven of thirteen. The fact that one betrayed him is irrelevant to the case; the Xtian God surrounded himself with a magical number, strongly suggesting that he was the head of a coven.

We know he was a man of high principles and advocated the identical teachings of love and tolerance that is typical of the Witches' creed, how little modern Xtians know of our ways, which run such a close parallel to the teachings of their own Messiah, and again we know he was a mystic. Witches are not anti-Xtian as they are so often accused, on the contrary their principals are the same. We regard the Xtian God as a great Magus, it is what his followers have perpetrated in his holy name that is the scourge of the modern-day Churches. Their holy man taught us all how to judge people, did he not utter the prophetic words" By their deeds shall ye Judge them". When you look back on the Genocides that have been waged in his name and the slaughter of whole nations over the centuries it does not say much for what followed in his footsteps.

The dreaded Inquisition with its exquisite instruments of torture, so loathsome and abominable in their application to the fair sex that I will not pollute these pages with descriptions of them. The fanatical fervour of the crusades in which whole cities were massacred, men, women, and children is now but a memory. But these were not the only murderous expeditions, far from it, I could fill pages. Where are the Albigensians and the Walbigensians now? Where are the Aztec, the Inca, and the Maya? Gone, they have vanished off the face of the earth thanks to the expeditions of Rome in its quest for gold.

Take the persecution, not only of ourselves over countless centuries, but also of the Jewish nation, another poor continuously persecuted people whose only crime was being Jewish - i.e. not Xtian. History has shown time and time again that when the Hebrews were subjugated and converted (usually at the point of a sword) even when they had become Messianic Jews for aeons of time, the were also amongst the first to be slaughtered in the eternal pogroms.

Druids, Kings, Countesses - and Magic Circles

So we know that Pagan practise and Wicca had started to raise their heads again in the early 1700s with Druidism and Masonry emerging together that same year. Masonry flourished and spread, and was emulated by newly-formed lodges in America and Ireland which the Grand Lodge of England refused to recognise.

Druidism also evolved further and in 1781 Henry Hurle formed the 'The Ancient Order of Druids, the same order that Winston Churchill belonged to. It is not widely known that the great wartime leader who steered us through the turbulent Second World War years, with the tremendous help and aid of our American cousins, was a Druid!

This specific Druid order was followed-up ten years later with the formation of the Iolo Morganwg. (Autodictat) by a Welshman named Edward Williams in1791; He formed the Welsh Gorsedd, which also promoted the preservation of the Welsh language by using it in all rituals. These three dominated the scene, and still do right up until a few years ago when the Order of Bards, Ovates, and Druids was born.

They say what goes around comes around, and it is my earnest belief that the birth of freemasonry was based on old occult practises and was in turn the background to Gardner's newly formulated Book of Shadows.

So now we are in a dilemma, on the one hand we see the re-establishment of the God and Goddess worldwide, an upsurge in all things green, ecological and conservation groups growing annually in strength. There is tacit acceptance now of the fact that we are not Satanists, and that the Lord Cernunnos is not the Devil invented by Xtians, that is indeed progress, great! But despite all this we are losing our roots as new rituals and practises are introduced as if they were ancient on an almost monthly basis as each new book appears on the market.

It is this very fact that prevents so much knowledge being passed on as many fear that if secrets are passed on with the upsurge in numbers, together with the inevitable backsliders then it would be but a matter of time before the knowledge would appear in print. Furthermore we have been plagued by a few unscrupulous individuals who have insidiously attempted to inveigle themselves into covens and groups with the express purpose of gaining knowledge for a book.

Fortunately we have expertise to-date in thwarting them having had notorious newspapers attempting to do the same in order to obtain a headline story for the national press, in fact in my book *The Last Bastion* I was delighted to be able to recount a most hilarious episode where a local poacher hoodwinked a freelance *News of the World* reporter into 'uncovering' a coven in the midst of a woodland where the local vicar was hosting a Halloween party.

Notwithstanding this, the wonderful resurgence of colourful Pagan gatherings such as the fabulous Green Man Festival held annually at Hastings in Sussex, mentioned earlier, continues to show the growing strength of Paganism.

We have had our fair share of persecution over the years but now in the 21st century we have the law of the realm on our side and other than the periodic attacks on us by the churches we have no real fears, unlike our North American native cousins. So many of their rituals run a close parallel to ours, The red man was taught the passing of the moon's phases from early life and was brought up with a respect for all fauna and flora, taking only what he needed from the land, the white race did to them what the Xtians did to us.

The simple yeoman and woman had the self-same knowledge, passed down from mother to son and father to daughter, it was not universally taught as far as we know. Each village outside of the wise women whose knowledge was vast had a leader, the one the Xtians called 'the man in black'. He would have glanced at the moon and silently the villagers would have made their way to secluded glens, carting their farmyard implements with them. If there was a possibility they should be discovered they would cut a new wand from the nearest hazel bush, a candle would be melted to form a roundel and they would mark it with the ancient sigils that were passed down from father to daughter and mother to son.

Xtianity started out as a pure teaching, it was founded by a simple unpretentious man who eschewed riches and preached that it was better to give than to receive, with a doctrine to turn the other cheek in what was a pacifist movement. He did not wear gaudy gold thread in his garments, as the High Priests did, together with their gold chains, but simple clothes (we can beat them there as we wear nothing) one up to Wicca!).

Compare this to the Catholic Church and its wealth, in fact all Xtian churches. Recall what I wrote about Italy and the poverty stricken village with no fresh water and open sewers and the villagers raising money at the instigation of the local Catholic priest to purchase a ruby for the centrepiece of the solid gold crucifix that lay to the front of the altar in the church.

So let us go back in time and see how new initiates were being educated into many of the old mysteries. If we turn the clock back we find that the tri-gradal system whereby the power was given at initiation, the old degrees being completely the reverse of what they are today. With the passing of the persecutions we evolved into the present age and allow three degrees of Witchcraft i.e. initiation into the very first of the mysteries, followed by a probationary period of an absolute minimum of a year and a day. Then, if they have learned to cast a circle from memory and perform minor magical rituals, plus learning the secret intonation of the words, they are elevated to the second degree where they will probably remain for many years, if not for all of their Witch life. Eventually those of outstanding ability will be honoured and subsequently elevated to the third degree, whereupon they would be expected to 'hive' and found another coven, and start all over again. At this stage they would be instructed in the inner mysteries and these would remain secret with them until they too had found over the coming year's suitable third degree Witches in turn.

This was Paganism pure and simple, the old lore of nature worship being performed 'en masse, and was not Wicca as such. An adage that seems to have become lost in the last few years is that yes - all Witches *are* Pagans, but all Pagans are not Witches, and therefore there is ample room in the new renaissance for Paganism pure and simple and does not require fancy titles.

Let us revert at this stage to the very word Pagan and what it means. First of all the word is Latin and was originally *Paganus* meaning a heathen, i.e. one who lives on the heath or in the countryside or woodlands. Nothing like the image of a bloodthirsty barbarian with which heathens have come to be associated, it was a term that applied to all who lived in the countryside and also became equated with 'peasant', all those who lived 'outside the pale'. (The pale was usually a wooden structure that enclosed a town to keep undesirables out and which also offered a degree of protection as it could be fortified if the town was attacked.)

Heathens of course were allowed into the towns, they spent money and supplied local produce for the inhabitants. Many years were to pass before these pagans/heathens were ostracised, it was only commerce that allowed them to be accepted and were it not for that I am sure that they would have been included in the list of undesirables as non-town dwellers. Criminals were forbidden entry to the town and beggars, gypsies, and any bad characters were evicted at nightfall, and usually refused re-admittance; those who were completely excluded and forbidden entry were described as 'beyond the pale'.

It was not long before Witches were 'beyond the pale' and they stayed well outside of the towns' boundaries practising their magical arts of healing both sick human and animal alike in villages and often isolated hovels. Wicca, and the Witches' art was a country practice then and the towns' sick and maimed would often prefer to seek the ancient wisdom of these Pagan wise ones who would gladly accept a loaf of bread in exchange for their healing skills or a half dozen eggs, as against the towns' apothecaries who demanded silver.

Again we see the roots of the persecutions commencing as the medical profession swiftly joined voice against these country Witches who were depriving them of a lucrative and often useless trade. Each and every ailment, the leeches of the day (doctors) decided, was caused by bad blood, and bleeding the patient became unilateral practice, often to the point of death. In studying Wiccan wise women's practises I have not even found one single instance of them using this useless treatment, leeches yes, they used these to remove subcutaneous haematomas for example, particularly in sensitive areas such as eye injuries, but that was the closest they ever got to the standard practise of the 'qualified surgeon' who was their competitor.

After the advent of Xtianity the new religion referred to so-called heathens as the 'un-enlightened' inasmuch as they refused to accept the new Xtian doctrine. But as the years passed the word came to take on a more sinister connotation and was swiftly identified with any warlike tribes who were swiftly dubbed Heathens!

So much for the meaning and origins of Paganism, now let us turn the clock back prior to the influx of the Flemish weavers and what followed on their heels and the impact they had on British Witchcraft. We find the present system of the grades of 1-2-3 was reversed to 3-2-1! The power being passed by sexual induction at the new Witch's initiation.

The reason in those days was both simple and practical, for if the coven were discovered by the ever-eager Witch takers and finders, then even if the coven was decimated as long as there was one solitary survivor with the knowledge and power then the craft would survive. Every new Witch learned these secrets and the power they could generate from the very beginning, with the persecutions at their height it was essential if the old ways were to survive for extinction loomed as the Xtian priests set out Hell bound to eliminate Paganism once and for all in a concerted effort of what was near genocide.

Imagine in this day and age if the power and inner secrets were to be passed to a new initiate as of old, who like many before him can violate his sacred oath secured on his very soul, can backslide and go public with all they have learned. When the Craft in England was less than a mere handful by comparison to now, and your confession to even having been a member of a coven was certain and painful death, then the secrets were safe.

Now with the Craft going into seven figures, maybe even eight worldwide, then the secrets can no longer be regarded as safe, as the spate of books written by many a so-called 'Witch' shows quite clearly. There are secrets within the Craft that are jealously guarded to this day, not least of these being ancient spells tried and tested and of great power. Take for example the infamous 'Sang d'amore' love spell of legend, now as far as I know virtually extinct and, I hesitate to say, rightly so. An old West Country Witch imparted it to me over thirty years ago, and said she had only known it to have been used once in her entire life time and vowed she would never ever perform it again, such being its power.

I have seen other so called sang d'amore spells loosely based on this one but they all lacked the basics. Can you imagine the commercial value of this if it was exploited? One is therefore faced with a dilemma, logically one day, probably long after I have passed to the Summerlands, those who would inherit my own Hand of Rite will see its secrets unfurled within its copious pages. So how long would it be before it became public knowledge? Remember it only takes ONE! And Artemis is over a hundred strong not counting the myriads that have hived from us over the years.

You may scoff at the very idea of such a spell existing still in the 21st century, and furthermore not understand why it cannot be broken, and I cannot tell you, but to draw a parallel imagine if someone was exposed to radioactivity then it would remain with them for ever, and all the medicine and science in the world could not remove it, such is the power of this ritual and what is used runs a close parallel.

Sadly I saw it used by one of my people who was my High Priestess for a time and we discussed its future at length many years ago. Foolishly she decided without telling me to try it out on a man she had set her cap at and whom she desired, within the passing of a moon he was bewitched and fell in love with her. Use magic wrongly and there is always a price to pay! The relationship was a disaster and she left him. That was over twenty-five years ago and he still yearns for her. He will never leave her alone, he phones, waits on street corners, and arranges to 'meet her', always accidentally of course. A blighted life! And all through her selfish action. For 25 years she has had to live with this and has vowed to take the secret of the spell to her grave with her, a salutary lesson indeed.

Should such ancient wisdom be destroyed? I have pondered long and hard on this issue, and am reluctant to consign this spell to history, but with the nefarious books I continuously see emerging I think that with sadness in my heart it must be destroyed soon as I grow ever closer to the beloved Summerlands. The spell was a subject of much debate during my lecture tour of America, and has been the subject of much correspondence since.

One thing I have found in America is that despite the commercialisation of the Craft there was a hard core of devotees who desperately wanted to go back to its fundamentals. In California at the end of a lecture the High Priest of a coven whose roots lay with the legendary Witch Queen of Kent approached me as to whether I knew her? I was delighted to be able to tell his group of how I had worked with both she and her High Priest on many a happy occasion, and upon my return to the UK was able to put them in touch with each other, it made yet another part of this memorable tour so satisfying.

I was able to regale them with tales of her ubiquitous nature and her wonderful and somewhat wicked sense of humour. Her house in Kent where the covenstead met was graced with a wonderful completely round cellar to cast the circle in and here, deep down in the very bowels of the earth, we celebrated the great Sabbats. What the unwary newcomer did not know was that this particular Witch's house lay alongside a tidal river and at a certain point at the end of the evening when the ceremony was closed and as we were about to partake in the cakes and wine agape, suddenly the high priestess would pull out the plug, and the water would rise waist high as it rushed in from the river. Try enjoying your cakes and wine with swirling water around you, and the odd eel! Then with a laugh she and her high priest would produce towels and the skyclad coven would dry themselves and retire to a beautifully heated room to get dressed and partake of the goodies she would arraign for us.

When the tide turned the water flowed out and she would replace the stopper – until next time and the next initiate! her water ritual was notorious, and many a time and oft we would invite an unsuspecting candidate from another coven to join us. I think that this light heartedness is one of the major factors in the craft with its great sense of humour at all times. Laughter and merriment is, and always has been a tenet of the Craft and makes such a contrast to the dreary and often doleful sermons we had inflicted on us in our early years before we saw the light so to speak. The sheer joyfulness of Sabbats and equinoxes contrasts so sharply to the dirges within the Church, with its emphasis on death and eternal punishment in hell fires that came from the Xtian priest's lips.

Many a famous Witch has passed through this famous cellar and lived to tell the tale, and our American brethren were delighted to have found their roots again. Here was a coven that had wonderful sound roots and we burned the midnight oil discussing much of the abysmal state that so much of the Craft had descended to in America, all male covens, all women covens, and an array of some bizarre covens stunned us. The Craft is essentially heterosexual with a union of both God and Goddess; there must essentially be a polarity to balance the forces of nature. I can accept that single sex groups exist and wish to become exclusively one sex or the other, but surely there is some room for compromise here to ensure that at least a degree of polarity exists.

If a coven of men only want to worship the old Gods then fine but they must essentially have at least one woman at the helm or the whole thing becomes a parody. Equally an all female coven must also by the same criteria have a man, well at least say once a year! My opinion only, but polarity of men and women has always been the criteria of the Old Ways. Naturally it is not possible to establish an equally sexed coven unless you restrict membership to an equality of numbers, but in so doing you would be exempting some admirable candidates seeking admission, and the Craft must continue to expand to survive.

Let us examine ancient ways, and explore the very roots of the Craft and analyse the origins where known. Beltane. Traditionally celebrated between May eve and May Day (April 31st - May 1st) but over the years the emphasis has been on May Day. Witches of old however spent the evening beforehand preparing the Beltane fire and preparing the maiden who would represent the Goddess with the coming of the dawn. The origins of the Beltane fire have been lost in history in England; celebratory fires were commonplace at all gatherings, but particular emphasis was laid on the Beltane fire. Fire disperses light and banishes darkness, and the symbolism is obvious.

Light traditionally represents purity and dark is representative of evil, real magic is often (quite wrongly) referred to as 'white' magic (again for the record all magic is essentially neutral) and those who follow the left-hand path are said to practise 'black' magic. This again is symbolised worldwide as right being symbolic of good - white and left to depict bad - black. Religions worldwide follow this cardinal tenet; the right hand is used for greeting and performing basic duties such as working and eating, while the more foul bodily functions are abluted with the left or unclean hand. Regretfully this led to left-handed people being ostracised and even persecuted years ago, and in my youth I clearly remember left-handed pupils being literally forced to use their right hand against their natural inclination.

Beltane was a great and symbolic fertility Sabbat. The maiden was symbolic of the Goddess incarnate, she was always young and beautiful and representative of the young Goddess's blooming fecundity. It was also a symbolic time when the Great Rite could be allowed for the creation of the legendary 'Child of Promise' in the hope that the birth would be a girl. It was also symbolised with the sacrificial mating of the Oak King for prosperity in the future for the villagers.

Xtians under the doctrine of replacement theology adapted this ritual by proclaiming a village girl as Queen of the May but its origins are pure Pagan. However the original background to the run of the mill balefire being referred to as Beltane fires most probably derives from Scotland, where balefires were always referred to as Beltane fires and undoubtedly the practise and name spread south.

April the 31st was May Eve and it was Scottish tradition for all fires to be suppressed that day while the Beltane Fires were prepared for the morrow. On the mountaintops clan would signal clan as they claimed their boundaries and marked the territories in mutual friendship no matter what the altercations may have been in the past. Beltane was a time of peace not unlike the Yule Sabbats when universal peace and love was the order of the day; a tradition taken up by Xtianity but regretfully ignored by them once the season of goodwill was over.

A large section of well-dried wood, usually from a sacred tree, traditionally oak, was drilled to several inches depth and very, very wide across, and a large piece of like wood preferably from the same tree called a 'wimble' would be tightly inserted into it symbolic of the sex act and new life. Records as to how the fire was commenced are few and far between, but the aboriginal art of using friction was the means of combustion we know. What we do not know is the size of the wooden piece itself but logically it was a tree stump for apparently a magical number of people would be used to create friction on a large scale, it would appear that 13 members of the clan would rotate the wimble deosil, but whether these were all men, or men and women is not clear, and again we are left to surmise how this was performed.

As we are talking of rituals here that commenced long before the dreaded burning days my analysis is that all the clan gathered openly to witness the creating of the sacred Beltane fire, and it was most likely to have been performed by men of the clan and not necessarily the Priesthood. We do know that a magical number of participants took part, and that the minimum number was three, and that nine a magical combination of three times three was used. This gives an indication as to just how big the Beltane sparking log must have been if it took nine burly men to rotate it!

Moss was added as the heat grew and eventually flared, some old Witches say dried fungi from birch trees were added to make fire. One legend that persists was that if any of those chosen to rotate the log was guilty of a crime, including adultery, then the fire would not kindle and a new set of rotators would be chosen. One can only speculate as to how the retiring rotatory team must have been viewed afterwards knowing that one of the nine, or more, had something to hide! Once the fire was ignited then the celebrations were identical to those Witch gatherings throughout the whole British Isles. Moon cakes in the form of the crescent and full moon would be consumed and elder wine from the previous year's elder flower and berries would be drunk and the Old Gods libated with liberal supplications to the Earth Mother as the villagers and coven poured their tributes of wine into the ground.

Couples would be betrothed and jump the fire in celebration, virgins would jump for prosperity of crops and a good season, followed by the rest of the coven, even the old and infirm would be ritually carried over it by a myriad of eager hands. All this accompanied by the echoing chant of "As high as we jump then the corn will grow as tall - Hail to the Goddess, the Goddess of them all". Those betrothed by the greenwood marriages would start the dance around the Maypole in a deosil dance step, meeting in the opposite direction alternate men and women as the ribbons became entwined. The maypole was a fine upright symbol of fecundity as a phallic symbol was worshipped as such. Beltane allowed sexual freedom and the woodland around the circle would echo to the giggles of the maidens as they gave up their virginity long after the final closing of the circle.

They would secrete nuts and sweetmeats in the undergrowth then set out to 'seek and find' - not just the nuts (that symbolised the testicles) but also a willing partner. When they met he would offer her the nuts with a meaningful look, and if the maiden found the youth to her liking she would offer him a handful of leaves in exchange, known in Wiccan lore as her gown of green (pubic area). Then, exchanging nuts for leaves they would softly slip away to consummate their newly-made arrangement. The maiden's gown became green where she lay on the ground!

A Beltane cake was produced and cut up and one section would have a silver coin inserted into it, this section was called a 'Carline' and woe betide the poor miscreant who found it!

Joyously he or she would be seized and carried to the Beltane fire where the carriers would pretend to throw the unfortunate in. This strange ritual was never dodged by the one who found the Carline as the gift of silver found within it signalled prosperity for the coming year.

Beltane, sometimes called Bealltainn, Rudemas, Cyntefyn, and Roodmass was celebrated worldwide where the traces of Celtic and Pagan ways were universally recognised. In Germany they called it Walpurgis Nacht, the name spread here and in many areas particularly in the north such as Lincolnshire in England the name was commonplace.

The song *The Lincolnshire Poacher* was sung right up to the present day in pubs and hostelries nationwide but is regarded almost as an anthem in Lincolnshire, and can still be heard reverberating through the night every Mayday in that old Pagan county. The words strangely enough have altered little with the passing of the years, and are full of innuendo that is pure Wiccan. Words such as - 'T'is my delight on a summer's night in the season of the year' was outwardly the song of a poacher and as such was smiled upon by the authorities even though they did not approve its contents - but no, this was the song of the old Witch calling them to a Sabbat. The song is known to Witches as the summoning song, sometimes called the entrancing song and has re-emerged in yet another new format in the 20th century, and still retains many of the original words. Now quite openly these can be sung at Beltane with both public house revellers singing *The Lincolnshire Poacher*, while the woods resound to the words such as "We pledge the wine, when Stars do shine unto the Gods of old - Nor shall there fail - the Witch wassail, or Beltane fire grow cold." At that point everybody present would pick up a piece of wood and 'feed the fire' so that the next morning when the ashes were shared they would contain part of their own contribution.

In olden days when the villagers gathered at the fire even children would be encouraged to toss a twig in and everyone anointed somebody of the opposite sex the next morning by rubbing a pinch of ash on their forehead, even a new-born baby would be anointed. This, I would presume, is a primitive or even original form of the 'gifu' practised by traditional covens and which has found its way into modern Witchcraft when the sacred oil is used in a purification rite before the ceremonies commence at each Sabbat, Solstice, and Equinox.

Once again we see this old custom echoed in the Xtian baptising of infants under the doctrine of replacement theology. When a Xtian cross is marked on a babies forehead replacing holy water for ash, how little they know! For long before they copied our ways and sought to alter them to their own doctrine we also anointed - somewhat differently as every initiated Witch is aware - with holy water from sacred springs and wells, blessed and additionally purified as only we know how. Recently I came upon a discourse amongst Xtian Priests who were e-mailing each other as to how they made water 'holy' and of course it was not long before it appeared in the press. It emerged that no matter where they trained to become Priests there was one missing ingredient – they were not taught how to make holy water and each individual Priest would 'Do his own thing' I marvelled at their ingenuity!

Could one of the simplest 'secrets' of the Craft, have survived the inquisition? Something that is so basic that it really is hardly regarded as a secret any more, almost any book on Witchcraft outlines the method, yet strangely enough this seems to have escaped the attention of the ecclesiastical authorities, but then I suppose Xtian priests are not allowed to read books on Witchcraft. Eagerly I watched the correspondence as each told of their own particular method of sanctification, ranging from saying a prayer over it, making the sign of the cross over it, or taking a chalice of eau to the altar and requesting benign blessing from above, I was highly amused to see they had no idea as to how to make it, yet they really were inventive.

The prize has to go to an elderly priest who wrote in stating that for years he had pondered on the problem without success and when he had approached the Bishop in his early days had received a disdainful look as if to say 'you should know' (clearly the Bishop did not either) and was ignored. Nonplussed he stated he would give the matter great thought and eventually, when asked how to create Holy Water, replied - "It's quite simple. I take ordinary water from the tap, and just boil the hell out it." - Stout fellow.

The origins of Walpurgis Night lay strangely enough in a Xtian saint, to wit St Walpurga, who was symbolic of good and became identified with German Witches who were alleged to practise the 'black' – i.e. Pagan arts in the Brocken, a peak in the Hartz mountains. Everywhere the Goddess would be worshipped in various forms, the most common of these being as Flora, Freya, Frigg, Holda, Held, Hilde, and Gaia, as well as Cerridwen. It celebrated the sun's coming up from the south and manifested the forces of spring, the growth of plants and crops, the fertility of cattle, sheep, and pigs, and of humankind. It is the third festival of the eight celebrations that are pure Pagan.

The God was also a significant factor in these celebrations and as the Goddess represented the silver moon so the God represented the sun in the form of Baal, Bel, Beli, Balor, Belenus, or Boab - hence Beltane being referred to in old texts, as Boabstime, Baal was known as the Bright one, And again the symbolism of the Beltane fires dispersing the powers of darkness is apparent. These were lit on the highest point for all to see in the pre burning days but once the persecutions started they were held in remote forests and woodlands away from prying Xtian eyes, usually when they searched over the coming days all they would find was a burned area where the Balefire had blazed, literally a 'scorched earth' policy, for at dawn even the cooled ashes would be gathered up and taken home and spread on the land as an offering, by returning the wood ash back to the earth as they prayed for good crops - and it worked!

It is amazing when we look back on those early days and how frequently the old ways are found to have a scientific basis, for we now know that wood ash is rich in potash and a fine fertiliser. This occurs over and over again when we find modern science has found that old cures contain all the elements of modern medicine and there are more to come for only now in the 21st century has herbalism come into its own, yet has been practised since time immemorial. (See '*The Last Bastion*' for a comprehensive study of old cures, and tree lore.)

There is a host of legends associated with Beltane and Stewart Farrar and I spent many happy hours discussing Beltane rituals and customs when we stayed with him and Janet in Ireland in 1981. It was amazing to compare and learn which customs were indigenous to each country and which were secular not only to a separate country but also to separate counties. Stewart regaled Audrey and I with the local and 'wicked' practice of water stealing by the locals. Immediately pictures of the wild west sprang to mind with water holes and watering places changing hands in fierce gunfights, after all stealing another man's water must be a very serious crime - but in Ireland it's a game of subterfuge and cunning. Apparently water stealing, or water skimming, as it is called was to acquire prosperity and success for the rest of the year for as the morning sun fell upon each well then miraculously the water became magically transformed as a luck bringer - but only the surface.

Each farmer would rise at the crack of dawn, Stewart said, and leaving his offspring or wife to safeguard his own well would immediately set off with a small skimming pan and receptacles to steal his neighbours' 'magic water'. Everybody skimmed the surface of everybody else's well to gather as much luck in as possible without getting caught. Every farmer who was seen to have bumper crops must have been regarded as a most accomplished thief, and those whose farms had not prospered had obviously had the well skimmed at dawn. Legend - yes, but based on historical fact - but all in a spirit of good fun, for if your own well was skimmed, then you skimmed someone else's. Note, this custom was peculiar to Ireland only.

Both England and Ireland indulged the early morning ritual of dew washing on May Day when the village maidens would rise with the dawn and either gather up the morning dew in little bottles or wash their faces in it to remain beautiful. If you could gather up enough dew in an hour after dawn you could use a little each day to rub in your face and grow more beautiful until May Day came around again.

Edward the Third, King of England was alleged to practise sorcery in the Round Tower of Windsor Castle, rumour in fact alleges that the famous Round Tower was built so that the original religion of this country could still be practised in safety. For although Xtianity now had a stranglehold on the country as a whole, it was rumoured that Royalty paid lip service to the Xtian priests submitting to their blandishments while still secretly worshipping the original old gods. It was a secret though that could not be contained, servants, courtiers, maids and ladies in waiting would be aware of who slipped off to the Round Tower periodically, and it would soon have been noted as more than coincidence these nocturnal visits coincided with old Pagan Sabbats plus New and Full Moons. Also the smell of incense would have wafted through the draughty corridors arousing more than just a passing curiosity to any passing by.

It was said that locals who went to work in the castle daily referred to it as the Devil's Tower, and never accepted work there. It certainly seems that a select body of still Pagan servants serviced the tower and kept everybody else out. It would seem that a large number of the Royal Court were Pagans keeping to the old ways and rumours were rife as the existence not only of royalist covens practising there, but of a coven supreme that consisted of the highest in the land. This seems not to have been without substance, and there seems a high possibility that Edward the Third was the High Priest.

An indication here is the close friendship Edward enjoyed with the Countess of Salisbury, and she certainly was a court favourite of his for he frequently danced with her at the royal balls. We all know of the memorable incident when a green leather or snakeskin garter fell off her leg while she was dancing with the king, not only the sign of a Witch, but of a Witch of the third degree, the highest attainment in Witchcraft! For only a Witch High Priestess would wear the Garter as a sign of her authority and rank. As already mentioned, I feel it was more than a gallant gesture when His Majesty picked up her garter and instead of returning it to her, placed it on his own leg with the now famous phrase he uttered at the time of "Honi Soit Qui Mal y Pense" and promptly formed the Order of the Garter which to this day is the supreme accolade in Royal circles.

Both Henry and the Countess were Plantagenet's, and I intend to do further research into the background and beliefs of them later in 2006, paying particular emphasis on their religious beliefs and outlook.

The Summer Solstice - Bygone Days and Tattybogles

So many books have been published over a span of years on Witchcraft ceremonies starting with Candlemass and ending with Yule, and from Stonehenge to the sacred gathering grounds frequented by Pagan and Witch alike, that it is unnecessary for me to elaborate upon a particular ritual. But the purpose of this book is to record the many old ways that are fast disappearing as you have seen, and therefore I must turn the clock back to the old ways that were universally part of the Summer Solstice on June the 21st.

It is generally known that this day when the great gathering takes place, where Witch covens who are in touch with each other select who will be the host coven, and arrange a great meeting where they will all eat, drink, and make merry after the Solstice ritual nuptials have been duly observed and celebrated by all present. The eldest Witch would be chosen to represent the hag, and would be revered for her wisdom, the earth mother would be the most powerful High Priestess present from those gathered, except of course if she was the Priestess of the host coven, in which case she would invite a guest coven to conduct the ceremonials. And finally a young and pretty Witch would be chosen to represent a virgin, which technically she should actually be.

Thus another maid and crone will be the centre point. On this day they will discuss what rituals they have conducted and any alterations they may have made to ceremonies, for remember that the craft is a wonderfully flexible religion that has no dogma, and new ideas and rituals can evolve. Spells will be swapped and old knowledge exchanged, but most importantly of all it was the great day that was open house to all who were sympathetic to the craft and were freely welcomed to attend.

We of Artemis are fortunate to have a beautiful coven site enclosed by swathes of rolling countryside. There, nestling in the centre of the woodland alongside an ancient wood once known as Jack's Patch after the God Cernunnos, is a magical Witches' circle that goes back centuries, and it is ours. I wrote at length about it and its origins in "*The Last Bastion* "in 2005. It is a mystical place, and it is here that many covens meet on this day and all the locals, particularly the farmers, join in the celebrations.

On the Solstice we naturally restrict the rituals to what the non initiated are allowed to see, but it gives them a taste of the world of Witchdom and many as a result are attracted and seek to join us; it is a good recruiting ground. Well this is the solstice of the Witches where many gather but what of those who used to observe the customs associated with it. In the days when strawberry vendors hawked their wares, the people would eat this fruit as a sign of love and luck, and the old strawberry man would wear a straw hat to announce his profession, on the day of the Solstice it was considered particularly important to eat the 'love fruit'.

Many professions could be identified by the caps or hats they wore years ago. I can recall the old coal merchant who poured coal down a specific opening known as the 'coalhole'; he wore a leather cap which stretched down to his waist to protect his back from the heavy and coarse coal bags, and this garb was copied by the dustbin men too who carried the heavy dustbins on their backs.

The sooty sweep by tradition wore a battered old top hat, and was a must at every wedding when he kissed the bride and dirtied her face and wished her and her husband a long and happy life, he would sell you back the soot as a fertiliser for the garden (essential if you want to grow good parsley).

The onion seller was always French and wore a distinctive black beret and striped jumper. He travelled from village to village with strings of onions plaited together over the handlebars of his bicycle. He could carry as many as twenty strings of these and would always sell out. I never did find out how he replenished his stock, but off he would trundle when he had sold out only to reappear later with copious strings of the onions once more.

They were halcyon days full of rich characters. I must mention 'en passant' that one of my memories is of my mother standing by the coal hole and counting the sacks as they went in (each sack was a hundredweight) and the usual order was a ton of coal - twenty sacks. It was an old trick for a coalman to slip an empty sack underneath the one he was carrying and deliver only nineteen bags, but when the householder came out to pay him he would meticulously count out twenty empty sacks before her as proof of what he had delivered. My mother would have none of it and would vigilantly stand there and count them in! By law he was obliged to carry a set of scales and you could demand to see each sack weighed. It was also a common practice then to remove a lump of coal from each one and the coalman could easily fill an extra sack from what he had filched.

People would gather in the streets on the solstice if the coalman was due, and would grab any piece of coal that fell off the sack or the coal lorry, spit on it, and throw it over their left shoulder for luck. This custom originated in Victorian times and was clearly a remnant of an older practice. Over the years this old rite is no longer associated with the Solstice and now a superstition has been born by whereby if you see a piece of coal you must pick it up, spit on it, and throw it over your left shoulder - but now it is supposed to be to frighten old Mephistopheles away (he's always just behind the unwary) and try to hit him in the eye.

Sorry if I digress but so much of a way of life has disappeared in my lifetime alone, it is little wonder that with the passing of the years old customs associated with the Witch have been forgotten, particularly when these old customs were suppressed by the Church and the pastors would preach to a packed audience every Sunday on the sins of the old customs. They had a captive audience as church attendance was compulsory, unless you were a shepherd. Men could be, and were, excused on condition that they gathered each Sunday morning on the village green and practised archery. Knowing the drollness of the pedantic sermons with their emphasis on Hell and damnation it is little wonder that England could sport the finest bowmen in the world in times of war!

I have seen outside of those mentioned above, the wonderful characters that so enriched our lives; the bread man who came wearing a brown coat and the milkman cruised the streets with his hand cart upon which he carried up to six churns of milk and a ladle with which he sold it in 'gills' not pints, now wait for it - it was bread that was sold in pints, and you would order a pint loaf etc.

The Walls ice cream man on a three-wheeled tricycle with its distinctive black and white squares was a daily feature, and only those of us who savoured it will ever know the delight of the snow fruit he sold, again long disappeared. It came in a triangular pack that had to be pushed up with your finger! He was usually followed by the Italian ice cream seller with his gaily painted hand cart who dispensed his wares in a scoop, He was known as the 'Hokey-Cokey' man, on account of his cry as he entered the street of "Hokey-Cokey, penny a lump", then sold you two large scoops for a ha'penny, in those heady days that was a mere 'four hundred and eightieth' of a pound sterling. (1/480th of a pound - (100pence)) what price inflation!

Every week the local washer woman came round and collected a topping wash, and the next day would return with your linen fresh and clean. Then there was the fishmonger and his assistant who physically pushed an enormous cart with huge blocks of ice on it and a selection of chilled ready to eat fish. It was amazingly cheap, and whole lobsters could be purchased for a pittance.

The muffin man came around only at weekends and was easily recognised by the astuteness with which he carried a giant tray of muffins on his head while ringing a brass bell, on his tail would come the crumpet man, almost identical with a head-held tray and bell as well, it was difficult to distinguish who was who.

The old rag and bone man came round weekly with a resounding cry of "Rag an' Bone" echoing through the street. He would give you a goldfish or a halfpenny for a bundle of rags and the week's 'H' bones. Children collected what they could to give him and were rewarded with a balloon. Everybody had H bones to sell him for the poor people's diet consisted of steak and prime beef at a penny a pound and the great bones in a haunch of beef were worth money, you could get a ha'pence for them alone. He also would pay a halfpenny for every bottle you returned which he would wash and sell back for a penny to the bottlers.

The rags were processed to make high quality paper. While old bones were stewed with a mixture of cow horns and horses' hooves to make glue, as strong as any you will buy today. The bones were then ground down to make bonemeal. Old leather-workers and snobs (boot and shoe repairers) always had a giant glue pot on the boil into which periodically they would toss a handful of horse hoof shavings. One visitor I used to love to see when I was probably knee high to a grasshopper was the old knife grinder; busily he would turn his wheel with his legs on a converted bicycle frame and crowds of us would gather round and try to catch the sparks as they flew. Gosh but the health and safety officer would have had a fit if he had been around.

Publicans were always glad to buy back the empty beer bottles at a penny a time, and beer bottle collecting was a major source of income for the boy scouts, as was collecting empty jam jars at four for a penny. More than one scout hall has been bought on the profits of these.

Gypsies would scour the dumps for discarded bottles and sell them back to the local inns at a penny each, and I remember a local pub that bought several dozen from a gypsy troupe and was delighted to get them. Equally so were the gypsies who assured him they could get more. True enough an hour later they returned with another even larger batch; followed by others. It was only at the end of the day when he went outside to his back yard that he realised he had been buying back his own empties all day long.

Gypsies were the major source of clothes pegs which they made from hazel sprigs by splitting them and binding the top, and would desperately try to increase their income by telling you your fortune - after you had 'crossed the palm with silver' in those days we had silver three penny bits and a cheap forecast could be obtained. Oh dear, you modern day Tarot readers had nothing on them. They had their own secret sigils when they traversed the villages selling their wares, and carried a piece of chalk with them with which they would mark the nearest post or gate. Each sign had its own distinctive meaning and would depict the temperament of the householders' reaction to gypsy folk.

This self-same ploy was used by the many itinerants who travelled from town to town and village to village begging a few coppers or a meal to keep body and soul together. This was long before social security came into the frame, and unless you stayed in one area and availed yourself of the charitable soup kitchens that abounded, or the Salvation Army, then you could well starve. These in turn had their own signs that they left behind and were more detailed. I have dwelt upon these in another chapter.

They were affectionately known as 'Gentlemen of the Road', or 'Milestone Men' - a reference to the stone markers they passed in their travels and upon which they left notes and signs for their own kind. In the towns they were called the 'rags and tatter' brigade. We regularly saw them and few begrudged them a copper. Mostly they were gentle folk, always polite with none of this aggression we associate with the 'got any change Guv' brigade of today, there was always the exception to the rule of course. To the general populace they were known as 'tramps', a name given to them as they 'tramped' from place to place, either seeking work, or more often begging.

Many a time an irate farmer would humorously complain that the 'tattybogle' in his cornfield had been robbed and undoubtedly a Milestone Man had stolen some of the clothing and, wearing his cast-off tweed jacket, was probably on his way to the next village.

For the uninitiated a tattybogle was the old country name for a scarecrow, a figure made of sticks and on which cast-off clothing would be placed to resemble a humanoid figure. A broad-brimmed hat was always secured on with twine afterwards to give the ever-thieving crows and rooks that scavenged the fields the impression that a human being was around. Two sticks bound together were often placed under one arm to give the impression of a shotgun which the birds knew to their cost.

Tractors were as rare as hens' teeth in those days, and as you travelled the highways the sight of giant dray horses pulling the plough was exhilarating. One of the great treats we frequently enjoyed was a charabanc trip, usually to the seaside. Modern coach trips somehow are not the same for the charabanc outing was a social outing of music, sandwiches and lemonade, culminating on the beach with the building of sandcastles with a bucket and spade we would purchase there on arrival. It was a great day out with ice cream for us and a treat of shellfish for our parents from the cockle and shrimp stall.

Every village had its washing woman, not to be confused with the washerwoman. This person was a layer out of the dead. She would arrive by appointment and lay out the deceased; carefully washing, shaving, and binding the corpse, and wrapping it in fresh linen. Only after this had been done would the undertaker be called to take the body away, it was a matter of pride.

We used to look forward to the hot potato man who stalked the streets with a great open brazier upon which he cooked great big potatoes, each one a meal in itself. He would cut a great slab of cheese and place it between the two halves. The more affluent of these sometimes had a hand-held wheeled oven with a big chimney on top and could produce large numbers of hot potatoes for fairs and parades. This mobile oven looked not unlike Stephenson's Rocket.

Equally welcomed was the hot chestnut man who did an enormous trade at Christmas and also traversed the streets with his wares. We had great open fires in those days and when he was not around we cooked sweet chestnuts in the glowing ashes. At nighttime the factories were guarded by an old night watchman who sat at the entrance with a burning brazier, and at every roadworks, long before the days of traffic cones, there was also a night watchman with a bag of coke and a great blazing brazier. After a good night out we would crowd around the glowing coals and warm ourselves in the winter, and it was a custom to bring the old boy a bottle of beer as a present. Quite often there would be a steamroller parked nearby awaiting its driver the next morning. Once more when we were young we adored the sight of this great monster trundling down the road flattening the gravel or tar surface, while a fire nearby kept a gigantic drum of hot tar bubbling in readiness.

Every town had its flower sellers usually by tradition selling sweet violets, a left-over from the days of plague and pestilence when it was thought that foul vapours were the cause of disease and that sweet scents were a protection. Although they sold a variety of flowers they still gave the traditional cry of "Violets, sweet violets".

The greengrocer would come round daily with a cart that was piled high with vegetables and fruit in intricate patterns, we watched in wonderment as he pulled out melons and marrows without losing the arrangements, usually in the shape of a giant pyramid or a long reversed 'V'.

In season the cherry men would come round selling their wares and would set up their stalls in each street with the cry of "ripe cherries". I remember when I was at veterinary college in Camden Town seeing the cherry men in the market selling cherries at sixpence and nine pence a pound. To my surprise I saw one pouring basket after basket onto his stall, then place a board down the centre and promptly mark one side at a tanner (6d - about two and a half pence nowadays) and the other at nine pence! One day I asked him how he got away with it; he gave a wink and said "Watch, come over here." Within minutes a woman customer appeared and her first question was, as predicted - "What's the difference?" "The nine penny ones are the best and sweeter, they have far more flavour, try one" he invited her.

The lady took one and savoured it then hesitated. "Now try the sixpenny ones" he invited. The same procedure ensued. Without hesitation she then ordered the dearer ones. After she had gone the trader said "The first one makes a real impact on your palate, just the first one, after that your juices have got used to it and the next is not quite the same", he laughed "It always works".

Well let's look at a few more old customs that are fast becoming just a memory, the vendors we loved have disappeared like snow in the morning sun, windmills no longer grind the corn, the old customs of rosemary and yarrow are no more, and dew is no longer sacred. Welcome to the 21st century - but let us not forget these are our roots, our ways, and must be recorded.

My time here was interrupted when I received my calling-up papers and went into the RAF. I was wished well and a safe return by a giant negro who I had got to know who was one of the sights there. He was a professional tipster who was a wonderful character as well and rejoiced in the name of Ras Prince Monolulu. He was a familiar sight at racetracks, garbed in his usual highly-coloured gowns and gigantic multicoloured headdresses of ostrich plumes, where his cry of "I've got a horse" could be heard. No-one had ever seen a black man in those days; they were as rare as snow in the Sahara, and he was a character who attracted people to him. His fame diminished with the war and the arrival of thousands of black GIs.

As I have said, those were colourful days enriched with these characters long-disappeared and taking with them a quality of life, often hard, but enriching in a time that was before television, and canned entertainment. A time when we gathered round the piano and had sing-songs, a time when the neighbours called in and partied with us. It was a time of our own home-made entertainment with Monopoly and card evenings, ludo and snakes and ladders, party games and quizzes. Wonderful times coupled with great simplicity, we lived dangerously! When you stole your first kiss in the dark playing 'Postman's Knock' to much merriment and giggling. Yes, this was your first sexual experience as a number was drawn and you slipped out blindfolded to kiss a mystery girl in the corridor and came back wondering who it was. I think that looking back on those carefree days of home entertainment that period was the greatest loss of all, for in my mind I still hear the tinkling of the piano and sounds of laughter, so long disappeared, and remember my first stolen kiss.

The following three years saw me posted as far away as Egypt, the Sudan, Saudi Arabia, and Aden where I learned much, but it was my service days that disenchanted me with Xtianity and laid the foundations for my subsequent conversion to the Pagan path. Looking back I realise it was the call of the woodland and all things green that singled me out as a Pagan-to-be, and after my demob it was not long in coming.

Strawberries, Solstice - and the Miller's Glory

When the strawberry man was seen he was joyously received, and his wares bought, then invariably he would be asked for a wish by the local girls, although men were not excluded. We know that you had to touch the strawberry man for the wish to come true, and the ritual of the strawberry man prevailed right up to the end of the 1800s, and still exists in a modified form today. The only difference is that now it is applied to any man wearing a straw hat, usually a boater, for that was the style worn by the strawberry vendor, but with the passing of the years only the image of the straw hat remains.

Tradition says you should approach him and say "Strawberry man, Strawberry man, give me a wish (or grant me a wish)" Then apparently you had to touch your left elbow with your right hand. Many an old gentleman has been surprised to be asked out of the blue for a wish, not realising the reason for the approach was his straw hat. Again, to the best of my knowledge the custom has died out completely, but the old custom that was once observed everywhere on the Summer Solstice has now been recorded here for prosperity.

Dalmatian dogs were as rare as snow in the Sahara, and were better known as 'spotted dick' dogs, and it was considered extremely lucky to see one or be able to touch one, and if it was on the Solstice, then prosperity was yours for the rest of the year

On this same day, when the Witches gathered for their great jamboree, those who were lucky enough to see a piebald horse were extra lucky it was widely believed, and in the days of the persecutions the villagers would scan the horizon to see at what position the sails of the windmill had ceased their revolutions, for the windmill had to come to a standstill of its own volition. On the Solstice they would hope the Gods would give them a sign and the sails stop in the form of the old Witch sign of the cruciform (Celtic) cross known as the 'Miller's Glory'. Remember the even-sided cross was an old Pagan symbol that gave the Xtians the perfect emblem to superimpose a modification on, as to what was soon to become a Xtian symbol instead under their doctrine of replacement theology.

The sighting of the Miller's Glory was not exclusive to the Summer Solstice, for if it was seen on a spring day the village women would go out 'en masse' and plant yarrow. The beans of the yarrow planted on this day were harvested and kept as magical beans, and every household would have a handful of magical beans around the house whereby prosperity would befall them, for many were the magical properties associated with them. There is every possibility that the old fairy story of Jack and the Beanstalk had its origins in this custom, and the early illustrations drawn for children's books show the beanstalk's leaves almost the same as yarrow leaves and not at all like runner bean leaves.

After the yarrow had been planted, the village women would next gather rosemary which had to be cut before midnight as the luck associated with the herb rosemary diminished at midnight, so it was always gathered in daylight hours on the 21st of June. There are contradictions here as another legend is that rosemary is both a magical and lucky herb at any time but that its luck force reached its maximum on the day of the Summer Solstice and so it was desirable to gather it on that day.

Rosemary however did not grow in many areas and therefore this old custom could not be observed universally as I gather it liked specific soils. Old records say that if rosemary did not grow in the area or if you lived in a town then you had to rise at the first glow of the sun in the sky on the dawning of the

Solstice day and seek out a red or scarlet rose that was wet with the morning dew upon it. This rose had to be carefully gathered with the dew still upon it and put on pure silver, usually a silver plate, that would be taken with you in case the dew should evaporate before you got it home. Alternatively it had to be placed in a silver goblet or utensil. Needless to say these items were usually borrowed from the better-off - who gladly loaned them in the belief that luck would come to those who provided the silver on the Solstice.

There are many, many legends associated with the Summer Solstice that have disappeared like snow in the early morning sun. Love spells were prevalent that could only be performed on this day, amongst them a most beautiful and moving ritual known as the 'ring spell'. Lovers would plait a few hairs of their betrothed into a short rope usually a few inches only and this would be knotted around a gold ring, (in all Witchcraft ceremonies it is the rule to always use silver as reminiscent of the Moon Goddess, and Witches wear the silver 'cladagh' to this day as a symbol of their beliefs) on the solstice however the ring would be gold presumably as this was the golden sun's supreme day when it reached its zenith.

Each of the lovers at one stage of the ritual would lower the ring holding the little rope made out of their partner's hair into a glass or goblet where it would be suspended. Once more, much of this ritual has been lost and I do not know if the rings were lowered into separate glasses or into one together, nor how long they were left there, but I do believe the ritual has been recorded somewhere and if anyone can help, or knows where it is recorded it would be appreciated.

Also on the Solstice it was customary to gather fern seeds, fern shoots and fern leaves and place them on a white handkerchief or square of white linen. After the moon had shed its light on them the evening of the solstice they would be gathered up and wrapped in white parchment or white paper to end a run of bad luck. Nowadays (for this spell is still known to Witches) the fern pieces are usually sealed in a white envelope and after a year (the day before the Summer Solstice i.e. the 20th of June) they are buried together with a libation of wine as a thank you to the Old Gods for their kindness. In Witchcraft a Witch always repays a favour and thanks the Old Ones as of old.

Fairies, Corn and Old Horny

I was puzzled, as a young man, right up to the end of the Second World War, to see the corn fields cut in a deosil circle, and, as the circle of corn grew ever-smaller, men with guns and dogs would gather around and secure a bunny rabbit dinner as the wild rabbits were driven into a circle of just a fragment of standing corn. By this time most of the gunmen had secured something for the pot as the more timid rabbits made a run for it.

It was invariably a rabbit that was bagged, though quite often it was a cock pheasant who would lose its nerve at the last minute as the harvester drew ever closer and would fly out with a wild clacking noise only to fall to the waiting guns. Everybody had a gun in those days and gun crime was almost unheard of. At this time the war was on and in the country we relied heavily on the odd bit of game, particularly rabbit, to supplement our meagre rations.

During the worst period of the war, our allowance was just two ounces of corned beef a week. There were no eggs, only imported egg powder, those were grim days, our lawns were dug up and we planted potatoes and cabbages. My Pagan instincts were still embryonic in those days, being torn between my love of nature and seeing my parents' faces when I presented them with a freshly-killed rabbit. The old lady in the village who was famous for her herbal cures said to me 'We were all hunter gatherers in the old days'; she taught me the hunters' prayer.

I take my gun unto the hill
And pray to the Gods, but this
I pray that when I shoot - I kill
And when I miss - I miss.

During those war years I honed my skills as a marksman, and supplemented my family's larder. I realised also just how much of the crops, particularly wheat, that the rabbits and pigeons destroyed. The merchant navy were risking their lives to bring wheat in from Canada to feed an increasingly hungry population. I did not have a conscience after that. I had learned a lesson though, and never fired unless I had a certain shot in my sights. Then I was conscripted into the Services, and emerged from my basic training as a marksman.

I remember buying my first gun license across the post office counter for the paltry sum of seven shillings and sixpence - 37 and a half pence in today's money.

One thing I noticed in those pre-war days was that the harvester never ever cut the small section in the centre of the field, but the driver would retire at this stage, and be given a rabbit or pheasant by one of the farmhands who had had a good bag, as a reward. By now the guns had would have fallen silent and probably only 3-4 square yards remained standing. At this point, all the hunters laid down their weapons and advanced on the remaining stalks with hand scythes and billhooks; then they would, rather messily, and most inefficiently fell the remaining stalks by throwing the blades etc at them from a distance, some after taking aim would shut their eyes as if ashamed of being the one to fell the last stalks inside which the all-powerful spirit of the corn resided, and finally when the last stalk had been felled they would gather them up and make a sheaf.

Everybody present, well all males at least, had to participate in the felling of the last remnants. Many would take home some of these last remaining stalks and I later learned that they and their wives and girlfriends would fashion these into corn dollies which they would hang above their doorways for prosperity over the coming year and until the next harvest when they would bury them together with a libation of ale. This was a generation who in the 20th century were still close to the land, and had been taught by their fathers to honour the Earth Mother.

One phenomenon was that as the last of the corn was felled, myriads of rabbits that had been driven into the ever-diminishing area by the thresher would suddenly make a bolt for it - unmolested. No-one present attempted to bag them and their dogs would be kept in check on leashes. It seems that old superstitions decreed that no blood should be shed when the last sheaf of was corn was felled. The legends associated with the last sheaf of corn are legion, and are too numerous to record here, but one thing is certain and that is the tremendous variation from county to county and north and south of the border.

All these legends have a common denominator however, and that was that the corn spirit was embodied in the last sheaf and had retreated there as all around him was decimated, but now, safe within this final sheaf, he remained inviolate. That was the reason that all those creatures who had sought sanctuary alongside of him were inviolate also. In some areas the entire last sheaf was made into corn dollies, but in Berkshire, where I spent my youth, it remained standing and revered throughout the following 12 months, and subsequently was ploughed back into the ground as a final sacrifice.

As you cycled through the lanes everywhere to both the left and the right, you would see one lonely sheaf of corn, starkly outlined on the horizon. But when we were embroiled in war, old customs went by the board and every last sheaf was harvested for food as the enemy blockaded our ships, and food supplies ran out. Despite this, it was difficult to completely get the country folk to obey government rulings, and in many a cottage, a miniature stack about nine inches high and three inches across would be made, and quietly placed in the centre of the field later. Old habits died hard, and though they seem now to have completely disappeared, I would like to know or hear, if this is kept up anywhere.

It was said that the fairies would be watching to ensure that the corn king was left safe, and no countryman or woman would dare upset the wee folk. It is rare to find this custom observed now as the giant combine harvesters reap every square yard, and a new generation of farmers have ripped up thousands of miles of hedgerows, creating a wilderness, destroying nesting sites and habitat for hedgehogs, mice and voles etc. Today a new God has emerged called Mammon.

Lammas was of great significance to the fairies, a fact I found of great interest as I could find no trace of any other Sabbat that coincided with Wiccano/fairy festivals. Certainly all the old records speak of intense fairy activity and their participation in all the Pagan Sabbats, but only Lughnasa was ultra-special to the fairy folk, and was sacred to them in their own right, for it was ruled by a fairy Goddess by the name of Aine. It was she who in her capacity as the fairy Goddess of the Harvest instructed the faerie people to gather in all the grain left after harvesting. The fairies were reputed to scour the fields before the flocks of pigeons arrived, and they would gather up all the corn that had been scattered to make fairy bread.

It was also said that if you watched the ancient tumuli where they were reputed to live, you might observe them moving away with all their possessions to another hillock and establishing themselves there. Sometimes these could be a considerable distance away, sometimes only a small number of fairies would leave and proceed to the newly-chosen site; their own way of hiving off to found a new group. If you were very careful in your observations you might be lucky enough to notice that each fairy carried a small light to see their way. Another legend says that on the eve of Lughnasa each fairy would pick up a glow-worm to take with them, presumably to see their way and afterwards to light up their homes.

With the nights growing ever darker we see the dawning of Hallowmas - the Samhain of old, and what has evolved into Hallowe'en to the chagrin of the Church who shudder at seeing their Xtian flock celebrating one of the most profound and sacred Pagan rituals as they emulate Witches, wizards and warlocks, as they see it. Good on them! Hallowmas is one of the most sacred times of the year next to Candlemass and the coven celebrates many rites as of old. This night we celebrate the union of the dead, talk to them, and invite them to return for just a passing phase that night. It is the night of the reunion of souls of our families and it falls on October the 31st every year.

This is the night Hecate, a much maligned Goddess, who was given a bad press as a result of the machinations of the Thessalonian Witches - quite undeservedly. This is the night when the Great Rite was enacted as a re-affirmation of the very life-force itself, it was an intense and solemn rite where, prior to the union of the Priest and Priestess, the High Priestess has to confront the God of Death and Resurrection prior to entering the underworld. It is a profound and moving ritual.

This ceremony culminating with the Great Rite is the most important festival of the great eight Sabbats when the affirmation of life following the death rituals is spent. It is also known as the Feast of the Dread Lord of the Shadows, and is sometimes called the Feast of the Dead, and the Night of the Dead. Do not be disturbed at this ceremony as it is moving and also involves great beauty, sometimes a maiden will perform the erotic phases of the moon ritual to lend a little enlightenment to it. I have elaborated on this in the following chapter - 'Same Moon - Same Sun - Old Ways.'

To the beat of tambourine and drum she will cavort skyclad, covered in a black velvet cloth, and perform the phases of each stage of the moon, showing an arm or leg, then half her body as she rhythmically mimes the moon's phases from just a mere fraction of her showing to represent new moon, until with a final swirl she casts off the cloth to stand as the star Goddess and full moon. She is showing that to all Witches and Pagans, death is no more than the passing of a particular phase of your development, and like the moon's phases as you are reborn into another stage of your existence but on the earthly plane.

This night is the celebration of eternal life and reincarnation, and the celebrating of the New Year to come. Hallowmas is the first festival of the Pagan year. There is another ritual again long-forgotten that was enacted prior to Hallowmas, and this was 'Eldmas' and was carried out with great intensity. Hallowmas followed in its wake and this in turn went into November, when Musemass, sometimes called Muse Mass came into its own between the 21st to 22nd of that self-same month. The following day is a cause of celebration to our coven, the Order of Artemis, as November the 23rd is the Festival of Artemis a most important date to us.

The actual day that is associated with our particular Goddess is the day of the Festival of Ekklesia, the family of our lady which includes all her earthly devotees plus all the Geniae and spirits of nature on earth. The list is all enveloping and absorbs all the Heras and Wise ones who once existed on earth and passed into perfection after entering the Summerlands plus the souls in different worlds and spirit planes who gave themselves to her, Artemis of Inanna who appears in the form of a huntress of souls. The word Ekklesia (pronounced Ek-kales-lees-eeah) means 'She who calls us out'. Artemis takes us out of the material realms into the ethereal realms of her very special family. Her arrows represent silver shafts derived from her mother's pure light which symbolically destroys darkness, the darkness in human hearts. Through Artemis we can achieve divine reality.

She holds the silver bow of power in the form of the crescent moon, symbolic of the moon's rays that are the first light to appear after darkness has fallen. To we of 'The Order of Artemis' she is our Goddess, guide, and protectress of all who worship her. She is the Maiden of the Silver Bow, and on her day we do not hold great ceremony, but instead the 23rd of November is a day of prayer and meditation. All Witches are at one with Artemis and her vast and glorious family - Hail unto Thee O Great Goddess!

At Faerie time, the world of the mystic world of the fairy could merge with the humanoid world at Samhain, and likewise the world of the human could easily slip in an unguarded moment into the 'otherworld' as they called it - the realm of Faerie and Faerie time, later to be called Fairyland. It was the overlap of the seasons as the 'other world of the unknown' came the closest to the world we know. After Samhain some fairies would emerge from their burrows, but Puck would keep a low profile deep in the warm bowels of the Earth and not venture forth until the first rays of sunshine appeared.

Puck was better known as Phooka in Ireland and was reputed to wreak havoc at Hallowmas, when he is alleged to spoil the blackberries, as a result no-one in Ireland will gather them after Samhain. In England the same superstition prevails but with a different slant, for here it is said the devil walks abroad this night and spits on the blackberries. In Wales all crops are spoilt at Hallowmas by the feared gryphons.

Countrymen said that fairy mounds often split at Hallowmas, and if you care to dare to venture forth on this day it is said that you can peer into the depths of the tumuli and get a glimpse of the world of the fairies. Close on the heels of this great festival there is what we call Hollantide which falls 11 days later on November the eleventh and is also known as the 'Old Samhain'. Also on this date those fairies known as moon fairies guard the blackthorn and will not allow it to be cut.

We have now come full cycle, and have reached what the Druids called Alban Arthan- better known as Yule. Once more this was taken from us by Xtians who superimposed the Christ Mass on this date the 21st of December then conveniently moved it to the 25th and renamed it Christmas. It was a holy day to the Vikings and the start of one mega feast that lasted for thirteen days - now that is what I call a real party! They also called these celebratory days Yule Tide which in turn passed into our language. To them it was the days of the return of the Sun, and the triumph of light over darkness.

Witches also celebrated the 21st as the rebirth, and return of the Sun, and the Sun God at this the Winter Solstice. This Sabbat day was sacred to Lucina and also to Astarte. The date for Yule has been a source of controversy over the years, mostly by the Church who continuously debated what was the correct day of their Messiah's birthday - not that this had anything to do with Yule anyway as apart from tradition this is astronomically the shortest day of the year – period!

Out of interest let us have a look at the controversy that has been generated between different factions of the Xtian church over the years, and how even the dear old Pagan festivals from the Egyptian Gods to the noble Druids affected their reasoning. In fact the Xmas celebrations as such are attributed to the Egyptian Goddess Isis. When her husband Osiris died, Isis and his sister proclaimed that Osiris was now a tree spirit, and after his death a dead tree stump miraculously sprang into life overnight as Osiris entered it and gave it new life.

It would appear that this over the years led to the traditional Xmas tree and established itself as a tradition in the European continent. It did not arrive in this country though until this, plus other Pagan Yule celebrations were introduced into Britain by Prince Albert, the husband, and consort of Queen Victoria, who brought with him the Yule celebrations that were part of the German heritage. With Albert came the practice of ornamenting one's abode with greenery such as holly, and evergreen branches; but once more this was part of the Roman Saturnalia celebrations, when the halls were garlanded with evergreens..

Germany was basically a predominately Xtian country and these old customs of greenery etc were very, very, Pagan. In fact it was an offence for which you could be excommunicated if any green branches or plants were found to be in the house - it's clearly laid down in the Bible. The idea of placing presents under the Xmas tree was originally gifts and libations to Osiris as a tree spirit.

Well, it was not to be, they had been playing around with the date, altering it continuously between 200-400 AD, and had finally decided on the Roman Saturnalia festival. It was not long before many Xtians were up in arms and accusing the Holy Roman Catholic Church of every crime imaginable from the worshipping of false idols, debauchery, and over imbibing of the grape on the back of it all.

Also remember that during Saturnalia you gave out little presents to everyone, well everyone you liked, you could tell who your friends were in those days by seeing who you didn't get a pressie from. These were often in the form of candied fruits called 'strenae' which meant lucky fruit; and represented wishing the recipient good luck over the next year. It was Osiris who was born on the 25th of December, not Jesus. If you study the Bible (not that this is my most favourite book) you will find a large number of clues pointing to the birth of the Xtian Messiah as varying from spring to autumn. The 25th of December was also sacred to the Persians whose main religion was Mithraism, and the Mithraic cult was a strong contender against Xtianity in those days.

To us Pagans Yule is synonymous with the birth of the Sun, and this became the Saturnalia of the Romans. Fun, parties, drinking and making merry all round - plus a little bit of naughties. With everyone shouting 'Jo Saturnalia' - guess nothing alters. So what happens next? The Western Churches decide this is the ideal date to place Christ's Mass, and proclaim it as such henceforth. Now this was not a case of the usual replacement theology for clearly it appealed to them. If only they had kept this up there could have been some hope for them!

Enter into the ecclesiastical fray now the strong Xtian community of Edessa, who threw in Moon and Sun worship as a further crime. His omnipotence the Pope though, had decided it would henceforth be celebrated for a full twelve days over this period, and as usual had his way. You know the scene; send in a highly motivated Xtian army to crush the dissenting Edessian Xtians, hand out a few crucifixions, and the vote suddenly is for you.

The 12 days of Xmas adopted by the Church was another little example of the subtle cannibalism they used, for this was based on the Mesopotamian festival of Zagmuck which by tradition lasted a full 12 days. The Mesopotamians had a whole pantheon of Gods and Goddesses, and at Yule they appointed one of their most powerful Gods, namely Marduk, to drive out the old year and all the elements of chaos existing within their country. He and the King sided with each other and went to war against the old year.

Regretfully at the end of the year, and with a New Year and prosperity dawning, the poor old King found he had to forfeit his own life as a sacrifice for enlisting Marduk's help. I would imagine that what happened next was probably the quickest abdication in history for the king would retire and hand over all powers to a newly appointed king who would replace him for a mere 12 days, now there's a coincidence!

Even the village idiot would not fall for this malarkey so a felon under sentence of death would be appointed as king. In return for a nice speedy execution as against some particularly nasty means of disposal they had planned for him, usually something drawn out and gruesome, he could live the life of Riley for nigh on a fortnight, and have a swift exit from this world by a swift stroke of the axe or sword at the end.

The Church loved these 12 days they had inherited. The churches collected alms, gave blessings, redeemed sins, and promised salvation in return, and everyone was happy (you get a better contribution from a tipsy old drunk needing redemption). Cromwell, a really old dyed-in-the-wool puritanical Xtian, abolished Xmas when he came to power in 1647, and everything to do with it, including the traditional 12 day revelry - including of course Father Xmas. No laughing, no revelry, no fun, no maypoles (a phallic fertility symbol) and sex was restricted to procreation only, it was forbidden to enjoy it - Big Mistake - Big Time!

After the Restoration Cromwell's decaying body was dug up and he was ceremonially hanged by the neck, not until dead though. This part of the legal proclamation was not read out. Afterwards his severed head became a museum piece; in fact Xmas virtually ceased to exist from then on right up to 1835. It was revived after the publication of '*A Xmas Carol*' by Charles Dickens in 1843. Prince Albert led the way with the Austro/German Pagan traditions he had brought with him and Victorian England followed his example.

The idea of a mock king being appointed for 12 days was not exactly a new idea; a reversal of roles was quite common for nigh on 2000 years. In Italy when the Romans ruled, half the world, even the emperor himself changed places with a slave and waited on him during the celebration of Saturnalia - mind you, only for one day, and masters everywhere changed places with their slaves for a day.

In many areas of Ireland this custom is practised to this day. A 'Lord of Misrule is appointed who would rule wickedly, albeit humorously, from sunrise to sunset - and woe betide any who crossed his path that day. This custom is prevalent in southern Ireland who continuously buck the holy Catholic Church with the electing of a Lord of Misrule, and on another occasion they elect a billy goat as king as a representative of Old Horny, and ignore all the hell-fire vitriol that comes from the mouths of their priests who continuously try to suppress this ancient custom as a form of Devil worship.

Ireland is a strange land of religious contrasts, for in the areas that are predominately Catholic, strong elements of Paganism prevail, these vary from the little tributes they offer to the 'little folk', to a reverence for Pagan sites etc. But the placing of an ornamented billy goat on a richly ornamented throne complete with garlands on his horns is a complete and utter outward worshipping of the Horned God himself.

If you are brought before the Lord of Misrule that day - and that can be for the slightest misdemeanour - real or imaginary, then you will probably be told that you will be let off lightly by a simple obeisance of kissing his foot. Alas as their lips touch the appendage, the victim is more than likely to find a cascade of ice cold water upon the back of their neck or a funnel passed into their trousers and a bucket of iced water cooling their ardour. I have even known someone who was commanded to push a pea across the road with his nose. Sometimes this powerful overlord, if he is loved enough, can be elected to rule from Yule until Oimelc (Candlemass).

The original word was Uil, and the word Yule evolved from it, it is believed it was from Old Norse or Gothic. The period from the 24th to the 25th was known as 'Modsunect' there are a variety of spellings associated with his 24hour period.

The election of the Lord of Misrule as stated is abhorred by the clergy, as it has a strong association with the Paganism of yesteryear. It is also associated with the Lord Cernunnos, although methinks the God Bacchus would sit as well in that favoured seat for the amount of alcohol that is sunk that day you could float a battleship on.

I know of one elected lord in Eire who was voted into the seat year after year, and his antics were sheer hilarity - so much so it that upset the clergy for starters, and they rounded upon him verbally from the pulpit for his Pagan ways. Well the conclusion to this tale was that he was henceforth elected by the villagers to rule from Yule until Candlemass thereafter; and promptly had his revenge by forbidding all and sundry to attend Mass or make confession upon pain of giving up tea, coffee, and beer for the whole period. Well the conclusion was that no-one went without their morning cuppa, and it was business as usual in the local hostelries, and no one went to church for a month, that'll teach 'em to mess with Old Horny.

There was not much I could find of reported fairy activity at this period, but I did not expect to do so, for we know they love the sunshine and abhor the cold. We do know that they are closely associated with the spinning wheel during this time, characterised by the turning of the cycles of the year, but the evidence is rather sketchy.

Folklore, says that fairies would target spinning wheels in particular and remove any spinning left unfinished, probably because the spinning wheel was associated with the cycles of the year and this was the Yule Solstice. The word 'solstice' means 'Sun stands still'. In some countries all spinning had to stop at Yule as a mark of respect, so maybe the fairies removed temptation and purloined anything still on the wheel - well it's a good enough story to tell your employer that the fairies must have taken it when there's a shortfall in your output, and if you had made something for your lover on the side girl, you could account for the dent in your housekeeping allowance for wool by telling your husband the fairies were responsible. Oh and make sure your lover does not turn up to clean your windows wearing a new woolly jumper.

In conclusion as I finish this chapter there have been a number of developments that I feel conclusively, and beyond all doubt show physical manifestations of these tiny spirits from what I presume is the Deva kingdom. When you take on the role of investigator you have essentially to be a sceptic. Whether I am investigating poltergeist activity, a haunting, a weird manifestation, or any form of occult activity the first thing I look for is facts, followed by hysteria, followed inevitably by vivid imaginations, exaggeration, genuine mistakes and finally fraud. It is only when all these possibilities have been researched and eliminated that you can begin to conclude that there is a case to answer.

I started on the fairy trail a born-again sceptic, resolutely determined to nail the fairy myth once and for all, my conversion so to speak, or shall we say the start of my conversion; started in Ireland as you have read. Essentially I had to look for everything from telegraph wires to electric pylons that could be transmitting the music, followed by checking grids later to trace any underground cables that could be the source of the phenomena. I swiftly eliminated hidden tape recorders or transmitters as the distance we both walked was several miles, and once you considered the time element involved then no ordinary tape could possibly last that long.

I also had to check ourselves, that we were not the unwitting victims of a hoax, and that we had not had something secreted on our persons. (I do not think Audrey has ever forgiven me for turning her handbag upside down in my search!) Upon reflection I dismissed this as no-one could possibly have known our movements to time it - we ourselves did not know until the day. The end result was I had to record the phenomena as 'unproven' but high on the list ranging from probable to 'almost certain'. Subsequent events have moved me more towards the affirmative.

It was years later, just after the publication of *The Last Bastion*, that people started, hesitantly may I add, to share their fairy experiences with me. The more I listened, the greater the evidence gathered. On one occasion I was invited to a so-called 'Fairy Glen' in Scotland where I was assured that once there any doubts that I still maintained would be quickly be dispersed.

Regretfully time, distance, and travel, have prevented my going at present, but a well-known and trusted psychic, who likewise was a sceptic, investigated regarding the assignment as a 'bit of a giggle; only to return suitably chastened and prepared to now accept the probability that what they had seen had no logical explanation.

Part of what was seen that evening was that simultaneously a crowd of small winged figures suddenly took off from the meadow they were observing. One thing that all testified to was, that unlike the popular image of the fairy in humanoid form, these creatures were shapeless, translucent, and winged. They left small vapour-like trails as they flew, like unto streaks of light. They hovered, danced, and flittered about. Described as 'not unlike the mating dance of butterflies'.

An examination of the area immediately after the aerial display by the light of torches revealed nothing whatsoever that could be associated with the phenomena, no winged insects, no fireflies, and no glow-worms. The only living things that appeared were a few small moths attracted by the torch lights. Locals sagely nodded their heads and had no doubts that there were certainly strange fairy-like activities there, but refused to be drawn further; once more it was obvious that the thought of being ridiculed prevailed.

I had met one fascinating lady, a local wise woman, at a Witchfest event who knew the area well and told me how as a young girl she had spent many an evening entranced by these little elementals' activities. Her description of them was absolutely identical. She had been branded a Witch by locals even as a young girl because of her activities, and was actually beaten on one occasion after spending time there.

A fellow occultist like myself also attributed stories of fairies as nothing more than folklore, but one day as a very chastened man he told me how he had observed a strange shapeless winged creature that was semi-translucent, and had a slight luminescence also. One of the strange things was the fact that he described it as at least 9-10 inches tall, far too big to be a goat moth or perhaps a death's head moth. This case has also been relegated to an ever-growing 'unexplained' file.

Leslie Price, a well-known investigator observed what he swore was a solitary strange fairy-like creature on Ditching Beacon on several occasions in Sussex, and I gather he selected three people to accompany him one day to attest to what he had seen. One of these was a local solicitor, who later made a sworn statement.

Sane, logical people of all trades and persuasions have come forward with tales of unexplained manifestations that are akin to fairies and fairy-like activities to such an extent, that there has to be something in it. My own conclusions are that they are elementals and as such can change shape. To me and to many hundreds of people I know, elementals are a fact of life, I have seen them like a sea of black beetles on a Witch's house floor, merrily scuttling around, completely oblivious to the human world around them.

I pondered long and hard as to whether to expand a chapter on the Deva kingdom, and the conclusions I had reached, but when I realised that they were an accepted form of life whose existence had never been doubted for over 1200 years, followed by the discovering of a law under Henry the Third protecting them, and making it a capital offence to harm them, that I relented.

The final phenomena came as I finished the chapter and sat back wondering as to whether I should include my theorems in this book, as I sat at the computer musing yeah or nay, I was suddenly aware of a movement in front of me. To my astonishment a small swirling winged entity floated down and landed on the keyboard of my computer. It landed absolutely central and as straight as a die. Looking down I observed it to be a small champagne glass, with a set of gossamer wings protruding from the stem, and a miniature false gemstone, not unlike a topaz, at its centre. I recognised it at once for I had last seen it on a congratulatory golden wedding card we had received some four months beforehand.

We had been married 50 years on November 5th 2004, and this phenomenon occurred on the 9th on March 2005. Where it appeared from, I do not know, except that it had been on a shelf nearby. My wife, impressed with its beauty, had saved it from the card as a souvenir, and had also last seen it on a shelf quite nearby. There was no draught of any description and no heating on that could have caused it to move, besides it was far too heavy to become airborne. On the one hand, and also there were far lighter objects such as tissue butterflies that had been in a letter sent to us from a fellow Witch, that were as light as gossamer. I immediately experimented with it dropping it at arm's length but each time it dropped like a stone.

I rest my case, if ever I needed a sign to include this chapter then this telekinetic activity was it, there was no logical reason as to how it had been teleported, but I was aware of a high energy field around me seconds after it occurred. As if to give a show of strength that evening, myriads of elementals started rushing around everywhere in a show of strength, we were quite used to seeing these little creatures, and were pleased to see their antics. It was as if they were agreeing with me and saying "Yes Ralph, they are as much a part of the Deva Kingdom as we are - and you unreservedly accept us." The result is I have included this chapter and now await even more reaction - I hope positive.

Recently, and just prior to publication of this book, I have received a number of communications as to sightings of small 'matchstick'-like creatures, particularly on ancient sites and stone circles. My immediate reaction was that these were the small beetle-like elementals that are well-known, but upon investigation the reports insisted that they were more humanoid in shape – a phenomena completely unknown to me. A trick of the light? Or another form of elemental? I do not know as I personally have never seen them, and thus cannot comment, however if anyone cares to correspond with opinions or independent witnessing of this phenomena then I would be delighted to hear of same, and of course be invited to witness such phenomena first-hand. My e-mail may be found at the front of this book.

One thing that has delighted me since I started writing this section was a newspaper report in '*The Times*'-no less! That was published on Monday the 21st of November 2005, to the effect that a building development in St. Fillans in Perthshire by the side of Loch Earn been abandoned after it was found to be the home of the local fairy colony. Normally the planners would probably have dismissed this as superstitious nonsense, as normally such projects can only be halted if it was the habitat of a rare orchid or lizard for example, but fairies?Unheard of! It seems the locals were enraged and gave vent to their feelings vehemently, besieging the local council and muttering dire warnings of what would happen to them if their traditional home was bulldozed. One thing was certain they said and that was that no good would come to the building company and bad luck would surely follow.

It seems that as soon as the diggers moved onto the site the alarm was raised by a villager shouting - running towards them shouting - 'Don't move that rock. You'll kill the fairies'. He stood his ground and the diggers backed off. Within days the village was aroused and public meetings called. E-mails and numerous phone calls ensued. The end result was a resounding victory for the villagers as an investigation confirmed that the large standing stone, the developers had intended to move was in fact standing above a fairy colony, and was protected by law - wonderful news.

The standing stone in question was of great historical significance as well, as traditionally the Kings of Perth were crowned upon it, dating right back to the 6th century. Plus the fact that local custom forbade the moving of any standing stone, so to hell with the 21st century and what was called progress, the standing stone and the fairy colony beneath was to be protected, and protected it was.

A local lady by the name of Betty Neish McInnis it appears had regretfully passed this world recently but had imparted to the villagers the many legends surrounding the standing stone and the fairies who dwelt beneath, going back into prehistory and old Pictish lore. The area is steeped in local superstitions, and the standing stones are revered and respected, that particular one was sacred, and the little folk beneath it must not be disturbed. So Mote It Be.

One thing I made special note of in the Planning Inspectorates report was that by law 'local customs and beliefs must be taken into consideration', a fact that we must remember if we Pagan ecologists see any other incursions into sites we hold sacred, for we can quote this as a legal precedent.

Rather 'tongue in cheek' the local planning authority quoted the above, mentioning 'en passant' that there were no specific guidelines with regard to fairies, but it seems that the evidence was overwhelming and the project accordingly halted. The latest news is that a development will now take place around it and the fairy colony will henceforth be preserved in the centre of a park.

On a final note, there is another phenomenon that seems to have become extinct, but this could be because of climate change. I remember as a child watching out for 'Pictures by Jack Frost' who would visit us in the middle of a cold icy winter's night and leave elaborate pictures on the window. Pentacles and floral patterns abounded, and were a source of great wonderment and entertainment, and as children Jack

Frost was as real to us as Father Xmas. Well we Witches know that Father Xmas is based on fact, and is an adoption of St. Nicholas, when the church made the God Cernunnos, better known as Nicholas (hence Old Nick) into a saint. Jack Frost, we were told was an Ice Spirit. Nowadays when I look at a frosted-up window I see no wondrous patterns. I have asked a number of people in my age group as to whether they remember looking at these pictures and they all unreservedly answer 'yes'. Is it because the temperature no longer drops low enough to form these patterns?

Water has profound magical qualities and as a result magical wells and streams became a historical fact, also a microscopical examination of ice crystals show these self-same patterns in miniature. Again perhaps someone from the still frozen wastes of northern Scotland will e-mail me to say the Ice spirit is still alive and well, and has simply emigrated farther north.

When one studies water magic I thoroughly recommend a book entitled '*The True Power of Water*' by Masaro Emoto. The magic of this wondrous liquid is thoroughly explored within its pages, and shows scientifically how the consistency of water is altered when subjected to ritual and incantation. The basis of all magic.

So Mote It Be.

Same Moon - Same Sun - Old Ways

What I am forced to wonder is would the skyclad peasant in the fields on days of yore have made of this' modernisation' of the Craft? Silver wands set with gemstones, beautiful robes etc. At the height of the persecutions and the dreadful burning days they would have glanced at the moon and silently the villagers would have made their way to a secluded glen, carting their farmyard implements with them. If there was a possibility they should be discovered they would cut a new wand from the nearest hazel bush, then a candle would be melted to form a roundel and they would mark it with the ancient sigils that was passed down and memorised from father to daughter and mother to son.

A stoneware drinking goblet would become the chalice and a piece of chalk would inscribe that too. They would NOT have formed a circle but would have marked out a square, the four corners, not quarters as such, would be marked by the very agricultural implements that they carried with them. A fork would mark one corner, and a spade thrust into the ground another, hoes, rakes and flails would follow until the square was formed. A young maiden, a virgin, a married mother with children and an old woman to represent the crone would disrobe and represent the moon's phases, here before the assembled villagers the ceremony would begin as the old Gods of England would be worshipped.

The Great Rite would not usually be performed unless a fecundity ritual was required after drought, poor crops, or perhaps a poor lambing season had occurred. The ritual was beyond sex and was of great spiritual significance. Contrary to popular belief such rituals were rare; if a female child were born as a result of the union she would be raised by the entire village and would never want for anything.

This was the legendary 'Child of Promise' worshipped as of yore, and would represent fertility in the years to come. At the first paying of her first 'tribute to the moon' she would enter into a whole new aspect of the village and the coven, but regretfully there is no records known as to what her role became as her menses started and she entered womanhood.

These people were close to the earth, the woodland glades were their churches and the canopy of the trees was their roof, they lived and were at one with nature. All their rituals were allied to the animals and birds of the forest in their love of the foliate God and Goddess.

Many of these ancient traditions have still come down to us in amended form. Take for example the phases of the moon ceremony, I have seen this in a modern-day book on Witchcraft and it does indeed run a close parallel to an ancient rite, I intend to contact the author as to where this lore upon which it is based came from, but usually I find these are oral traditions. In this particular one the Priestess would come into the circle clad from head to foot in a long black cloak and as the rite commenced would re-enact the phases of the moon. The shrouded figure representing initially 'dark moon' then as each quarter passed she would shed one fourth of the cloak revealing a fraction more of herself each time, ending up completely sky-clad in the star Goddess pose as 'Full Moon'.

In another they would take the roles of animals and birds and play out scenarios embracing the very elements of nature, together with portraying the dances and calls of birds, and the rutting of the deer. This style of ritual should be very dear to Americans as the indigenous natives emulated these in such rites as the Buffalo dance, and many bird dances as can be seen in Hopi ceremonies.

In the English woodlands the villagers and covenors together would wear animal and bird masks, and then re-enact the role of each - cats would chase mice, hawks and falcons would chase the mice back, eagles chased rabbits while wolves chased the deer (wolf always lost in ancient tradition when he chased 'stag' who was of course the God incarnate. This ancient re-enactment has passed down in much amended form in a beautiful ritual part of which reads "and I shall go (to the Sabbat) as a wren in spring, with sorrow and sighing on silent wing", to which would come the rejoinder "Aye, and I will go in our Lady's name, Aye till I home again".

There is much evidence that this style of ritual was enacted with everybody emulating their chosen animal by leaping around joyously, and perhaps even attempting to fly, which gave rise to the popular 'flying' adage so beloved of the Xtians in their prosecution of alleged Witches. The basic truth of the matter is that they did believe they had flown after they had anointed themselves with magical unguents and had drunk magical potions before the dance; usually the drink contained a number of hallucinogenic ingredients derived from magic mushrooms and other fungi not named here. The salve they applied would also be a concoction of herbs and plants that could produce near identical effects such as belladonna.

Thus this was old-style ritual as was practised centuries ago, it was an era when the people were completely and utterly devoted to the land, to husbandry, to nature herself and to the Old Gods they associated with them, It was pure, it was simplistic and it was sincere. The Pagan roots of Witchcraft are essentially simplistic, admittedly they did indulge in practices that would be anathema to society today, or would it be so rejected one is forced to ask?

I refer to of course the taking of hallucinogenic drugs and salves that were used on occasions, and I do mean just occasionally and for specific ritual, Again when one looks around at the cannabis-ridden society of today and the lax attitude that is taken to it by the authorities then would it be so alien in this day and age? One thing regarding this is certain however, and that is at least these were imbibed for a purpose, at especial Sabbats; and drugs played no part of their everyday life: when the farm worker needed to keep a clear head at all times. They were not used socially.

The other practice, of course is the raising of the 'Child of Promise' in other words the raising of a professional bastard in Xtian eyes> This child was revered and taught all the virtues and none of the vices. Reading through old annals a clear pattern emerges that tend to show that this child is the original Queen of the May, or the May Queen that we see openly practised by Xtian folks. She depicted the eternal virgin at rituals and was exalted as the living personification of the Goddess herself. History does not record what became of her as she approached marriage, the Xtians in this country have succeeded in destroying or eradicating much of our old roots over centuries of suppression and blind persecution. We only know that with the doctrine of replacement theology i.e. if you cannot beat them join them, that the village maiden who we know was the predicted child of promise evolved into the carnival queen we see today.

This doctrine of replacement theology has had many strange repercussions over the years, and we see this continuously. St Augustine decreed that to suppress the Sabbatical practices of the people they the Xtians should superimpose their own festival days upon them to quite deliberately coincide with their holy dates - not always successfully may I add.

They succeeded at Easter by imposing it on the great Sabbat of the Goddess Eostre, known as Beltane, but still set it by the moon as of old. They got it quite hopelessly mixed up with the vernal equinox (Spring Equinox) hoping in one sell swoop to wipe out the two Sabbats in one go. All they knew in the in Xtian eyes was that the Hearth day was March the 21st, and that the ritual must be conducted during the period of the

Vernal equinox which was between the 20th to 23rd of March. In actual fact it was this Sabbat that is more closely associated with Eostre or Eostar as she also became known, and in setting Easter it is clear that they never understood the purpose of Vermas, which fell on March the 31st.

The fact that a whole pantheon of Goddesses were associated with these events only made them all the more zealous to suppress them as these were female orientated rituals and the emancipation of womanhood played no part in the Xtian doctrine as decreed by St Paul whose anti feminist Xtian stance is legendary

They undoubtedly knew that both Demeter and Persephone were closely associated with spring when the two Goddesses were shown in contrast in the invocation of light festival, and it was at this specific period that the old Pagan Festival of Trees took place.

To them the suppression of Beltane was a must in their eyes with its separate pantheon of Goddesses. The mere fact alone that the Goddess Frigg was involved was enough to send shivers down their puritanical backs, add Freya, Holda, Hilde,and others and it becomes a feminine hierarchy. They seem to have completely overlooked the fact that Beltane originally was known as Boalstime, sometimes called Boabstime - a God! And gave its name to the traditional Fire God, associated with the lighting of the Bale fires.

I mention 'en passant' that between May Eve and May Day (April 30th and May 1st) many have forgotten the ancient searching for a hag stone or Witch stone, these are usually found on sea shores or in gravel pits and are stones that have a naturally weathered hole in them, and are avidly collected over the years.

In Britain farmers would regularly search out a Witch stone and add it to a growing collection of them on their farm entrance gate to ward off evil, encourage fertility of crops and animals, and bring luck to the land. A new piece of rope or twine would be brought and the newly found hag stone added to it annually, as a young man I was fascinated to see these stone necklaces tied to farm gates in Berkshire and Wiltshire in particular.

Sadly at the height of the persecutions between the late 1500s and 1700s the stones became associated as charms to ward off the depredations of Witches as the Xtian propaganda machine eroded all the ancient beliefs, I am happy to say that in the 20th century and now into the 21st century this old tradition is being restored, but they have disappeared off farm gates and instead are avidly collected by local Witches. I have however seen them hanging in barns.

Many covens have them hanging over their altars, and I have see skyclad Priestesses displaying necklaces of small hag stones collected from the seashore, instead of acorns! Tongue in cheek they are of course far more durable than acorns as these tend to dry and crack over a period and fall off. In my early coven at fertility rites the High Priest would present the High Priestess with a 'new dress' for her to wear at Candlemass, a newly gathered necklace of acorns he had lovingly collected the previous autumn.

One senses the sadness when you sit amongst the old Witches still alive; we mourn the passing of so many of the old school, and see the modern ones with a sense of trepidation. Quo Vadis is the cry, will they return to the old ways at the end of the day, or will the new age revolution dominate and form a completely new and modernised form of Paganism over the coming years?, only time will tell, it is in the hands of the Gods. Whatever the outcome, what we do know is with its inherent love of all things green and of nature; it will be a welcome relief to the all cloying hypocritical shackles of Xtianity.

It is this very fact that prevents new initiates being educated into many of the mysteries by the older covens. If we turn the clock back we find that the tri-gradal system whereby the power was given at initiation-the old degrees being completely the reverse of what they are today. With the passing of the persecutions we evolved into the present age and allow three degrees of Witchcraft i.e. Initiation into the very first of the mysteries, followed by a probationary period of an absolute minimum of a year and a day, and then if they have learned to cast a circle from memory, and perform minor magical rituals –plus learning the secret intonation of the words,

Only then are they are elevated to the second degree where they will probably remain for many years if not forever, for many are quite happy to stay as simply supporters, eventually those of outstanding ability will be honoured and subsequently elevated to the third degree, whereupon then would be expected to 'hive' and found another coven, and start all over again. At this stage they would be instructed in the inner mysteries and these would remain secret with them until they too had found over the coming years suitable third degree Witches in turn, many third degrees have often elected to stay with us and have helped us to establish a powerful inner healing group.

Thus it is now, but turn the clock back prior to the influx of the Flemish weavers and what followed on their heels and we find the present system of 1-2-3 was reversed to 3-2-1! The power being passed by sexual induction, at the new Witch's initiation. The reason in those days was both simple and practical, for if the coven were discovered by the ever-eager Witch takers and finders, then even if the coven was decimated as long as there was one solitary survivor with the knowledge and power then the craft would survive.

Imagine in this day and age if the power and inner secrets were to be passed to a new initiate, who like many before him can violate his sacred oath secured on his very soul, can backslide and go public with all they have learned. When the craft in

England was less than a mere handful by comparison to now, and your confession to even having been a member of a coven was certain and painful death - then the secrets were safe.

Now with the Craft going into seven figures, maybe even eight worldwide, then the secrets can no longer be regarded as safe, as the spate of books by 'a Witch' shows quite clearly. There are secrets within the craft that are jealously guarded to this day, not least of these being ancient spells tried and tested and of great power. Take for example the infamous 'Sang d'amore' love spell of legend, now as far as I know virtually extinct and I hesitate to say, rightly so. An old West Country Witch imparted it to me over thirty years ago, and said she had only known it to have been used once in her entire life time and vowed she would never ever perform it again, such being its power.

I have seen other so-called 'Sang d'Amore' spells loosely based on this one but they all lacked the basics. Can you imagine the commercial value of this if it was exploited? One is therefore faced with a dilemma, logically one day probably long after I have passed to the Summerlands then those who would inherit my own Hand of Rite will see its secrets unfurled within its copious pages.

So how long would it be before it became public knowledge? Remember it only takes one person! And Artemis is over a hundred strong not counting the myriads that have hived from us over the years. I have been extremely selective as to who was admitted to Artemis over the years, screening each and every candidate, and only admitting them when not only I, but the entire coven, and council of elders were satisfied as to their eligibility.

Sadly with the passing of time I find that despite the most stringent checks I have made mistakes, -and encountered a mystery in the process. Luckily the bad eggs were all discovered while they were first degree Witches and further advancement was barred to them, they soon got the message and left, of the first hundred to enter Artemis there were only three, but that is three too many. Of the first hundred women there were three again. I suppose 3% is not bad going so we Witches are not perfect. One thing I feel I must say, and that is with these backsliders their crimes were their avidness for power, and to their credit, not a single one has ever ventured onto the left hand path.

You are probably wondering what the great mystery is I referred to with one of the candidates, and it is intriguing I must admit. It was in the early 1970s when I was approached by a young Jewish woman seeking initiation. Of all the people I have met and initiated over the years she was outstanding in her thirst for knowledge and her desire for Witchdom. I met her family who told me that despite their orthodox Jewish belief their daughter had dreamed of being a Witch ever since she was a little girl, For countless years she was obsessed with being initiated and joining a coven, and starting on the long road to attaining the power. Everything, she said, showed she was the right sort of person, she adored animals, kept frogs and toads in the garden, and had befriended birds and animals to the point of tameness. Her ambition was to learn healing spells and be able to heal and help the afflicted.

Here in one person I had found the perfect High Priestess to be. She danced skyclad under the moon, and sat for hours in woodland glades communing with nature. She had been on the scene ever since she was a mere sixteen summers, and had to wait a full two years to start her year and a day of meetings and discussions before she could even be considered for acceptance.

True to form, such was her eagerness, that she turned up on my doorstep on her eighteenth birthday with her birth certificate in one hand and a letter from her mother giving her consent in the other. Even so a whole year of study would have to pass before her initiation; In fact it was eighteen months before the big day when she was nineteen and a half. Such are our ways.

Eventually she was accepted and the big day came, when she arrived she was bubbling with excitement, no nerves, she was on a euphoric high. The initiation ceremony was a great success and we knew the Old Ones had accepted a new acolyte. Afterwards she rushed around telling everyone it was the culmination of her dreams to become a fully fledged Witch, she could hardly contain her excitement and threw herself into my arms sobbing "Thank you, thank you - that was a most beautiful experience.

During the Agape, the traditional love feast that follows a ritual, she kept asking what the next stage was, when could she learn spell-making, what was the first healing ritual she could master etc. At the end of the evening when she went home in all my years in the Craft I swear I have never seen a happier little bunny. The next day brought a phone call from her parents - an orthodox Jewish couple, saying she had arrived home on a high and was still on it the following morning.

The following day she sent me a bottle of brandy and a large bouquet of flowers for my wife, and asked the date of the next meeting, which was just a few days away, being a full moon. She wanted to know what the secret signs were to carve on her athame, and told me how she had bought a silver chalice for the holy wine etc, and was having a green robe made and hoped it would be ready in time for the full moon - and how much she was looking forward to it and seeing a full moon rite.

On the date in question she was late in coming and after an hour we had to start without her, keeping an ear cocked for the doorbell in case she was delayed, but no, she did not arrive. We phoned the next day to ensure she was not ill and were told by her father that she was fine and mentioned 'en passant' that she had spent the evening indoors watching television!

She never ever came to us after that wondrous evening. I wrote and thanked her for the brandy and flowers, and she phoned me to say thank you. She was friendly and polite, re-affirming to me it was a memory she would treasure for ever and stating she had purchased a lovely Goddess figurine. Our paths often passed over the years, if she saw me she would hurry over and give me the traditional Witch's kiss she had learned and would indulge in polite conversation on every topic imaginable, except the Craft, which once dominated her conversation, and we are talking of close-on three years since we first met.

The years have passed, she has never married and is still lovely now in her 50s, and I am still greeted enthusiastically when we meet, and her hug has real warmth in it. But no mention is ever made of Witchcraft, although I have since learned she openly professes to be Pagan on her forms where it says 'religion' etc, so her mother told me, and said she had a Pagan altar in her room, and burned candles and incense to the Old Ones. I have never asked why she never came again, and I never will. It will remain a mystery.

Naturally it is not possible to establish an equally sexed coven unless you restrict membership to an equality of numbers, but in so doing you would be exempting some admirable candidates seeking admission, and the Craft must continue to expand to survive. We at Artemis have always been top heavy with women over a period of over fifty years on a ratio of approximately two to one, the top 100 of Artemis at present numbers seventy one women to twenty nine men, in 2004 it was 67 women and 33 men, but we always ensure that the inner circle in dances etc contain six of each sex plus the lord over all in the shape of the High Priestess (As High Priest I get delegated to one of the six when Ma'am - She who must be obeyed is in charge).

It is difficult for me to judge in the modern world when I see all sex covens, I myself am 77 years old now, and have spent a lifetime with the standards I was brought up to Craft-wise, and I would therefore hesitate to condemn any group, but the world is changing, the Craft is expanding and a new morality and outlook has crept in. As I have said it is not for me to judge, but to me the perfect coven must have a polarity, and be a representation of both sexes. There can be no God without the Goddess, and no Goddess can be complete without her consort the God.

Legends and Lore, Graves and Ostlers

There is a legend often found on gravestones that reads as follows

'Here lies a weak and sinful worm,
The vilest of her race,
Saved through Gods electing love,
His free and sovereign grace'

This is alleged to have started universally as a rebuke to all sinners, but it is worth noting that in the old churchyard at Pitsea Mount near Basildon in Essex there is a grave of one Ann Freeman who died March 20th 1879. Local legend has it that Ann Freeman was the last Witch to be put to death in England. but this historically is not true, Witchcraft executions had long been outlawed by this date, and there is no evidence that Ann was ever a Witch anyway. It would seem that this legend has arisen as a result of the inscription.

Search old graveyards and you will swiftly find this inscription on more than one headstone, for it was frequently inscribed at the dictate of the local vicar as a rebuke after death to absolutely anyone who was considered in his eyes to have been less than devout in their worship of God, or who had not attended church regularly.

It did not take much to be labelled a Witch even under Queen Victoria, especially in rural areas, and it seems Ann Freeman was a bit of a herbalist, was also a bit eccentric, and most telling of all, she had a black cat. One can imagine that as she grew old she probably grew even more eccentric, and it only needed her to look at someone, and then for them to sprain their ankle, cut themselves, or something within a few days - and suspicions are confirmed, the local old one is the cause of it all, in the burning days or the days of the hempen rope as they have become known would have led to a lynching, or testing, and inevitably death. This epitaph was used widely by the Church on the grave of anyone who was not sufficiently in awe of its power, a final chastisement even in death.

There is a record of a so-called Witch being killed in 1895, but that was in Ireland and apparently was an accident. This again relates to the resolute belief in fairies in Ireland that is still deeply ingrained in them to this day. Irish women believed strongly that fairies stole baby boys and raised them within the fairy colony to serve the Fairy Queen for seven years, or to serve in fairyland for three years. To avoid this they would refer to them at all times, until they could walk and talk, by girls' names, and dress them in girls' clothes. This way they said the fairies would be fooled. It was also believed that fairies could abduct young women as happened in the1895 Bridget McLeary case. The stealing of babies was apparently restricted to boy babies only; as these were strong and could serve the near all-female fairy colony. Fairies found difficulty, it would appear raising elves, (Humans were much easier) so an elf child would be substituted in the cot. Irish women were mightily a-feared of their boy babes being stolen and that they were raising an elf child in its stead.

These babies were known as 'changelings' and any child that stood out to be different to the rest would be looked at askance and with deep suspicion as to whether he was really human. In the case of Bridget, her husband and all the neighbours found her behaviour odd after she had just been ill. They mutually decided that the real Bridget had been abducted as a baby at the time of her mother giving birth and that the woman who came out of hospital was in fact a fairy - or a Witch.

Contemporary reports state she was Bridget McLeary in all aspects and looks, but she was behaving oddly suddenly. Reading these old reports it is quite clear to us in the 21st century that she was suffering from what is now recognised as depression. The end result was that whether it was by accident or design she was set alight while being interrogated by her husband and neighbours, and perished. Unperturbed at their callous act the whole village gathered on the hillside the next morning awaiting his real wife to return as tradition stated, riding on a snow white horse. Come nightfall and no Bridget on the horizon they all returned home, but by now the local Garda (Irish police force) had been alerted and mass arrests followed this act. The subsequent trial handed down appropriate sentences for involuntary manslaughter, and many villagers and her husband served sentences. My grandmother said the case was headline news at the time. When you realise that this happened in 1895 it is staggering that such beliefs still existed as we approached the 20th century. But oh no, in Eire in 1973 the changeling fallacy was still dominant, and many country women dressed their male babes in girls' clothes and gave them girls' names until they were three years old.

Purely out of interest the poor newt, that featured so strongly in Shakespearean plays, particularly *Macbeth* (superstition says you must never ever mention it by name but refer to it as 'that Scottish play' was an essential ingredient for any magic potion together with bat's blood, tongue of frog, and hairy spiders according to ancient chroniclers. No bearing in history to substantiate this whatsoever may I add (though I did find one where you had to hold a live frog in your mouth as a cure for a croaky cough, five minutes inside and the cough was transferred to the amphibian - simple, and a good example of sympathetic magic widely believed in at the time as a cure for whooping cough.

I found one old reference to horses' urine being used as a cure, but so far I have not been able to discover what for, (not that I was going to recommend it). But there was a reference to the effect that a newt would know which horse was the best one and could obtain it from a suitable mare coming into season. Frankly I cannot fathom how one could possibly catch a mare's urine in a pot unscathed but I must wonder if what the newt provided was the genuine thing and not the result of a quick visit to the nearest bush with a bottle in one's hand. I can read your minds asking "How can a newt do this", so let me explain.

Well, I do not know when the word newt first appeared in the English language as the amphibian we all know, for nigh on every record of them refer to them by their correct name of efts. The word newt is the old name for anyone who rode with their masters in a variety of trades on his coach, they were known by the collective name of newts. These stable lads were not the most savoury of characters and gave their name to that old adage as to being as 'drunk as a newt' - ostlers and horse boys were given this name in the 17th and 18th centuries by their gentlemen masters who guarded their horses and coaches when their employers went drinking, wenching, and making merry in the nearest tavern

Drink would be sent out periodically to these servants, who would also spend their wages on drink at the same time; so when there masters eventually emerged from their revelry their 'newts' i.e. postillions, grooms and ostlers would have to be bundled onto the back of the coach, they being so inebriated hence the expression that has passed into history to be 'drunk as a newt'.

'Keep it at bay' refers to bay trees which were considered lucky. Bay leaves were worn during outbreaks of plagues and pestilences as a protection - hence the expression 'to keep it at bay'. It was also regarded as a charm to avoid being struck by lightning as I gather there is no record of a bay tree having ever been struck by lightning - but I guess there is always a first time.

Even More Fairy Lore - and Much, Much, More

When *'The Last Bastion'* was published in 2005 most of the correspondence I received, strangely enough, was on one particular chapter which greatly surprised me, and that was the section entitled 'Fairy Lore - and more! It constituted a mere eight pages and had been included mainly out of interest; it turned out to be 'Pandora's Box'.

Had it not been for a strange and inexplicable encounter in a valley in County Wexford in Eire in 1981 when my wife and I were guests of Lord and Lady Strathlock at Clonegal Castle, the Headquarters of the Fellowship of Isis run by the hon. Olivia Robertson, then I would never have put pen to paper to record what transpired. For as an adult man, I hesitated to mention what can only be explained away as a 'faerie' encounter for fear of ridicule; but since having sojourned in Ireland I have altered my whole outlook on fairy sightings and phenomena.

In England people would look askance at you, and regard you as 'a bit odd' if you should confess to believing in fairies, but I found quite the reverse in Ireland where you were regarded as a bit strange if you did NOT believe in fairies! Fairies, or the sidhe as they are known, are part of their heritage and you have only to bring the subject up in a rural pub in the Emerald Isles to be immediately regaled with tales of encounters with the wee folk by all and sundry.

They dwell they say beneath the old burial mounds and ancient tumuli, and these raised earthworks were called by a variety of names from the simplistic 'otherworld', to the 'dragon hills', 'the hills of faerie', 'fairy hill', or 'hollow hills'.

The volumes of names by which the fairy folk are referred to is endless, and range from 'the barrow people'; (from being associated with old tumuli i.e. barrows.) to 'the wee folk', the hidden ones', 'the little people', 'the good people', 'mothers' blessings', our 'good neighbours, 'the people of the hollow hills' and most reverently of all - as 'the gentry'. One thing they warned me was, if you see them, do not speak to them or acknowledge that you can see them, particularly if they are helping you. Later you can leave little libations of milk, or sweetmeats especially honey, out for them, and they will simply accept these, but still not acknowledge you directly.

Irish covens in the main believe in their existence implicitly, and in many cases hold their outdoor meetings on both what they describe as 'active' fairy rings and deserted and dormant fairy rings to be found in southern Eire. These hold their Sabbats in woodland glades that are steeped in legends of fairy pheno-mena.

They are all extremely secretive with regard to their activities but from all the investigations I made into fairy lore in Ireland and from interviews with the adherents of the Pookarian persuasion their sincerity came over loud and clear - fairies were an integral part of their beliefs and were highly respected by them. It soon became clear that one did not just 'happen' upon fairies, but had to invoke them, much the same as we have to invoke our own Gods and Goddesses in ceremony, albeit by 'stirring and summoning' them - but with fairies it was quite a different matter, it took much meditation on their part, in what I can only describe as one of the gentlest rituals I have ever come across. Also it was extremely time consuming, for if you intended to see fairies then you had to be prepared to spend long sojourns coaxing them to appear and convincing them as to your sincerity.

There were also specific libations and gifts of natural foods that you enticed them with, plus always a final gift of something shiny or glittering. All the people I have met, and spoken too, while gathering evidence as to the truth of the existence once of fairies, or the possibility that some remnants may have survived, told exactly the same story.

It was many people, Wiccans, locals, farmers and even the constabulary, who continuously provided the strongest evidence of their continued existence, and absolute proof that they were not extinct, albeit rare, and what today we would call an endangered species. I must also mention that the descriptions given to me, which I promised not to publish, of what they call 'fairies' are nothing like the fairies we identify with and which richly ornament children's books.

These scantily clad young maidens in translucent robes and sporting gossamer wings of all the colours of the rainbow are a strictly Victorian invention. My own belief is that this depiction of them is slightly erotic, and was meant to be so in the moral straightjacket of Victorian society, hypocritical as it was. This belief is further strengthened when I came across books such as the '*Fairy Erotica*' and the '*Erotic Book of Fairies*' common in Victorian men's smoking clubs.

From around most of the barrows or tumuli in areas around Cork, the local museums have a number of so called 'elf bolts', allegedly the tips of elves' arrows that they would shoot at intruders, or at those who had offended them. Once more this is just legend for we now know that these are Neolithic arrow heads used by our ancestors for hunting, and most of these have been brought to the surface by rabbits burrowing into the old Neolithic chambers, for the dead were often interred with hunting weapons and knives. But then, of such stuff are legends born.

Farmers in Ireland, to this day, always plough around these tumuli, and give a far wider margin than the law protecting them as ancient monuments states. If you talk to them they will tell you that their fathers and their grandfathers afore them always respected the hollow hills, and would not intrude on 'the little ones', in fact they would not plough up the fairy rings, or build or erect barns or dwellings, near or on a fairy path - old customs die hard even in the 21st century. But let us look at some recorded facts over the years.

One trial for Witchcraft took place in Dorset in 1566, and this involved fairies. The accused was one John Walsh, and on analysis there does not seem much doubt that he was a Witch, and a proficient one at that. Long before he was arrested and arraigned on a charge of practising Witchcraft, he was well known as a healer, and was proficient with the knife and scalpel as well, a rare qualification in those days of early and primitive surgery. Under examination they reported he did not know a 'hot' herb from a 'cold' one, come to think of it neither do I, or any of my herbalist friends, so if there is anyone out there who can tell me what a hot or cold herb is I would be grateful. Thank goodness we did not live in the 1500s.

I gathered from old records, that he was knowledgeable with the correct casting of the magic circle, having been taught the correct technique by his master Sir Robert Drayton, to whom he had been a manservant for seven years. He was a typical countryman of the time, ill educated and uncouth in manners but expert in his craft; alas he was no match for the skill of the interrogator.

Sir Robert was well known locally to have been a sorcerer and occultist, but he was dead and gone, and well beyond the reach of the law now. Walsh was alleged to have been seen 'consorting with fairies' and under questioning and clearly seeing no offence in so doing, readily admitted it. Once again it would appear that the existence of fairies was considered as natural, as the presence of birds or bees. They were just a part of nature and accepted as such. He gave explicit details of how he approached the fairies, and stated that it essentially had to be between noon and one hour after, or at midnight. Again this ties in with contemporary reports, although I could find no evidence of his having given the traditional three knocks in a secret and certain way to summon them, which is well recorded. I can only assume this was a secret even then, for he never disclosed it.

Amazingly, this evidence and confession in one was passed over by the judge, as 'being of no consequence', no-one in their right mind, he said, doubted the existence of the little folk, no, they were a fact of life - the prosecutors should be more concerned over his having a toad as a familiar.

The reason I quote this trial in particular is because of the casual way the fairy incursions were regarded. When he referred to one of the 'great heaps of earth' where the fairies dwelt he nonchalantly offered to prove his point and take them there. The bench decided it was not necessary, which seems once more that such a fact as to the existence of fairies was accepted without question. The Walsh case is unique not only because of the fairy element but also that Walsh was acquitted on the grounds of insufficient evidence.

I feel I must enter a paragraph or so, on the famous Cottingly case. There is no possible doubt now that the fairy photographs that fooled none other than the famous Sir Arthur Conan Doyle were undoubtedly fakes, and the subsequent 'confessions' of the two girls when in their twilight years substantiated this. But one thing still remained, for although they admitted to using cut-outs of fairies from a children's book to substantiate their story, and as we all know, then photographing them with a simple box Brownie, they never ever withdrew their stories that they had met and conversed with fairies on a number of occasions. Surely, if you are going to admit your fraud, when you are in your late 80s, and are getting closer to meeting your maker, you would want to make a completely clean breast of it, so why admit to the one and not the other? To me the answer is obvious; the fact that they had met and conversed with the faerie folk would appear to be true, while the photos they took of them were rigged as they admitted.

Was it sheer frustration that forced two little girls who continuously implored their parents to visit the fairy glen and 'see for themselves' that they were not fibbing, to go out of their way and decide that if the elders would not come to the fairies then they would bring the fairies to them - which they did, with outstanding results.

Their photos were authenticated, and the Cottingly fairies passed in, and out, of history. Why Oh why, I ask, did after all this, no-one ever visit the glen as further substantiation, or once the furore started did the Cottingly fairies go to ground once more, never to materialise before human eyes ever again? I guess we will never know; but one thing is certain; children in the sheer simplicity of their beautiful, undeveloped minds are far more likely to be accepted by the little folk and appear before them than we are, except those Witches who have formed a rapport with them, as outwardly the Pook covens have.

As an investigator you must forgive me for being a sceptic, but that is the nature of the job, therefore for me to hesitate to write an analysis of my findings was natural, but from the volume of correspondence that flowed in I decided to rewrite the chapter in a different format for this book.

For the record I mention 'en passant' that I spent eleven years in law, specialising in ancient and antiquated laws that were still enforceable in the 20th century, and in this capacity I was often consulted on ancient and remote precedents in law that could still be quoted, and enforced, they having never been repealed. It was in this capacity I was referred to in law circles as 'The Devils Advocate'. You can therefore imagine my surprise at finding since I wrote *The Last Bastion* that a law was still in existence, and un-repealed, making it a capital offence to kill a fairy!

The death penalty is now history, but up to then only two crimes remained on the statute book for which the penalty could be death, although undoubtedly in this day and age they would be commuted, and these were for treason (beware Tony Blair it's still on the statute books!) and for starting a fire in Her Majesty's shipyards. Now in 2005 I had discovered this law of Henry the III in 1135 making it a capital offence to afford any harm to a denizen of the Faerie Kingdom, such was the regard that the populace had for them.

Now laws are not passed without reason, there has to be a large degree of substance before an issue is legislated against, so why were fairies as such suddenly protected by law?

The Church was prone to condemn anything that even remotely suggested any form of supernatural or occult activity, but never against fairies, never to my knowledge was there any attack on them by the Church. In all the archives I scoured the closest I ever came was in one reference to them - where they were described by a churchman as 'Angels expelled from Heaven'. (I am not sure what their crime was, but they must have trodden on some ecclesiastical toes) mostly they were referred to somewhat benevolently as the 'Handmaidens of Nature'. But once more, please note that their existence was again a matter of fact at the time.

Accepting that the Church, to say the least, tolerated them, it is interesting to note nevertheless that the Maid of Orleans, the legendary Joan of Arc was charged with Witchcraft as we know; and suffered the supreme penalty. One of the accusations against her was that 'she did consort with fairies and did dance with them'. Technically this was an unsafe accusation in law, for this in itself was not an offence - well certainly not in England.

Fairies as we know were accepted as a part of nature, but furthermore, I feel I should include the fact that the law referred to, protecting fairies, was passed in 1400 under the auspices of Henry the Third, who was on the throne for 56 years, I quote the law here as it was originally written, I do not think a translation is really necessary, but I will give it just in case some foreign reader should be confused by the 'Olde Worlde' spelling. It reads as follows and proscribes death as being the penalty for:-

The"Killinge, wowndynge, or mamynge of a faerie" (The Killing, wounding, or maiming of a fairy.)

Currently I am searching through old archives to find evidence of prosecutions, why the law was passed, and what evidence, i.e. a dead fairy being produced as part of the prosecution, or some one who had stood trial charged with this crime - a daunting job.

It was not until the 1700s that a pogrom commenced chastising the country populace for dancing around old burial barrows, offering libations to wee folk, fairies, and elves, or having fairy charms on houses and barns. The Church avidly sought to discourage country folk from inviting these little people of the hills to enter human habitations, no matter how benevolent these goblins or elves might be.

The strange thought here is that the discouraging of farmers and villagers from consorting with gnomes etc was not much more than being protective of the people, and does not seem to infer any great fears of these troglodytes; it was no more than putting them in the same category as gypsies.

One clergyman went as far as preaching to the congregation that he was perturbed at the fact that local children had been seen 'cavorting with elves' by the old burial mounds and playing with gypsy children as well. He preached to the effect that he was strongly against this practice and urged parents to keep their offspring away from them.

One thing that comes over loud and clear is the rapport that seems to have existed between fairies and the local Witches. Isobel Halfgane, a Scottish Witch, alleged that it was the fairies who taught her, her calling. To this day modern Witches visit and worship the Old Gods in the valleys and mounds that were reputed to have been the homes of fairies.

These two have been closely associated with each other from the beginning of time itself, and when the extermination of the Witches began in the burning days and the wise women started to disappear, so also in synchronisation do the fairy colonies start to disappear. Local churchmen made reports peripatetically on the local colonies; and it makes interesting reading, but most of all the casual manner of their reports are interesting in their quiet acceptance of the colonies, some going as far as actually studying them.

One clergyman's diary reads in the 1790s that he 'fears the local fairy colony is dying out, for upon traversing some rather undulating country to visit the colony with a flagon of ale and some victuals for the journey - suggesting it was quite a hike, he comments on their scarcity. Some years later in 1796 he reports his sorrow at there being no more than a score of fairies there now, and the following report two years later in 1798 writes that at his last observation there were but six left. His last and final report (undated) states the colony is no more and that upon his last visit it was overgrown with bramble and nettles, he had not seen a fairy there for many a year.

Local villagers reported seeing a fairy funeral at Pulborough Mount, and concerned, called in the local vicar to authenticate it. He wrote this up in confirmation of what he had seen, the date? 1800! Right up to this date they existed according to old records in great profusion throughout the country, it is only as we approach 1800 that they seem to rapidly die out, notwithstanding the fact that there have been reports of them being seen, albeit in small numbers or even singly, right up to the present day.

Leslie Philips a well known researcher of the paranormal reported seeing a fairy on Chanctonbury Ring on All Hallow's

Day, the day of the sacred Hallowmas to us, this would have been around the 1960s to 70s. The exact date is not recorded but apparently he called up a number of witnesses to verify the sighting. In the late 1800s the famous Witch Biddy Earl, was reputed to have received her powers from the fairies, and it is said that they bestowed on her a wondrous elixir, in a translucent bottle of light blue glass. When she died in 1873 locals threw her wonder bottle into a nearby lake and it was seen no more - it probably awaits discovery by a scuba diver one day.

The last official sighting and recording of a fairy colony is at Harrow Hill at Patching in Sussex, and with this it appears that the age of the faerie folk was over, the faerie people overnight, were no more, and were virtually declared extinct. Or are they? If this extinction is factual, then I will say it is only in parts of England they have in theory disappeared, for rumours still persist as to sightings, particularly in the West Country. The last report I was told of was in 2005, but regretfully remains unsubstantiated. Like UFOs, there's far too much evidence to dismiss these out of hand.

How many of these sightings are hysteria or a vivid imagination is difficult to ascertain, but those who testify to this are invariably quite rational people and I cannot dismiss their reports out of hand. I mentioned that my whole outlook with regard to the world of faerie altered overnight after an amazing incident in Ireland in 1981 which I will recount for the record here and subsequently attempt to analyse this phenomena.

At the time my wife Audrey and myself were the guests of Lord and Lady Strathlock at Huntingdon Castle in Clonegal, County Wexford, and our hostess there was the Rt Hon Olivia Robertson who is the head of the Fellowship of Isis. We had been invited to spend a month with them in June of that self-same year, and also for Audrey's initiation into the inner Isian mysteries which were to be held deep down in the subterranean depths of the castle where the throne of both Isis and the black Isis were erected. This was performed with local Druids and mystics present on the 2nd of August 1981; the Priestess Grainne was also ordained that day. I note that it was after Audrey's ordination and installation as a High Priestess that the phenomena referred to occurred.

It was some two or three days after this wondrous event that we had gone exploring the local countryside as was our wont. On this particular occasion we had decided to start off extra early and head for a great mountain range that was some three hours drive away.

Audrey packed sandwiches and buns and with flasks of coffee and tea we set off. Some three and a half hours later about midday we were coursing the ravines and valleys along unmade roads and paths when we saw a little valley snaking upwards into the hills with a small waterfall cascading into a stream. Such a delightful place was ideal for our picnic, the sun was shining and there was a great air of peace and tranquillity in the air. We parked the car on a nearby stretch of ground and slowly made our way into the valley. The waterfall was farther away than we had expected and we had almost decided not to try to get there when we saw a small and somewhat rickety old bridge spanning the stream. This we decided would be our picnic spot and we laid out a fresh tablecloth by the streamside and prepared our repast to the twinkling of the waterfall in the background.

Suddenly as we were eating we heard the most beautiful ethereal music I had ever encountered. It was composed of strings, what I would describe as little bells, cymbals, flutes and harps; it is not easy to describe it but it had a distinct mediaeval air to it not unlike the music of '*Greensleeves*'. We sat in rapture as this little 'faerie' orchestra circumambulated around us continuously playing throughout our picnic. We were absolutely enthralled and immediately looked around to see where it could have been coming from - there were no wires of any description overhead, no electric pylons, no telegraph poles to be seen - Rien! - nothing.

Eventually we packed up the utensils, hid the picnic hamper in the bushes to pick up later and went for a walk, meandering along the stream bed and nearby ponds and meadows. The area was a wildlife sanctuary of activity. Butterflies, dragonflies and mayflies abounded everywhere, and wild flowers of every description grew profusely along the banks. We were followed, the whole while by the invisible orchestra. Later on we picked up the hamper and started back to the car, the faerie orchestra still following all the while with this ethereal music. There was a slight difference now though, as it was rising and diminishing in little crescendos.

Eventually we reached the road and immediately the sound was all around us for a few fleeting seconds then wafted away, oh so lightly, and gradually in the wind, then it was gone. It was one of the greatest experiences of my life and the exquisite memory of it remains to this day some 25 years later, and is still as vivid as the day it happened.

It was the following morning back at Huntingdon castle. We were breakfasting as was our custom with Derry (Lord Strathlock) and Poppy (Lady Strathlock, and our dear host Olivia who were always inquisitive as to where we had been the day before. We told them of the wondrous valley we had discovered and where it was. There was an immediate silence as they all looked at each other in a common understanding. Derry was the first to speak, and in a low voice asked gently "Did anything happen when you were there?" We then unfolded what had occurred and they were all overjoyed, Poppy was clapping her hands together, and Olivia was jubilant - then Derry announced - "That was the fairy glen you saw, the music was the fairies showing they had accepted you, it is so rare for them to make themselves apparent to strangers" Olivia was beaming. "Oh Ralph and Audrey" she exclaimed "It means you have been accepted by the little folk, we are so pleased.

To everyone at Huntingdon castle it was a good omen for our stay there, and far from being ridiculed; our hosts were overjoyed, and in celebration opened a bottle of vintage claret. At the end of the day we followed them into the castle grounds where we observed them pouring the last drop of the vintage wine into the Earth as a libation to the Earth Mother, and then put out little sweetmeats etc for the wee folk.

I have recounted the facts as they happened - no, we did not see fairies, all we saw was butterflies and dragonflies in profusion, together with the sound of wondrous music. What did happen that day? We had no radio with us, nor in the car, there were no telegraph poles to hum, and no pylons for miles, but whenever we mentioned the incident locally people beamed and said "we know - that is where the Sidhe live, we call them the Daoine Sidhe, this being the Irish for fairy folk, and pronounced Theena Shee.

We made another discovery on our return to England, and that was the magic associated with primroses and fairies; it was a widespread belief that if you ate primroses you would be able to see the fairy folk. It was particularly practised by village children. It would be interesting to note if a primrose contains hallucinogens, we know for a certainty they have healing powers, for in the New Forest the woodsmen there had healing unguents made from primroses and lard which they used to heal any wounds they suffered. Scientists please note, this is yet another field for you to research.

On May Day, when we Witches were supposed to be particularly active, bunches of primroses would be placed on the doorways of barns and cottages to prevent our entry. There are many superstitions associated with Witches and primroses, one is that if you pick these beautiful flowers for a posy, then make sure you pick at least thirteen, anything under is to invite bad luck. One wicked custom that country folk would perpetrate was to give a child a single primrose to take home and thereby blight their neighbour's hens into ceasing laying.

Fairies were reputed to cavort amongst primroses, harebells, and bluebells and could be seen dancing joyously amongst them as they heralded spring and the warm summer months. Legend says these little ones were remnants of the ones known as the Tuatha de Danaan the little people of the Goddess Dana.

Since Ireland my whole outlook has altered and now when I am asked if I really believe that fairies exist then my answer has to come down on the positive side and I answer yes! Please understand that what I am about to record is purely my own personal opinion, but the evidence over the years I feel of fairy phenomena is overwhelming, and their existence was never doubted for a thousand years, they are part of our history and part of our heritage.

I do not mean the little humanoids that fly around on gossamer wings in iridescent colours like butterflies, no, that is not my conception of what a fairy is, I put them in the same category as elementals which I know to exist beyond any doubt whatsoever. Rare is the house that does not have a number of elementals within it, and Witches' houses abound with them. One Witch I know has a house that simply swarms with them; they scurry around her floor like hundreds of black beetles. Be honest and answer truthfully, but have you not seen little dark patches flit across the floor and wondered what it was? Well undoubtedly it was an elemental.

Fairies are exactly that, elementals, that are a part of the mysterious Deva kingdom, little wood spirits that can be seen flitting across little glades where the sacred ladies smock and bluebells abound, in woodlands where the harebell grows side by side with the flower known as milkmaids flourishes. The pigeons eye flower is called the Fairies Flower in the countryside, and has always been associated with the 'little ones'. Do not pick the Fairy Flower however, for you will have robbed the little ones, and they will sour your milk.

Use a little imagination now, you see the flash of elementals as they flit from their never-ending tasks, you see butterflies of wondrous hues playing tag in their unique mating dances; throw in the wonder of dragonflies and their scintillating colours, add the mayfly and the lacewing to the scene, and then as dusk falls let the glow-worm light up, and the fairy legend is born.

Fairies are just that, elementals that are more attuned to some people as against others. Did those that lived close to the land all those years ago have a greater rapport with these elementals, I think they did. As we advanced in technology and the people abandoned the land of their fathers so the fairy folk died out. Their demise started with the industrial revolution as humanity poured out great smog clouds and the all-polluting sulphur from coal fires.

Mechanical shovels and excavators destroyed many of the old sites and fearfully the little wood spirits have moved out, bewildered at the sudden intrusion into their territory. Suddenly the world no longer respected them, and now they harbour themselves in the homes of Witches and Pagans who open up both their homes and their gardens to them as new sanctuaries.

Any area of one's garden can be set aside for secret moonlight lone rituals so beloved of all Witches, and it will not be long before this same area will attract all forms of elementals it is said, including the faerie folk. The best method of all is to simply adapt a section of natural beauty like an old gnarled tree, or overgrown patch and simply enhance it, do not clear away the natural debris of nature such as decaying leaves and fallen branches.

We are not speaking of one's old back yard here, but a place of beauty where fern and flowers abound, and where if possible there is a pond. West Country lore stated that where the gadfly and fireflies and the dragonflies swoop 'neath the willow, the little ones soon colonise it. Why you may ask can one not attract them into a less prestigious area? The answer is simple, everything in the realm of Deva is clean and orderly, and few back yards are. Remember they are creatures of the open air and wild, wide open spaces, but they still love dark hollows and fallen trees, what nature has discarded becomes their home. But in the villages and within suburbia where gardens are things of beauty they will survive,they say.

Now when you meet a Witch, and they tell you they have fairies at the bottom of their garden, well they probably really have, for in the form of elementals they do still live. They are the wildfolk spirits we know so well, some say they are tree spirits, while old legends say are the souls of Druids who have died as heathens, refusing to bow the knee to Xtianity, and doomed to the world of faerie for ever, most often as pixies though if male, and as fairies if female.

Evil Words and Sticks'n Stones

'Sticks 'n Stones may break my bones but names will never hurt me' - so the old adage goes but what a misnomer there is with what a Witch is. The feminine aspect seems to be pretty clear but our men folk are often and erroneously referred to as Wizards and Warlocks. Well, for the record, both male and female are Witches - period. The wizards of history are either alchemists or ritual magicians, Witches they certainly are not. Neither are our men Warlocks although there is a degree of truth in this.

In the days of the persecutions there was a law that stated "No coven shall know where the next coven abideth" and this was strictly enforced as far as it could be applied. If the members of a coven did not know who their compatriots were in the next village then all the torture in the world could not make them tell what they did not know. Yet communication between covens was essential for their own safety, the summoning to the great Sabbats, and the mutual exchange of esoteric knowledge, spells, and magic.

This task fell to one single person within the coven who was known as 'the communicator'. This appointee was always a male and would be chosen for his strength, ability to fight if neces-sary, speed of foot, and local knowledge. Not infrequently he was an ex soldier. This man was the Guardian of the coven, he would usually be of the rank of 3rd degree, and if the coven was decimated he was in a position to teach, but his main task was the preservation of the coven for teaching really lay in the hands of the Priestesses.

At coven meetings when they were forced to hold the Sabbats in secret, usually on a sacred site or in a sacred grove then he would mount guard, sword in hand and watch out for any war parties, or Witchfinders. Escape plans would already have been laid out in a contingency plan should the coven be set upon. Fortunately there are scant records of an entire coven ever being taken so obviously the 'modus operandii' was successful.

The communicator would always wear black so that he could disappear in the night if called upon to do so, but there was a far more practical purpose to this for he was the only one within the coven who knew where the next coven was, hence his fitness to elude any pursuit and his ability to fight out of a situation should it arise. His chances of survival were good, and the likelihood of his being taken was remote, and his nocturnal activities outside of Sabbats, and full moon meetings was literally to 'communicate'.

His name within the coven was the lookout man, and as his duties as an observer was that of looking for any aggressive activity when the coven met and he was universally known as the 'War-look' which over the years became 'warlock'. The name came to be identified as a male Witch which is not correct, for only one man within a coven was the warlock, and as a coven was by tradition a minimum of 13, of which at least half would be men, then his chances of survival were good. It is a matter of historical fact that most Witches arrested and arraigned were single and usually women, and sadly for them were not even Witches.

Because of the popular concept of a Witch any poor old woman in the throes of senility could be taken for a Witch together with any physical abnormality such as a gob tooth, a squint, a caste in the eye, a stutter, or even a wart just to give a few examples. Those who were mentally impaired, or were mongoloid, or had been unfortunate enough to have been born with a club foot, a hunch back or withered limb would also be a natural target for the mob for the pure and simple reason that they were different to the majority. It is also the war-look/ communicator that came to be identified as the feared 'man in black' - a fear and misnomer that existed right up to the 20th century as was seen in the famous Orkney Island case when the villagers had their children seized by social workers and forcibly put into care for months on end for having been reported to having been seen in clandestine meetings with a 'Man in Black'. The cry of so-called Satanic activity echoed in the national press as even more social workers descended on the Islands and tried, unsuccessfully, to uncover Witch covens and traces of Black Magic. All protestations by eminent occultists to the effect that Black Magic and Satanism had no part whatsoever in Wiccan practices fell on deaf ears

Remember this was in the 1980s long after the Witchcraft Act had been repealed in 1951. Even if the allegations had been true there was no case to answer for Witchcraft was not a crime, and no children are allowed to attend Sabbats anyway as anyone could have told them who was reasonably informed. No-one can be initiated until they are 18 years old anyway - that is the absolute minimum age we will consider! The months passed, the children pined away, desolated at the sudden and forced separation from the parents they loved, and all this time the fathers and mothers cried vainly for justice and compassion for their suffering little ones, but to no avail; the social workers were hell-bent on uncovering occult activity on the Islands, and tracking down the 'man in black' - and they succeeded!

After months of probing and collecting enough statements to fill a warehouse they ran him to earth. The legendary man in black who had triggered the investigation turned out to be the local vicar, suitably attired in his raiment's of black and dog collar of white, giving evening classes and Bible studies. Results egg on faces all round and a resounding victory for justice and common sense eventually. Vindicated, the villagers awaited the return of their offspring whom had been incommunicado for several months. Were they now released? Were they hell! For some inexplicable reason they were still held and all overtures for their release back into the community were ignored.

By now the national press had taken up cudgels and were running a national campaign for justice, but behind the scenes the social services were doing everything in their power to prove their case continuously interrogating the children and even confronting them with male and female dolls to prove some form of sexual activity must have occurred, but naturally they could not prove what was not there. Eventually they were summoned to the High Court who ordered their immediate release, justice had prevailed, but over a year had passed and the children, now heavily traumatized, were returned. The psychological scars of their being torn from their parents in the middle of the night undoubtedly would remain with them for a long period, if not for ever.

Well, we have examined the meaning of the warlock, but let us have a look at the many names we have been called over the centuries. There has been a degree of controversy over the years regarding Wiccans - is Wiccan another name for Witch? Well historically the answer is yes, although with the passing of the years New Age Pagans and Wiccans have tended to distance themselves from the traditional Witches, particularly those who decline to change as we come into the 21st century.

I personally am sympathetic to those who steadfastly stick to the old ways. Logically of course we must conform to modernism and there is room amongst both traditionalist and hereditary Witches to amend old rituals, and by and large we have, but there is a limit to which we can go before we lose our identity and therefore many of us resist the new age trends which owe more to pseudo American Witchcraft than to old values.

If we cast our minds back to those early days when we, together with sorcerers, were called Strix or Strias, while in Italy they were known as Stregas or Strigas these were Witches in all senses. Those who saw the future, divined or were soothsayers were known as Sortiarus or Strigimaga and some records refer to them as *masca*. A word I believe that evolved into 'mask' for these Witches were in the habit of performing their rites while wearing animal and birds masks. This is found to this day when the 'chasing' ritual is performed and the High Priestess, skyclad (nude), dances around the circle, while the covenors attempt to catch her. In this guise she will mimic an animal or bird of the chase while the coven will imitate the predators. Part of the rituals run as follows as she merrily eludes them (they always by tradition fail to catch her).

"Oh I shall go as a wren in Spring, with sorrow and sighing on silent wing" etc while the coven chant "And we shall follow as falcons grey, and hunt thee cruelly as our prey", followed by "Then I shall go as a mouse in May. in fields by night, in cellars by day" and the coven recite "And we shall follow as black tom cats and chase thee through the corn and vats" etc while this chain dance is enacted the covenors would wear the masks of the animal they represent.

Lamia was sometimes used but this was really more associated with vampirism. All it needed to start a ball rolling was one of these rituals to be seen - or even rumoured - we never ever get a good press, a couple of bats are seen in the area, someone dies of tuberculosis and looks drained of blood, a poacher is seen and runs into a thicket, and minutes later a startled wolf makes a run for it, and we get the blame as always, guess we can't win.

Maleficus, now that is one that stuck long before Wicca came into the equation, simply it means 'one who works magic for evil purposes'. You would think it would stop there, but oh no, next in line was to call us scobax, for some reason it means a screech owl. Now to call us male Witches a scobax is the greatest indignity, but if it had been some ladies I know, well... Sometimes and heavens only know how this evolved into a scoba - literally a broom. Strange are the ways of the Xtians.

It was not long before we find ourselves described as 'gazarius', probably because we were regarded as heretics, but technically it should only be applied to Cathars who currently were also being persecuted, but if you can catch a Witch in the net as well, then let's go for it. It always was a no win situation as far as the poor Pagan was concerned.

The next stage was to refer to us as 'waudensis' or waudensians, same old theme, and still heretics. This overlapped with the persecution of the Waldensians, so maybe they couldn't spell; but this time not a Cathar hunt, but a Waldensian one, their only crime was worshipping the Xtian messiah by a new church service that was not in step with Catholic thinking. For this the punishment was to be burnt hideously at the stake without the benefit of strangulation beforehand. Is there no limit to their iniquity? Applied today it would send every Methodist, Baptist, and Church of England minister or follower to the stake. This gives an idea of the power of the Holy Catholic Church at the time.

Well, about this time they seem to have softened up a little bit for suddenly the records are referring to all followers of the Old Religion as 'herbarius'. Now that one was acceptable for this time it was a true depiction of the old wise women and healers of the time; it meant 'the herb gatherers'. Perhaps there was a glimmer of light at the end of the tunnel we thought, let's see what comes next.

Well it was not long in coming for they now reverted to the old divining edition and decided that all those who told fortunes or saw the future were 'pythonissa'. Since when were we fortune tellers I ask you? That is a modern development that abounds at psychic fairs currently, but not Wicca! Yes we do, do scrying but that is never in public and is confined to individuals seeking guidance themselves. Fortune telling was the calling of the travelling gypsies, certainly not us, but it was not a burning offence - yet. Next in line was a reference to us as being 'factura' derived from the Latin 'factus', meaning a maker of spells.

Alright then, guess we have to plead guilty to that one, so perhaps we could not be too perturbed, but overnight they were back on the old divination bandwagon and this time calling us 'divinators' (wait for it 'Witch' is coming) then still on the old diviner theme we next are called 'mathematicus', swiftly followed by 'necromanticus'. I will not dwell on what we are alleged to do with rotting corpses, and how we used them, I will only say that making love to a month old corpse does not seem very appealing. I only wonder how on earth they dreamed this one up. Within a short space of time this became corrupted to 'nigromanticus' (still committing indescribable acts with the dead!).

Well, the powers-that-be decided that the next stage was 'veneficus', those who made potions, salves, and unguents, well that seems fair enough. But in no time at all this became more associated with poisons, than easing arthritis, all it needed was some poor old dear being given a mixture of lotio plumbi (a lead lotion) most effective for aches and sprains right up to the end of the Second World War, and instead of rubbing it in as directed probably mixed it with the local gin and promptly turned up their toes; from that point onwards veneficus took on a whole new meaning alas.

It must have been about the time of James the first of England (James the sixth of Scotland), the same one who accused us of trying to drown him in his ship while we sailed around it in eggshells raising storm and tempest; who gave us the name 'tempestarius' meaning those who raise storms. Now that would be real power I must admit. I remember old Mabs who was my wife's High Priestess for many years, now she was a dab hand at whistling up a wind to dry her washing, but was a little bit missing on the power to stop it, so I know it can be done, and I have seen Audrey do a wizard little rain dance to chase the rain clouds away, no do not ask me how she does it, but she does and it works, but sinking a ship - I ask you!

Incantator was to follow meaning one who made incantations to order, I suppose I cannot say much in our defence, as this is an essential part of Witchdom. Then came the resurgence of the old Anglo Saxon Wicce or Wicca you have all been patiently waiting for until now, but I thought you should know the many references we had endured over the centuries. This time it meant those who cast spells, made magic, worked miracles, healed the sick and lame and cured gout, and got rid of worms, well something like that, but at least they got it right this time.

Just for the record, technically Wicca is masculine and Wicce is feminine so all you macho girls out there calling yourselves Wiccans - think!! I do not know when the word hex or hexing entered into our language, but we do know it came from the old German word *Hexe*, based on what was known as 'Old High German' to wit *hagazussa*, although this had many connotation and varied from aspects of cannibalism to sorcery and night spirits. Somewhere along the line the Hun invaders in the form of the Saxon hordes who invaded us for centuries probably brought it with them.

An Analysis of the Power of the Witch, and an Experiment

What I am explaining in this chapter is the power of the Witch, at the end of which I think you will understand why we do not recruit people or try to convert them to our ways. Firstly we are not evangelists, and do not recruit. And thus, secondly, we are highly selective as to who we admit to our covens, and who ultimately are taught how to acquire the ability to control what is known in the Craft as 'the power'.

I am often asked why Witchcraft nowadays is such a secretive society, and what do we have to hide, and the answer is nothing. We are secretive for a number of reasons, and these are manifest. They can range from the fact that many of our rituals are conducted skyclad, down to the fact that the world has changed so much since the old days of the Craft. For instance the media can be our friend, or our enemy, according to how they depict us, and show our rituals to the world.

Television and radio in the main are benign towards us, as are the local media in the form of local papers, but certain opportunistic and sensationalistic elements of the national press, loosely known as the gutter press are not interested in true facts regarding the Craft, but only what they can exploit and exaggerate. Therefore we are wary as to who joins us as there has been many an attempt by the press, and one newspaper in particular to infiltrate our ranks and expose us from the inside. Could you imagine what would happen if they learned the art of 'the power'?

Sometimes we are not sure of whether a particularly eager acolyte is genuine, so as is our custom we invite them to what is loosely called 'open evenings' a weekly gathering of acolytes, neophytes, established Witches and sorcerers who meet to discuss and examine all applicants, teach the basics and principles of the Craft that any future entrant must obey, and thereby to learn what we stand for and, most importantly, believe in.

As soon as a 'spy' (usually a female one) realises that that they must keep this up for a minimum of a year and a day before they can even be considered for admission, they swiftly fade away and we hear no more from them.

Even those who are admitted are not given these high rituals for some considerable time, they have to earn them, and prove they will not ever misuse them. Giving all and sundry the power would be like allowing everyone to have a gun; you know that eventually someone will misuse it. This is why we gave a three stage structure of elevation within Witchcraft, after you have graduated through your acolyte and neophyte stages prior to initiation.

These in order, are initially initiation of the first degree, after a year and a day - eligibility for elevation to the second degree (not automatically given please note). It is at this point, the elevation to the second degree where the power is given, the candidate having proved their worthiness during the previous year plus. A period of some years may now elapse before the final accolade is given, when what is known as the power supreme is transferred at this the final elevation. The Witch, now a third degree, can perform mighty magic if he or she has been trained properly.

When this is done, the Witch will have learned the basis of power, and most importantly its control. Power, like strength can be used for good or bad, the hand that can gently lift a child up from its cradle, or pick up someone who has fallen down, is using its strength for good, but that self-same hand can strike you! Strength is neutral, so is magic! This is why with the acquisition of power that Witches achieve once initiated, they are monitored closely by the elders that it is to a fit and proper person who is joining the coven and will not misuse their training, nor ever misuse the power.

It is therefore important to note that there is no such thing as black and white Witchcraft. It annoys me intensely when people ask, or state "I gather you are a White Witch". "No, I am not! I am a Witch - period", I retort, and by the very vows I took at my initiation - essentially white, for that is the basic tenet of the Craft's calling, to help and to heal.

The training referred to is important for another very good reason, and that is that anyone who has the power, or who acquires it, can use it subconsciously or even subliminally to hurt someone. On more than one occasion I have found myself bristling under a particular indignity such as when a particularly obnoxious drunk offended a friend of mine in my presence. Although I successfully pushed him off I was seething as he shouted out obscenities as we left, at that moment my guard was down, and subliminally I realised the degree of my fury at him. I heard the screech of brakes as a car veered away from him as he staggered into the road, and immediately willed all to be well. A somewhat chastened drunk was hauled back to safety by one of his companions. This is mind power and how it works.

I have known people suffering from a grave injustice, or who have been robbed and received no justice from the courts, people who have seen a thief walk free and make an obscene gesture at them as he walks away with no more than a slap on the wrist. Oh how foolish that miscreant was to have done that, for days later he was apprehended in a bungled burglary when he found himself trapped in the very house he had burgled. The sheer simplicity of it is staggering. Apparently the lock to the cellars had seized after he had gone down to investigate and rifle the area, and to add insult to injury the wooden ladder which reached up to the door snapped in the centre, so now he could not reach up to even attempt to force it.

The owner, who was an antique dealer, returned two days later to hear feeble cries for help coming from the cellar where he stored his antique china and coin collection. When the police arrived they found a very sorry miscreant who was just sitting there with only the crumbs of a packet of biscuits the owner had left in a desk, and an empty can that the owner had placed there to catch a slow drip of water that threatened his books. Our housebreaker had survived on these. The lock was less than a year old and found to be in perfect working order having been changed after a series of break-ins in the area. This time there was no acquittal. Coincidence? Well you cannot eliminate it, but time and time again Witches and those who have 'the power' tell of numerous events that strongly suggest that the sheer volume and number of incidents, has to be more than sheer coincidence. This is the 'eye' at work, and can of course react instantaneously, when an individual is angered.

The Witch of course, reacts exactly the same as anyone else, but because of the law of 'An ye harm none' has to immediately throw up a mind block to prevent harm coming to the offender. I have come across a large number of people who are convinced that they 'make things happen.'

My own wife Audrey found at a very early age that if she really concentrated on something she wanted it would come to her. In this case we see the power being used benignly, but it was there from a very early age. Over the years it only needed honing. Strangely she went on to become a Sunday school teacher in the Baptist church, and sang in the choir there as well, Previously having been baptised by total immersion, for the record she was born into the Church of England, and christened there. This is unique in itself for someone to have been christened, baptised, ended up in the choir and become a Sunday school teacher and from there to have gone on to become a High Priestess in Witchcraft and, to have been initiated into the rites of Isis at Huntingdon Castle in Eire, by Lord and Lady Strathlock, and the hon. Olivia Robertson as well as a Priestess of Isis.

This conversion did not come easily to her; 51 years ago, we met, fell in love and married. A strange relationship for in those early heady days I was heavily involved in Ritual Magic, not having entered the Craft at this stage. Audrey had long been disenchanted with the doctrine of the Church, her mother was a 'Hell Fire and Damnation' Xtian and it was she who had steered her daughter onto the Xtian path, persuading her to become a Baptist and teacher.

Audrey's whole environment as a child had been one of psalm singing, and Xtian rhetoric, for she, an only child, had been born into a devout Xtian family with a history of devotion. Audrey fondly recalls her grandmother, a kind and loving soul, as one of the few real Xtians she has ever met. But outside of that she was astounded at the hypocrisy she encountered within the church, and increasingly wanted no part of it as she matured.

Audrey was extremely tolerant of my early experiments in magic and looking back I now realise what a contrast her new way of life was to her. I had a room where all the paraphernalia of magical equipment was arraigned, and it was here within its confines that my early experiments into the world of the occult commenced. It was not long before I decided to concentrate on the three 'tele' sciences, to wit. Teleportation, Telekinesis, and Telepathy, with astounding results.

The art of telepathic transference came to me easily, and it was not long before I was engaged in comparatively simple telepathic experiments. These were initially the transmitting of simple commands to see if they worked and that Audrey picked them up. It was not long before I realised that conscious transmitting was only partially successful; the period and length of time involved was onerous and I was on the verge of abandoning this particular experiment when I made one of the first of a number of major discoveries, a pattern that was shortly about to emerge with telekinetic experiments too. Conscious thought-forms are weak, and do not work well, although they are partially successful provided enough time and concentration are devoted to them.

The secret of these forms of magic I discovered lay in subliminal thought, and was deeply enshrined within the subconscious. The results now were staggering, as I went about mundane and ordinary chores outside of my magical chamber, I would get a flash of inspiration, or something would instantaneously cross my mind and within a minute Audrey would appear and repeat a whole message just as if I had spoken. The sheer diverseness of this was amazing.

Distance was no barrier, that was the first discovery. Audrey could be out shopping and suddenly I would think of something that I needed and which outwardly she would not have the faintest idea I would require, only to return with the words "I had a feeling you would want this" and then produce it. As the years have gone by, (we celebrated our golden wedding last year - 50 years - November 2005) this telepathic bond has grown ever stronger, and we both now have the power to read each other's minds at will. I have found that other couples who have a strong emotional tie, and have a strong affinity, also develop this self-same ability. Audrey and I often jokingly remark when we both say the identical expression at the same time "Hey, get out of my mind". All either of us requires is for a thought to flash through their head in a split instant and the other absorbs it loud and clear.

Many friends and acquaintances of mine, many of whom would later be converted to Wicca, were also particularly interested in my research, but one of them, Mary O'Brien, was outstanding. We could communicate telepathically over long distances at will; it was almost as if we had a direct telephone link to each other. Many a time and oft we would be astounded at the most simplistic of happenings that would occur, minor incursions into our minds that were infinitesimal in proportion to what they related to.

A typical example of this as example was one day at home my wife Audrey phoned to say she was ready to be picked up from a shopping trip in Brighton, and that she was heavily loaded with Xmas shopping, asking me to rendezvous with her on a certain corner. I went out to the car only to find the battery was completely and utterly flat. Mary, who worked only a couple of blocks away, I knew would help me out of my predicament and I rushed back indoors to phone her. Mary was manageress of a large bedding store and I knew she would normally be able to break away to help.

In my panic I could not find my diary, and neither could I remember her telephone number, and Audrey was waiting for me not knowing my predicament. I was going through the telephone book for a taxi when the doorbell rang – and there was Mary, 'before I could speak to her first words were "Jump in, and tell me where she is as we go along." Telepathically she knew Audrey was stranded and I had no car. She eventually joined my coven and became a Witch of great ability; she is with me to this day.

Telekinesis was to have a profound effect on our lives in exactly the same way, it was once again the subliminal thoughts that generated the power at the beginning, and to this day that still prevails. The main difference being that whereas telepathy worked perfectly once in the subconscious, conscious transmitting was patchy at the very least. With telekinesis, conscious thought and concentration works when willing an object to move, but takes hours, and frankly I found it unproductive and not worth the effort.

My initial failures in these experiments went on for nigh on two years. The amount of time I would spend concentrating on an object, usually something small and light initially such as a matchbox, in an attempt to move it across a designated area, or to levitate it even for a few seconds. The results initially were abysmal, and often the amount of movement was at most an inch or two, and eventually I would have to admit failure, and unwind later with a record player to the airs of Chopin or Beethoven.

It would be at that moment as I relaxed, that things would really begin to happen, for within a few minutes you would think we had a poltergeist loose in the house. Whatever the last objects were that I had failed to move, or moved only fractionally, would now be floating merrily around the room, not infrequently when we had guests as if feeding on their energy. These incidents always happened when my guard was down and I had dismissed the matter from my mind, delegating it to the subconscious yet again.

What I had inadvertently done, having spent countless hours emitting an energy force that was going nowhere, was that I had built up a highly concentrated power that suddenly erupted like a volcano! Certainly from the phenomena that often accompanied these manifestations I could not ignore the possibility of other occult forces being at work here, and they in turn added to the mayhem for a malicious occult sense of humour seemed to have seeped in at this stage, which was extremely disturbing. My advice to those interested in taking this path is - don't. I have been down it and it is not worth the risk unless you are highly competent, and for what? Unless you can harness the power for good as you can in Wicca, then why risk taking a chance on what you may quite inadvertently conjure up.

Many a time objects that had no connection whatsoever with my experiments I had undertaken would be involved, often much larger and heavier ones at that. The only common factor would be that everything I had used in these experiments of levitation, and kinesis, would be there as well.

It was at this stage I realised that I had in actual fact succeeded in raising power, albeit from an unknown source, but was unable to either control or master it. A highly dangerous situation. By this time I was highly involved in Wicca, and the sheer and beautiful simplicity of this nature religion grew in dominance.

I decided I could not in reality serve two masters, but was reluctant to abandon my research into telekinesis. Also, I had virtually pulled away from my third study, which was experimenting with teleportation for reasons I prefer not to publish. It took much soul-searching, and I eventually decided I could not leave the task uncompleted though I would continue with the research into telekinesis. It was too dangerous to abandon it and leave unknown forces loose, plus I could see that the power of ritual magic, if carefully applied, could be incorporated to a certain degree into Witchcraft.

For those interested and who know how; I am of course referring to rituals of High Magic such as the Lesser and Greater Ritual of the Pentagram to be found in the Golden Dawn, and in some instance as the Lesser and Greater Ritual of the Hexagram.

To anyone who is experienced enough to perform this rite, may I strongly advocate that unless they have studied Ritual Magic, and are at least an Adeptus Major, even then, do not attempt the High Magic of the Hexagram, but perform the Lower Ritual of the Pentagram which is far more compatible to Wicca. Another recommendation I would make is that it be performed outdoors in woodland, and rehearsal should essentially be in sections until one is competent. Those within Witchcraft who have reached the 3rd degree, if they prepare themselves thoroughly, and have rehearsed the ritual in sections as stated, should then be able to perform this rite safely and competently.

Please note that I have emphasised 'in sections' it is most important not to perform this right the way through in case you make a mistake and leave a summoning suspended in the air, so do not complete nor perform these rituals until you feel confident and can do so from A to Z without stopping.

I would also strongly recommend they go through the Asana (Postures) Pranayama (Regulation of one's breathing) and most important of all Dharana (The control of thought). These are the first stages in becoming adept in Ritual Magic, and the lower rituals can be used within a Wiccan circle for major rituals where a great power source is required. Use the ritual of the double consecration of the circle, which is a safeguard, I cannot go into detail but practitioners will understand if I simply say perform the ritual of the wise eagle, the lion, the serpent, and the bull - in that order, they will know.

It was shortly afterwards that I met a Master at a meeting, who lectured on Kabbala. A friendship ensued, and he taught me much. As a result of his guidance I was able to quell the strange forces at work at home. Looking back I realise he always guided me, but never really helped, I cannot recall a single occasion he ever visited me to see the phenomena for himself, but without him and his advice I doubt if I could have succeeded.

My task was now over, and other than the lower grades I turned my back on Ritual Magic to the utter relief of my wife. By now though she had become fascinated with Wicca, and unreservedly decided to be initiated. In our particular tradition a man does not initiate his wife or vice versa, so Audrey became a Gardnerian within the confines of the Acorn coven. Sadly, as I recorded in my book '*The Last Bastion*' the High Priestess and High Priest who were married, split up, and the coven disintegrated. Audrey was still only a first degree at the time and it was a blow to her as she was making great strides. It was at this stage that the finger of fate was to step into the equation and propel her onto an even firmer path.

I spent eleven years in the legal profession, and was delighted to discover how many eminent members of this profession were often Masons and Witches also. During this period I met a number of police officers as well who were unafraid to admit their religious faith as followers of the Old Religion. These were such people as Dave Taylor who completed a TV documentary with me, and appeared in the show in his police uniform, and was seen by hundreds of thousands on television - and not a murmur from the powers that be. Not surprising really, for many within the Kent police force where he served were full Craft members. Dave incidentally married Sally Taylor an eminent Kentish Witch who was fondly referred to as the Witch Queen of Kent. Two others were Tom Penfold, a police sergeant, and his wife Mabs who held a high position at the Law Courts in the Strand in London. They were the High Priest and High Priestess of a very powerful coven in Sussex.

Unhesitatingly they embraced Audrey into their midst, and it was at Tom's hand she received her 2nd and 3rd degrees. This coven was a great training coven for Tom had been initiated by Rae Bone, one of Gerald Gardner's High Priestesses, and Mabs was initiated in that self-same coven. Some time later I was also reinitiated by Mabs into the Gardnerian persuasion, and in turn I initiated Mabs into the realms of traditional magic and into Artemis a sort of Wiccan 'quid pro quo'.

From that point onwards we often worked as one, joining the two covens together in many most powerful rituals. Sadly, they have both gone to the Summerlands, where one day we will meet again. Audrey had now lost two covens as there was no one to take the helm, and at this point she entered the Order of Artemis which she serves to this day; but has never accepted the mantle of power and been High Priestess although it has been offered. Lyn Baylis took the reins alongside me and I can say with alacrity is the finest High Priestess a man could have had. She also was employed in the legal profession, and currently is a Wiccan prison and hospital chaplain in her spare time.

In finishing this chapter I will recount a somewhat contradictory event centring on a power ritual; that was based on a hypothesis to the effect that 'could a spirit be created. This was many years ago and is well recorded throughout. The whole idea was based on the theory that spirits were energy, and if so could be created. We know that poltergeist manifestation is an energy form able to perform enormous feats of telekinetic activity, and these have been identified as spherical balls of energy that flit around room moving objects at will.

Some of the most eminent scientists and philosophers of their day decided to create a spirit while they were either in a trance like state, meditating, or in séance. With this combination of mighty intellectuals they felt sure of success. The format would be quite simple. Each member of the circle would create a particular aspect of the spirit to be conjured and contribute to its formation. Eventually ten leading intellectuals and scientists were gathered together and the first séance commenced. These, it was decided, would now be performed at regular intervals, over the coming twelve months.

A leader was elected and a formula worked out. Each in turn now made absolutely independent of each other to make their own singular contribution to what would be conjured. The first was asked to simply state the sex of the spirit to be conjured and they replied male, (at this point I should tell you I do not know all the details that were submitted but they ran close to what I am about to unfold - my intention is to therefore present as accurate a picture as I can as to what happened).

The next thing to establish was the intended age of his death, and this was submitted say for instance by the next man there, say 35. The third one present had to give his trade, and decided he would be a cobbler, His marital status was established by the fourth who deemed him to be married, while the fifth named his wife as one Rebecca, the sixth one present gave the spirit to have the simplistic name of John, and added the surname of, for example Taylor. The next two gave the names and sexes of his children as a girl of eight named Connie and a boy of ten named Robert, Eight people had now created a non existent entity, together with a mythical family. The ninth person present now added where he lived - say Nottingham, while the tenth decided how he could have died. As a result of much thought he decided it would be a riding accident, whereby he broke his neck and departed this life two days afterwards.

The séance now started!

These meetings gathered in intensity over the coming year, as they concentrated in a near catalytic state to create the spirit they had 'designed' to order. Interesting, well yes very. But the end result was an absolutely negative response; for the greatest scientific names in the land had achieved nothing, not even a whisper or movement from the ether. As they collectively sent their thoughts into the void - rien - nothing. After persevering for a whole year they were forced to admit the whole experiment had been a complete and utter waste of time, and that they had failed miserably - C'est la Vie!

The whole project died the death and the little group abandoned it, but still continued to meet and carry on with other lines of occult research. It was nigh on a year later that the most amazing phenomena ever recorded took place leaving occultists to debate and argue the sequence over the coming years. The scenario was a hotel room in London, well away from the rural confines where the original experiments had taken place. The experiment on this occasion was performed by a visiting medium I gather. Inexplicably in the middle of the meeting they became aware of a presence, and chillingly, a laugh. It was the non-existent John Taylor, their non-existent entity who they had attempted to create out of sheer energy and give credence to - a full twelve month later had manifested!

When questioned he confirmed the year he had died, and the exact date of his death, he was able to give accurate details of his trade as a cobbler, where his children had been born and his marriage. Close examination of the newly-created spirit enabled them to collect much detailed knowledge that they had sought. But the end result was that what they had thought to be an absolute disaster from the initial experiments had now unexpectedly paid off. Here at last was proof positive; they had made the monumental discovery that a spirit force could be created. They were overjoyed and at the end of the meeting set off, each to write their own little scientific paper on their findings.

It was the following day one of them convened an urgent meeting. The experiment he declared was a complete and utter failure after all! The intellectuals reconvened and re-analysed their findings; for some of the greatest brains in the land had overlooked one major factor. What if they had conjured a malevolent spirit force - one which had been privy to their early experiments and had then maliciously impersonated the very entity they were seeking? The findings could now never be conclusive.

It was another of the group though who threw the final spanner into the works when he announced that in his opinion John Taylor did exist - and furthermore he always had. He reminded the assembly that prior to the conjuration experiment the whole group, some months beforehand, had also conducted research into telepathy. How do we not know, he stated that John Taylor was not, or rather had been a real person right from the beginning? Could he not he argued, have telepathically communicated true facts about himself to each individual present, after all, their minds were completely open, as they were in a soporific state at the time, and thus were ideal receptacles for such a transmission.

The truth will never be known obviously, but the one overriding factor is that even though the whole idea turned out to be a failure, as it had left more questions unanswered, than it answered. It was at the same time proof absolute of occult forces that ran a parallel existence alongside this world. Like we Witches, they had crossed the barriers of time and space, and entered into the realms of the old ones. To quote the famous words that have been passed do us "There are more things in Heaven and Earth than we shall ever know Horatio.

Turning the Goddess on Her Head!

Just over 50 years ago the infamous Witchcraft Act was repealed and a new renaissance of the Old Religion was born. Overnight the old ways suppressed for years came to the fore once again.

Many practitioners of the Old Religion of Britain held back, not really believing that their newfound freedom would last. But as the years passed, they realised that it was here to stay and they had nothing to fear other than occasional social ostracism. Then, and then only, did they slowly come forward and declare the ancient beliefs of their forbears that they had been taught.

It was as recently as 2001 that I finally tracked down an old Witch family who still lingered in the shadows, having kept a low profile for the last 50 years, and their knowledge was immense. They had regarded the rebirth of the Old Religion as a positive step forward in the 20th century, but abjured the publicity surrounding its birth, and those who came to the fore, posing for the gutter press who were more interested in photographing a nubile young priestess in the nude than publishing the purpose behind the rite.

The real and true 'new age' was born from the loins of Gerald Broussec Gardner who is regarded as the father of modern Witchcraft, and within a number of year, running alongside him, having founded another so called path, we also saw a 'king' rise and fall into semi-oblivion. There was one who vainly tried to pick up the crown on his death, and place it on his own head, but other than gaining the title of 'rent a Witch' by the paparazzi, failed to make any real impact on the Wiccan scene. At the end of the day there were only two greats, and they essentially was Gerald Gardner and his protégé Doreen Valiente.

With the passing of the years many who had initially flocked to the 'king's' banner abandoned his teachings, and embraced Gardnerianism which had led the occult and esoteric revolution that was rising throughout Britain, as they 'swept away the cobwebs' of the past and brought Witchcraft into the 20th century on a wave of new found respectability. With Gardner's renaissance the image of the evil Witch was fading at last.

We saw the rise of his acolyte, Doreen Valiente who was the mother of modern Witchcraft even as Gerald was the father. With the tragic passing of Doreen we regretfully will not see the equal of her again in our lifetime, but she was not alone for there were many, many, more. I have refrained from mentioning them by name lest perchance I should leave anybody out and as a result they could be offended by my excluding them, but I am sure they would all join me in affording an accolade to dear departed Doreen.

Book after book has been written on the Old Religion since then, and basically the initial publications in those first heady days were based on truth and facts as to what we would regard as 'true Craft'. I could write at length on the rituals that were expounded in Gerald's Book of Shadows with its strong overtones of Masonic practice, and naturally this must essentially give rise to speculation as to just how much masonry was incorporated into his writings. But I have referred to this aspect in an earlier chapter.

Many years have passed and slowly and inexorably we have started to see a sad decline in standards laid down by the greats of the early fifties, when we all adopted a basic and tried format of magic, the purist period as I call it. The very digressions from a common base that had destroyed the base values of the Xtian church from its founding as a simplistic religion based on the teachings of a simple man who presaged a quasi-Pagan edict of 'An ye harm none', is happening to Pagans right now..

Within two hundred years the rot had set in Xtianity, and continued to do so for the next 2000 as it split into sects and schisms as they broke away from the Holy Roman Catholic Church We have seen Baptists Ana-Baptists, Brethren, Plymouth Brethren, Exclusive Brethren, Jehovah's Witnesses, Presbyterians, Methodists, Seventh Day Adventists, - you name it, the sects of Xtianity are fragmented into hundreds of persuasions. The list is endless.

Is there not a lesson to be learned there? And is it not sad that we see a new age emerging from our own basis, the emerging of the self-same destructive force that has all but destroyed the new religion of Xtianity, with its empty churches - and has already with the new age renaissance, started to destroy the very fabric now of the Old Religion; split, as we see new groups springing up worldwide under a panoply of different names and practices; many of which have only a semblance to ancient Witchcraft.

The Old Religion spread to America and is a major religion there now it has established its roots, but is it the Old Religion, as we know it? Practised in the old ways? No, quite often it is not. Sincere yes, but true simplistic Witchcraft - no. What often happens is that a group decide to 'form a coven' and the first step is they 'get a book' usually spurious with about as much connection to ancient Witchcraft as a bottle labelled; Napoleon brandy has to the French Emperor.

So with the first books obtained, they start a group, no background, no tradition, no training, no history to guide them - nothing. A practice that our American cousins call 'boot-strapping, and its practitioners are called 'bootstrappers' as you will see expounded in another chapter. Would-be occultists, most of them very sincere and usually pertaining to be Witches, are marred by an increasing number of people who formulate covens and invent practices that are anathema to true followers.

The main body of Witches in America see the new spread potentially threatening to discredit the Craft as these people hit the newspapers and press time after time. But to revert to this articles headline, what they all find particularly anathema to them is a practice that has arrived there and which has originated here in the old country and spread there. The ritual they refer to as 'turning the Goddess on her Head'.

I am of course referring to the erroneous teachings that have been published in a number of otherwise most excellent books originating here in England, but which often include a chapter depicting the Pentacle of Magic, symbolic of good, upside down to represent the left-hand path and the symbol of evil! Why? Where did this practice originate? It has no part of ancient practice. The five points of the pentacle have always been identified as (from the top, the head, arms, and legs of the Goddess in the Star Goddess position, so just who in their wildest imagination decided to turn her upside down? And identify the practice with the second degree?

The answer I gather goes back to Solomonic magic and the old depiction of the pentacle of brass, originally wax, as we all know, that is engraved with 8 sigils of the Craft, with the circular plate representing the mystical 9th sigil. The centre of the pentacle is dominated by the largest sigil of all, which is the Pentacle of Power, followed deosil around it by further sigils. When you get to the top right-hand corner we see a small pentacle reversed! And it is this symbol that has evolved into wrongly being identified as second-degree magic.

It is a matter of deep regret to me that I too adopted this blindly and wrote it into my earliest book of shadows; one must remember that I am turning the clock back to over 50 years ago. I am 77 years old at the time of writing this book, and as I have learned and studied over the years, so I have corrected and altered what I consider to be incorrect. Over these years as I studied I came to deplore this reversing of the pentacle which has crept into so many books, and unwittingly found its way into so many covens over the years. One dear friend of mine, who is a leading Wiccan, also writes books, and she decided to follow the self-same path and make sure in her next publication that the pentacle, allegedly of the second degree, was corrected. To her horror when the book was published she found that the printers in their ignorance had printed a reversed pentacle as a header on every chapter, thus perpetuating the myth. It seems the typesetter had simply been told that a star had to be printed of a certain size, and had no idea that a true star had to be aligned in a certain way. It was not possible economically to reprint the book.

So why has the pentacle been reversed over the years? As I mentioned, the answer lies within Solomonic magic. The centre large 'correct' pentacle represents the Macrocosm, and the much smaller reversed pentacle represents the Microcosm under the ancient adage of; "As above, so below", showing there are two sides to everything, the dominant light is countered by dark, goodness by evil, life itself by death!, but it shows that the former of each comparison is always the dominant feature, not the opposite.

I have encountered a number of compatriots who have reversed the pentacle and feel their lives have been affected adversely as a result. So surely there is a lesson surely to be learned here - if you reverse the Goddess and 'turn her on her head' then do not be surprised if your own life is equally turned upside down for you will have taken that first, albeit unknowing, first step onto the left-hand path.

Throughout history the reversed pentacle has always symbolised evil, and this dangerous new, albeit, unwitting, trend, must cease. It has no part in Witchcraft, past, present, or future.

Epilogue

The Sleeping Goddess Awakes – and Heralds a New Wiccan Dawn

I am the Sleeping Goddess, the beloved of the God with whom I once ruled, I was loved and revered by all humankind through all the Aeons of time.

It was a Golden Age.

Then came the Xtians and destroyed all we loved.

New Gods had arrived. Gods without substance that were conjured from the depth of the mind of their false priests. They sat themselves on lofty pedestals away from the people and claimed supreme power over all, and offered their own God as a salve to man's conscience. A God who would expurgate their sins for them.

Gone were the days of laughter and joy when youths and maidens frolicked naked together, and we Gods and Goddesses of nature were worshipped in ancient groves beneath the Sun, Stars, and the Moon. Instead, sombre black priests give droll sermons of a mythical hell in houses of stone where once our sacred sites had stood. Gone were the trees and bushes we loved and the earth was now covered. The Old Ways were gone and we the Old Ones wept.

Forsaken by the world and rejected I descended into slumber. The world now being dead unto me, so henceforth was I dead to the world.

Centuries have passed, and mankind has made his own way.

But do I hear a faint cry from my dying Earth? Raising me from my slumber? Who disturbeth me now? Who are they that wish to awake we Old Ones once more?

I stir, for I am the Earth Mother, and the cry of man and womankind is as a baby mewling for its mother, and as a mother I respond.

Hundreds of years have passed since I went into primordial trance, and I cannot believe what I see. My cloak of green has gone. My blanket of immortality has been destroyed. I see parched lands and deserts where once I bestowed life. Great craters lie upon the Earth's surface like gaping wounds, the very bowels of the Earth now lay upon its surface.

My lifeblood is now putrescence; where once it flowed over the land crystal clear and clean; the all giving life-force of the world. My oceans were clean and saline with the all-purifying salts.

My Earth has been raped and robbed of her riches and even as I watch the Earth is dying. The Old Gods are no longer loved, and we are no longer worshipped; and so I go to return to my primordial and eternal sleep once more - unloved. But a stirring from below will not let me rest. I must awake and return to my realm again to see those who seek me.

My spirit floats through cities where once giant forests stood and I see the degradation of man and woman. Where flowers once bloomed profusely there is now filth and squalor. In the towns I see the exploitation of my sexuality prostituted out of the fertility of my creed.

Surely there can be no salvation. I cannot return for all is lost, and darkness is the lot of mankind. Yet I cannot rest, for Earth was my creation and I miss the serenity of its woods and groves where I once walked. But hearken! Do I sense a stirring whereby it can be redeemed?

Yes! Faintly audible I hear the invocations of a few - gathering in intensity, like a wind blowing forth. My heart surges with new life and pumps with joy, for my creed is not dead. In every city I find those who are returning to the old ways as a new enlightenment heralds a fresh beginning.

My spirit is glad. I commune once more as of old with the Lords of the Outer Spaces and tell them that in a new renaissance there are still those who have kept faith and still practise the ancient arts. A new youthful generation is suddenly arising like a phoenix from the ashes and I seek to preserve my realm and protect my offspring. All lifeforms are sacred unto me and are revered by those who are returning to the Old Religion. And so as they call unto me I return unto Earth once more, for I am She the all merciful and loving Goddess who was with you at the beginning of time itself and will be with you at times ending.

Blessed be the Old Ones.

Blessed be the New Age

And Blessed Be the Hidden Children of the Goddess.

I will bestow love and blessing on all those who turn once more to the Ancient Ones. I will bless all those who love nature, and whose hearts are truly Pagan.

My hand will stretch out and make the crops grow bountiful once more. The ears of wheat shall ripen with the warmth bestowed by my partner Sol and my lifegiving and crystalline blood, sparkling and effervescent will descend from Nirvana and the deserts shall bloom again.

I will heal Earth's scars with a blanket of pure emerald and the woodlands shall echo to the song of the birds once more.

I am the Moon and my Lord is the Sun and we will warm the hearts of my people and return joy to the world.

The old age of Pisces shall henceforth fade away and Aquarius shall herald the new age to come with the dawn of the Pagan heritage.

We the Old Ones have returned, and tomorrow Mother Earth shall bloom again.

Blessed be the faithful.

A selection of other titles from Capall Bann Publishing

Lid Off The Cauldron - A Handbook For Witches

Patricia Crowther

We are delighted to make this classic book available again. Patricia Crowther, a practising witch since 1960, lifts the lid off the cauldron of witchcraft and reveals some fascinating ingredients. She explores the history of the Craft and the methods and theory behind magic and initiation. Patricia details spells, chants, prayers, methods of divination and ancient symbols, combined with the wisdom and experience of a leading, knowledgeable witch who has had a high standing in witchcraft since the time of the revival in the early '60s. ISBN 186163 032 8 £10.95

HerbCraft - A Guide to the Shamanic and Ritual Use of Herbs

Susan Lavender and Anna Franklin

"I would highly recommend this publication...a must for your bookshelf" *Beltane Fire* ***"....an excellent and truly comprehensive work, an essential reference and invaluable companion for everyone interested in the use of herbs for magic and ritual. Highly recommended"*** *Prediction*

"most comprehensive book...The sheer amount of information in this book is staggering...books with this kind of collated information are rare treasures." *Manchester Pagan Wheel*

Moves beyond herb folklore and examines their true magical nature, showing how power plants can be employed for the transformation of Self and consciousness, according to the teachings of Native Pagan Tradition. Detailed descriptions of herbs, cultivating them for magical purposes, their traditional uses, explanations of lore, the art of herb simples and traditional recipes. Correspondences - animal totems, magical tools, deities, planets, elements and festivals. Set out in alphabetical order, with appendices designed to help each individual with their own personal development. ISBN 1898307 57 1 £19.95

The Book of Dowsing and Divining **Sue Phillips**

MOST PEOPLE CAN DOWSE, it's simply a question of learning how. This book will teach you to find out all kinds of things from health problems to buried treasure; from ley lines to what colour you should wear to enhance your energies. Packed with illustrations, The Book of Dowsing and Divining contains clear step by step instructions for divining with forked twigs, dowsing rods and pendulums. There are easy instructions for making your own dowsing tools, too, even if you have no practical experience or money; and ideas for improvisation when you simply have to dowse, but have left your equipment at home. Sue Phillips is a dowser and healer of many years' experience and has distilled her knowledge to bring you this highly readable and entertaining How-to book. ISBN 186163 1200 £7.95

FREE DETAILED CATALOGUE

Earth Dance - A Year of Pagan Rituals, Jan Brodie
Earth Harmony - Places of Power, Holiness & Healing, Nigel Pennick
Earth Magic, Margaret McArthur
Egyptian Animals - Guardians & Gateways of the Gods, Akkadia Ford
Eildon Tree (The) Romany Language & Lore, Michael Hoadley
Enchanted Forest - The Magical Lore of Trees, Yvonne Aburrow
Eternal Priestess, Sage Weston
Eternally Yours Faithfully, Roy Radford & Evelyn Gregory
Everything You Always Wanted To Know About Your Body, But So Far
Nobody's Been Able To Tell You, Chris Thomas & D Baker
Experiencing the Green Man, Rob Hardy & Teresa Moorey
Face of the Deep - Healing Body & Soul, Penny Allen
Fairies and Nature Spirits, Teresa Moorey
Fairies in the Irish Tradition, Molly Gowen
Familiars - Animal Powers of Britain, Anna Franklin
Flower Wisdom, Katherine Kear
Fool's First Steps, (The) Chris Thomas
Forest Paths - Tree Divination, Brian Harrison, Ill. S. Rouse
From Past to Future Life, Dr Roger Webber
From Stagecraft To Witchcraft, , Patricia Crowther
Gardening For Wildlife Ron Wilson
God Year, The, Nigel Pennick & Helen Field
Goddess on the Cross, Dr George Young
Goddess Year, The, Nigel Pennick & Helen Field
Goddesses, Guardians & Groves, Jack Gale
Handbook For Pagan Healers, Liz Joan
Handbook of Fairies, Ronan Coghlan
Healing Book, The, Chris Thomas and Diane Baker
Healing Homes, Jennifer Dent
Healing Journeys, Paul Williamson
Healing Stones, Sue Philips
Herb Craft - Shamanic & Ritual Use of Herbs, Lavender & Franklin
Hidden Heritage - Exploring Ancient Essex, Terry Johnson
Hub of the Wheel, Skytoucher
In and Out the Windows, Dilys Gator
In Search of Herne the Hunter, Eric Fitch
In Search of the Green Man, Peter Hill
Inner Celtia, Alan Richardson & David Annwn
Inner Mysteries of the Goths, Nigel Pennick
Inner Space Workbook - Develop Through Tarot, Cat Summers & Julian Vayne
In Search of Pagan Gods, Teresa Moorey
Intuitive Journey, Ann Walker Isis - African Queen, Akkadia Ford
Journey Home, The, Chris Thomas
Kecks, Keddles & Kesh - Celtic Lang & The Cog Almanac, Bayley
Language of the Psycards, Berenice
Legend of Robin Hood, The, Richard Rutherford-Moore

Lid Off the Cauldron, Patricia Crowther
Light From the Shadows - Modern Traditional Witchcraft, Gwyn
Living Tarot, Ann Walker
Lore of the Sacred Horse, Marion Davies
Lost Lands & Sunken Cities (2nd ed.), Nigel Pennick
The Magic and Mystery of Trees, Teresa Moorey
Magic For the Next 1,000 Years, Jack Gale
Magic of Herbs - A Complete Home Herbal, Rhiannon Ryall
Magical Guardians - Exploring the Spirit and Nature of Trees, Philip Heselton
Magical History of the Horse, Janet Farrar & Virginia Russell
Magical Lore of Animals, Yvonne Aburrow
Magical Lore of Cats, Marion Davies
Magical Lore of Herbs, Marion Davies
Magick Without Peers, Ariadne Rainbird & David Rankine
Masks of Misrule - Horned God & His Cult in Europe, Nigel Jackson
Medicine For The Coming Age, Lisa Sand MD
Medium Rare - Reminiscences of a Clairvoyant, Muriel Renard
Menopausal Woman on the Run, Jaki da Costa
Mind Massage - 60 Creative Visualisations, Marlene Maundrill
Mirrors of Magic - Evoking the Spirit of the Dewponds, P Heselton
The Moon and You, Teresa Moorey
Moon Mysteries, Jan Brodie
Mysteries of the Runes, Michael Howard
Mystic Life of Animals, Ann Walker
Nature's Children, Rachel Mayatt
New Celtic Oracle The, Nigel Pennick & Nigel Jackson
Oracle of Geomancy, Nigel Pennick
Pagan Feasts - Seasonal Food for the 8 Festivals, Franklin & Phillips
Patchwork of Magic - Living in a Pagan World, Julia Day
Pathworking - A Practical Book of Guided Meditations, Pete Jennings
Personal Power, Anna Franklin
Pickingill Papers - The Origins of Gardnerian Wicca, Bill Liddell
Pillars of Tubal Cain, Nigel Jackson
Places of Pilgrimage and Healing, Adrian Cooper
Planet Earth - The Universe's Experiment, Chris Thomas
Practical Divining, Richard Foord
Practical Meditation, Steve Hounsome
Practical Spirituality, Steve Hounsome
Psychic Self Defence - Real Solutions, Jan Brodie
Real Fairies, David Tame
Reality - How It Works & Why It Mostly Doesn't, Rik Dent
Romany Tapestry, Michael Houghton
Runic Astrology, Nigel Pennick
Sacred Animals, Gordon MacLellan
Sacred Celtic Animals, Marion Davies, Ill. Simon Rouse
Sacred Dorset - On the Path of the Dragon, Peter Knight

Sacred Grove - The Mysteries of the Forest, Yvonne Aburrow
Sacred Geometry, Nigel Pennick
Sacred Nature, Ancient Wisdom & Modern Meanings, A Cooper
Sacred Ring - Pagan Origins of British Folk Festivals, M. Howard
Season of Sorcery - On Becoming a Wisewoman, Poppy Palin
Seasonal Magic - Diary of a Village Witch, Paddy Slade
Secret Places of the Goddess, Philip Heselton
Secret Signs & Sigils, Nigel Pennick
The Secrets of East Anglian Magic, Nigel Pennick
A Seeker's Guide To Past Lives, Paul Williamson
Seeking Pagan Gods, Teresa Moorey
A Seer's Guide To Crystal Divination, Gale Halloran
Self Enlightenment, Mayan O'Brien
Spirits of the Earth, Jaq D Hawkins
Spirits of the Air, Jaq D Hawkins
Spirits of the Aether, Jaq D Hawkins
Spirits of the Water, Jaq D Hawkins
Spirits of the Aether, Jaq D Hawkins
Stony Gaze, Investigating Celtic Heads John Billingsley
Stumbling Through the Undergrowth , Mark Kirwan-Heyhoe
Subterranean Kingdom, The, revised 2nd ed, Nigel Pennick
Symbols of Ancient Gods, Rhiannon Ryall
Talking to the Earth, Gordon MacLellan
Talking With Nature, Julie Hood
Taming the Wolf - Full Moon Meditations, Steve Hounsome
Teachings of the Wisewomen, Rhiannon Ryall
The Other Kingdoms Speak, Helena Hawley
Transformation of Housework, Ben Bushill
Tree: Essence of Healing, Simon & Sue Lilly
Tree: Essence, Spirit & Teacher, Simon & Sue Lilly
Tree Seer, Simon & Sue Lilly
Through the Veil, Peter Paddon
Torch and the Spear, Patrick Regan
Understanding Chaos Magic, Jaq D Hawkins
Understanding Past Lives, Dilys Gater
Understanding Second Sight, Dilys Gater
Understanding Spirit Guides, Dilys Gater
Understanding Star Children, Dilys Gater
The Urban Shaman, Dilys Gater
Vortex - The End of History, Mary Russell
Warp and Weft - In Search of the I-Ching, William de Fancourt
Warriors at the Edge of Time, Jan Fry
Water Witches, Tony Steele
Way of the Magus, Michael Howard
Weaving a Web of Magic, Rhiannon Ryall
West Country Wicca, Rhiannon Ryall

What's Your Poison? vol 1, Tina Tarrant
Wheel of the Year, Teresa Moorey & Jane Brideson
Wildwitch - The Craft of the Natural Psychic, Poppy Palin
Wildwood King , Philip Kane
A Wisewoman's Book of Tea Leaf Reading, Pat Barki
The Witching Path, Moira Stirland
The Witch's Kitchen, Val Thomas
The Witches' Heart, Eileen Smith
Witches of Oz, Matthew & Julia Philips
Wondrous Land - The Faery Faith of Ireland by Dr Kay Mullin
Working With Crystals, Shirley o'Donoghue
Working With Natural Energy, Shirley o'Donoghue
Working With the Merlin, Geoff Hughes
Your Talking Pet, Ann Walker
The Zodiac Experience, Patricia Crowther

FREE detailed catalogue and FREE 'Inspiration' magazine

Contact: Capall Bann Publishing, Auton Farm, Milverton, Somerset, TA4 1NE